THE FINAL RUSH HOUR

RICHARD WILLOWS

Introduction

Consciousness. Ecstatic spiritual epiphany. Intense paranoia. Suicidal thoughts. The guilty pleasure of going off the rails. The watercolour world of skunk. Losing identity. Falling inexorably into my unconscious like a black hole. Psychological and sexual abuse. Profound inner peace. Reality bending beyond all recognition. Facing demons. Fighting. Giving up. Living to tell the tale.

I decided, sometime in mid 2015, to write my own mental health memoir. There are, of course, a great many such books by others who've chosen to tell their own tale, in ways both moving and illuminating. In such a rapidly-growing genre, what on earth could the USP (Unique Selling Point) of my own story be? None of the conditions I have or tribulations I've endured are unheard of. In fact, they're spoken of increasingly often, and rightly so. What could I add to the public conversation that could be either new or of value, let alone interesting? After some thought, it hit me: A Phenomenalist approach.

I knew I could write the story of my mental health struggles in a number of ways but wanted, emphatically, to do something a little different. It had to be something more than just a chronological memoir or informative explanation of certain conditions. I wanted to convey a compelling *story*, in as evocative and creative a way as possible while still, of course, recalling the truth of my own experiences. Something informative, yes, but also epic and, hopefully, engaging. But how best to approach said task?

I've been fascinated by consciousness for as long as I can remember. It was a few years prior to beginning this book that I became aware of the philosophical movement known as Phenomenology. Its inception is attributed to German philosopher Edmund Husserl and is, in a nutshell, the study of the Subjective. The slippery, intangible domain of private, subjective experience. Its principle approach and, indeed, challenge, is often explained via the question 'What is it like to be a bat?', first posed by American philosopher Thomas Nagel in 1974. We know bats can't see very well, have highly sensitive ears and find their way around using echolocation (sonar). Scientists know a great deal about their biological constitution. But we really have no idea what flying around, precision-navigating with *sound* instead of sight is actually *like*. What's it like to 'hear' your way around the world? What's it like to be a bat? This simple question can be applied to any animal and, ultimately, any other person. It's a relatively little-known fact that we all see colours ever so slightly differently. What 'red' is like for you may be quite different to how I experience it. It may be very similar. We just don't know.

Explanations of the concept of Phenomenology tend to use everyday sense-data, or 'Qualia' (from the term 'Qualitative' as opposed to quantitative) as illustrative examples. "Redness", "Coldness", "Wetness" and the like, are often used as they're simple examples most of us can relate to. But these seem, to my mind at least, to represent the shallow end of our experience. What *really* characterises our lived-experience is the deeper, even more slippery realm where thought, emotion and sensation at once coexist; the level at which we experience everything from excitement and frustration to melancholy, joy and much, much more. This is, for my money, the really engaging, nitty-gritty stuff of human experience where the challenges of phenomenology and language itself present an incredible and exhilarating dilemma. It seemed the ideal way to approach this book.

That, then, was the task I set myself. To not only tell the story of my mental health struggles, but try damn hard to take the reader *inside* those lived-experiences. To actually describe the lived-experience while telling a (hopefully) compelling story. The list with which this introduction began represents some of the many qualia that would have to be described.

With these objectives in mind it made sense to focus entirely on my pre-diagnosis days, without reference to specific psychiatric labels (those come in the final chapter), as that period, undiagnosed and utterly perplexed, seemed to offer the most fertile material for the task at hand. The strange, bewildering and dramatic world undiagnosed mental health problems, *as experienced*.

Memory is a notoriously selective phenomenon. Prior to taking medication, my memory for life events was among the best of anyone I knew. A friend might say, "remember when we got drunk on the racecourse?" to which I could instantly reply, "Yes, that was a school night in late April, 1996." Since medicating, however, that level of detail is harder to come by with regard to my post-diagnosis life but, curiously, not events beforehand. They remain quite accessible, so far as memory goes. What follows are first-hand accounts of key moments in the journey, that I've recalled to mind as vividly as possible and described with all honesty. Given the significance of these events in my life, they remain a clear as memories can be.

The story is structured as a series of flashbacks, experienced as I drove to work one March morning in 2007, simultaneously elated and terrified; almost completely convinced I was about to be brutally killed for something I hadn't done, at once resigned, overwhelmed, mortified and even glad. It was without a doubt the weirdest day of my life. Although I've obviously had to embellish the amount of detail contained in the flashbacks, and their chosen order, both the drive itself and all of the flashbacks were real experiences I've lived through. Each flashback represents either the best pre-diagnosis example of a given condition or else what I believe to be the cause of a given problem. In some cases, both. All conditions and issues are elucidated in the final chapter.

And finally a word about style: in describing conscious experience, I've tried to be as creative-yet-concise with language as I can. Metaphors, adjectives and analogies abound. I've taken more than a few liberties with grammatical style, but only where absolutely necessary. Readers will notice, at certain key points, that I suddenly switch from past to present tense, whenever the drama really heightens. This is quite deliberate. It's my hope that within these pages, Consciousness itself is, at times, a character. The broader story is told in past-tense; scenes set and themes developed but, each time I switch to present, the intention is to bring consciousness to life and escort my readers directly into the eye of the experiential-storm. This book is something of an experiment in creative writing, phenomenology and mental health awareness. It's also my own, very bizarre story…

The Final Rush Hour, Part I

The shrill electric shriek of my old Nokia screams out at seven AM, piercing sleep, eardrums and the morning itself in an instant. Another day has dawned. Quite possibly the last I'll ever see.

I haul myself out of bed and stagger across the room to the furthest shelf, where I always leave my phone, so I have to get out from under the covers to turn off the alarm, rather than 'snoozing' it for a good hour and stumbling into work late. That won't happen today. After just two hours of taut slumber, I'm exhausted, but very much awake, body aching with a weary-tension I've grown grimly used to. I've been running on empty for months now: muscles weak, shaky and overwrought from incessant tension, poor diet and lack of proper rest; eyeballs sore beneath perpetually drooping lids; head pounding, mouth dry, shoulders forever clenched up to my ears, and the constant, sickly taste of reflux in the back of my throat. It's like this, Every. Single. Day. In the midst of this zombie-stupor, I'm constantly hyper-alert; there's an intrusive brightness to everything that rapidly ascends each morning as I emerge from the forgetful bliss of morning-grogginess. Not today. Today I'm wide awake the second the alarm goes off, as though a firework has just exploded beside my bead. Emerging from frugal slumber, the familiar mixture of exhausted-alertness is there straightaway and in droves, but, this morning…*this* morning…there's something else there, glowing brilliantly, somewhere inside the usual mental shit-storm…

Just a moment ago, I inhabited a High Definition, profoundly resonant dream. On the small field at the end of our road – the field in which I climbed trees and played hide-and-seek as a child, and later, as a lonely teenager would sit for hours alone instead of going to school – I was locked in a death-struggle with a giant, evil, mutant-Spiderman creature.

Much bigger than me and far stronger, he quickly and repeatedly defeats me but for reasons unknown can't quite finish me off. I keep getting back up and giving it all I've got. It's a holding pattern: I can't win but I'm not giving up; he can't quite vanquish me or allow my escape. It's him or me. As we grapple over and over again I'm almost completely lucid, and aware of two things: first, this mutant-beast is the very presence and embodiment of so many deep, complex fears and perhaps even Death itself and second, that there's a brilliant fire blazing within, one I was sure burnt out long ago. And there's something else: a strange intimacy between us, as though we're both somehow destined for this endless bout; inexorably set upon one another by unseen forces, beyond either of our control.

I fumble into my dressing gown, slide on my slippers and shuffle out of the bedroom. As I descend the stairs, I'm myself lost in the same bewildering tempest from last night. Exhilaration. Joy. An immeasurable bliss radiating from deep within my bones – as though a blazing light has switched on in my very soul; all the sweet, rapturous textures of existence suddenly reborn, after years of emotional deadness. And I'm terrified. No, horrified. Near-paralysing dread, thundering anxiety, apocalyptic fear. A sizzling cocktail of toxic waste and hallucinogenic poison rips through my veins. A brain, machine-gunned through with acid bullets and splintered metal arrows. Muscle and bone pressure-cooked to a blackened, powdery crisp. All of it. All at once. Elated, despairing, terrified and *everything* in between.

I can't be absolutely certain, but I'm fairly convinced this will be my last day on earth. I think I'm probably heading to work today to be brutally and publically humiliated before being murdered, for something I haven't done. And I'm not even sure I care.

The usual desperate-tiredness is familiar enough, as is the hopeless anxiety and inconsolable sadness. But the lighter stuff, that's new. An exquisite and unexpected side-effect of the events of the past few days; one might expect the beautiful brightness to have swept all before it in a restorative transformation. It's done nothing of the sort. I finally let go of everything, in the hope of being at last freed from this mental hell, but instead of sweet release, everything's just gone off the scale. I'm a loose, out-of-control speck of debris flailing about in the eye of an near-supernatural storm. Up may well be down; day could be night – the swirling of impossibly intense sensations seems close to obliterating any notion of context whatsoever. I can scarcely think straight. I'm beyond trying to understand what on earth is going on, and really have no idea what to do other than try to continue on as normal. How could I explain this insanity to anyone? Surely they'd think I was a complete lunatic. That's certainly what I think.

At the bottom of the stairs, the muted-spluttering sound of the shower tells me Dad's in there, as is his routine. I trudge, trancelike into the kitchen and sit down at the counter to find Mum's laid all out the usual breakfast paraphernalia. Through the steady, grumbling crescendo of the kettle comes the routine rhetorical question:

"D'you want tea?"

"Yes, please."

"Did you sleep alright?"

"Not really. At least today's the last day of training. I can start my normal hours next week."

I make small talk with Mum while staring blankly at the Breakfast News on the little kitchen-TV, still haunted by last night's dream. Please don't let it be a sign. It might as well be, given everything that happened over the weekend. I've unleashed a process that can't be halted now; the dam has burst, finally and irrevocably, they're probably going to kill me. Nothing to be done about it. Hands tied; fate sealed. All bets are off. All I can do is wait. Dad emerges from the shower. More small talk. Most days, I'm painfully distant from polite conversation but today I appreciate it in a new way: this could be the last breakfast I ever have with Mum and Dad. Or anyone. Part of me doesn't care. I'm burning up inside, terror threatening to consume me whole. I don't fight it. My newly liberated heart glows with the brightness of a thousand suns. I'm settled, joyful, rejoicing. Ambivalence swirls within: despair, fear, freedom, foreboding, elation, helplessness, optimism, desperation, buoyant light. Cornflakes. Tea. God only knows what will happen today. I want to tell Mum and Dad what's going on in my head, but I no longer have the strength or words. Besides, I'm tired of endlessly fighting to resolve these baffling, mortifying problems in my messed up brain. Beyond tired. Beyond sick of it. I have to go into work today and confront them, head on. The breath of life tingles throughout my body. It's invigorating. They're going to kill me. Slowly. Inch by inch by inch. Or not. I'm weak with fear. I hope it's all in my head. I don't know anymore. There's nowhere left to run. One way or another, I want it over. My nerves feel like they're about to tear themselves apart.

One disorienting hour later and I'm 'ready' for the day ahead, ostensibly at least: fully dressed and dosed up on caffeine, nicotine and sugar. Second cup of tea shakily drank; teeth brushed while stomach did bungee jumps. Nothing left to do before leaving the house. No more stalling. Time to go. Face the salivating horde. There's a football-sized lump in my throat as I open the front door and shout "Bye" with as much nonchalance as I can muster. No knowing if I'll see my family again, I want to tell them I love them. It's not a phrase we use often – if said now, they could suspect something's wrong. The front door closes behind me and I walk tentatively to the car, as though led to the gallows by an unseen executioner, blinking in the cruel, unflinching glare of the morning sun. Each inward breath is an exquisite rush of luscious fresh air, filling me with sensual joys and fanning the flames of this mortifying terror. Nerves fire high octane fight-or-flight signals to every muscle as they burn with taut readiness. And yet the bright hues of life mingle amongst the darkness like carefree butterflies. I'm finally free, but it might just cost me my life.

Open the car door, climb inside, pull the seat belt across body. Click. It seems almost comical – the idea this little strap of material might be enough to protect fragile flesh on a day like today. Maybe there'll be a fatal crash on the way this morning; something quick and relatively painless. That'd be nice. At least then I won't have to endure the one thing I've been running from all this time. Seems unlikely. Luck went AWOL a long time ago. No surprise return expected today.

Key in ignition. I can't believe this is happening. Turn. Engine struggles to life. Oh god. Reverse off the drive, and the journey begins. Breathing not too shallow. Yet. Will be later. I don't fight the bone-terror, panic, joy or exhilaration, or even attempt to control any of it. It's far, far, *far* too late for that. The point of no return was finally passed at the weekend; something monumental is coming to an absolute end today. That's all I know. As I drive up the hill out of the suburban crescent that's been my home for most of the last twenty five years, bits and pieces of memory from all the years of mental health problems flash across my mind as, terrified, I smell the sweet roses. Bracing terror and quiet calm. All at once. What the hell is happening to me? How did things get this messed up? Where did it all begin?

I've been fighting the feeling that some kind of unavoidable confrontation was on the cards for about six months now…it started when I was living in Scotland, late last year…

...Keep on Moving...

Keep on Moving

Late one hazy, August afternoon in 2006, and I'm rattling along the northernmost stretch of the M6 in my old, red Ford Fiesta, at eighty miles an hour. I've been on the road since mid morning, so must be at least two hundred miles from home by now. Rolling over the endless stretch of concrete and hypnotically-repeating white lines, my tired eyes clock a couple of signs growing in the distance. The road's quieter now. I crawled through heavy traffic somewhere near Birmingham, sailed on past exit signs for Liverpool, Manchester and Preston, before stopping for lunch at a motorway services in the Lake District a few hours back.. Now, there are just a handful of other vehicles still heading north. Speed brings the signs looming into view: 'Services 5 miles' and 'Scotland 15 miles'. The latter sign elicits a feeling of sudden unease, or at least, a new *kind* of unease, mixing in with all the usual crap. Something important suddenly and rudely, dawns: although the feeling of leaving my 'life' in Worcester behind has proved a mild tonic for all the usual, grimly-familiar despair and desperation, I realise I don't actually want to arrive in Scotland. Or anywhere. I could just keep driving until I fall off the edge of the map. Better take another break. I drift into the left hand lane, slow to sixty and tail along behind a huge, thundering HGV. This sudden realisation is quite alarming, almost dizzying – best to take it slow until I reach the services. Why does my brain always turn these weird tricks?

The countryside rolls by as if on a repetitive blue-screen-loop, and another sign looms: 'Services 1 mile'. Scotland is now just eleven miles away. I don't want to arrive. Don't want to have to talk to people while being afraid of each and every one of them; to frantically navigate the endless taunts and threats from my brain; make small talk while trying to veil suicidal desperation. I hate it. It seems unlikely that the last four years private hell will suddenly, magically evaporate in some cinematic big city montage. But I don't know what else to do. Ask for help? No. Not a chance. Far too much at stake. Still, time for a rain-check before going any further.

The slip road rises into view, racing up to meet the car as I glide off the motorway, ease off the accelerator and let the engine run itself down a little before applying the breaks. White lines, painted arrows and bright blue signs convey me to the landscaped purgatory of the parking area in yet another retail park pit stop.

Rain Check

Five minutes later, sitting halfway out of the open car door, nursing a coke and smoking a roll up, I rub my aching eyes and wonder if I should go any further. Or if I even have a choice. I have about four hundred pounds to my name, no job lined up and absolutely no connections this far north. A few nights' accommodation booked in a hostel dormitory in Glasgow city centre. That's it. And I've just realised I don't really want to get there at all. I could happily continue driving forever. I just don't know what to do.

I go over the same old ground for the millionth time. I'm dead inside. Four years ago, while working at a local factory, out of nowhere, horrendous, unspeakable intrusive thoughts began tearing into my mind with a horrifying vividness and frequency that brought me to my knees. That's where I've been ever since. They poison my every waking moment: each thought, emotion and sensation. There's never a time they're not there. A relentless internal torture. I can't discuss them with anyone. Ever. Not properly or in any kind of detail. They're beyond horrible. Not the kind of thing you discuss with anyone. Under any circumstances. But…I *need* to. They stalk and traumatise every waking moment and I just can't cope with them by myself. And yet, I'm *so* viscerally afraid of what could happen if I ever confide in someone, that 'coping' alone is what I've been doing, very badly, for the last four years. Then there's the blushing. If I blush at precisely the wrong moment, as I'm sometimes prone to, I'll be violently lynched, torn apart, hung, drawn and quartered by a baying mob. I can barely bring myself to think about that one.

When it all first erupted, the emotional terror involved was such that it felt like my very humanity was shutting down; all sensations of human emotion coagulating, first into sore scabs and eventually, as the horrors continued unabated, into cold, hard, concrete. A physically-tangible feeling of inner-deadness. Lifelessness. Cold, dark and unbearably heavy. These days it's hard to feel much of anything beyond anxiety, sadness or panic – the rest is frozen solid, deep, deep down inside the concrete blocks that weigh down my gut, covered in pungent dust. Someone might pass by with a cute baby or an adorable puppy and I'll feel nothing – I hear of people I used to know getting married, having kids, even dying, and none of it registers in the slightest. Or rather, it registers for a few nanoseconds before being absorbed into the solidified visceral mass within. It weighs me down everywhere I go. Sometimes I can almost *see* the concrete obtruding into my mind's eye…and feel *tiny* tremors of emotion struggling to move within it: the encased remains of dangerous humanity and emotion…or perhaps no more than a dying gasp? I can't tell. It's frightening just how numb and zombie-like I've become. And, ever since that fateful day back at the factory four years ago, a haunting sense that I just can't outrun the problem haunts every movement and thought; as though a slow-motion nuclear aftershock pursues me wherever I go, whatever I do, inching every closer. And I'm getting tired. *Really* tired. Soon I won't be able to run. There's a constant, throbbing knot in my solar plexus – sometimes the discomfort of it even wakes me in the middle of the night. It's scary to even think about any of this. And the vile intrusive thoughts bombard consciousness every hateful, fearful step of the way.

I finish my rollup and make myself another while going over it all in my head. How have I found myself in this weird horror-story? I have no idea. I tried changing my diet, giving up weed, different 'spiritual' outlooks, distancing myself from others, keeping busy, not doing too much, trying to figure it all out rationally and talking *very* vaguely with others about the problem in ways that were superficial and non-committal. Nothing worked. If anything, the problem has only deteriorated. Which leaves three options: stop resisting all the intrusions and terror and see what happens – absolutely out of the question – or tell someone my terrible secret. This second option has always carried an uncomfortable resonance. I know in my heart of hearts it's what must be done, but whenever I envision myself actually describing the intrusions to someone else, my imagination ignites like petrol as my mind's eye fills with images – sketchy and vague in detail but crystal clear in their unmistakable sense of danger – faces turning in disgust, voices raised in abject hatred and a chain of events that would surely bring about a most, violent, untimely demise. The third option is what I've been doing for the past four years: keep running and hope against hope that I can either wait it out or figure it all out, one way or another. Carry on dragging this concrete-laden carcass around, barely sleeping and suffer the worrying tension-headaches in the left side of my brain. Something in there wants to push through, to process, to release, something dangerous. The hope with this third option is that I can somehow avoid the first two; find a way to make it all just stop. I wish I could risk confidence in someone…anyone…but the fears that swell with the thought of said risk are so profound and blood-curdling that I'm quickly back on the motorway, heading north at ninety miles an hour.

Somewhere in the back of my mind, I know that when I arrive in Glasgow it'll just be the same old crap: having to talk to others through a shitstorm of disgusting, distracting intrusions, the paranoia and that haunting feeling of danger that never leaves my thoughts. Going through the motions, acting calm while petrified; struggling to sleep; not wanting to eat, wash, talk, socialise…live. Maybe the bright lights of a big, unknown city, so far from home, will snap me out of it just long enough to find a way forward? Maybe. But I know, deep down inside, this is all just another hopeless twist in the never ending game of cat and mouse between me and this intractable problem. I'll have to face it sooner or later. Which is a shame. Because I can't.

An Unwelcome Guest

Driving through Glasgow city centre at sunset, the growing unease and sense that I don't want to arrive both skyrocket. I feel like someone stepping onto an ice rink for the first time. An ice rink on a cruise ship. In stormy seas. With broken skates. I'm hoping the excitement of the unknown will provide exhilaration and renewal: enough to sweep all the mental troubles aside, or at least take my mind off them for a good long while. Some folk back home said I was being brave; others, foolhardy. All I'm really doing is running from the nuclear blast, the heat of its swelling threshold ever-hotter on the back of my neck.

The orange hue of sunset gives way to the sterile, copper-glare of a thousand streetlights, as I finally arrive at an inner city street of Victorian terraces. I park the car and drag my suitcase and tired cadaver along the pavement to the location on my printed-map. Approaching the hostel, accelerating-anxiety gathers pace, racing for the sound barrier, threatening to push to new, hellish heights.

"150MPH."

"This will be the one. The time. The place. The people. This is where it all finally goes wrong. Someone will notice. You'll blush, they'll think you're a killer and tear you apart. It's what you want."

Shutupshutupshutup.

As I reach the address, my brain is a sizzling chip pan. I grit my teeth and push it all down with everything I've got. This kind of thing goes on inside me *all* the time, but today, it's that much worse. Anxiety is starting to feel almost like some kind of demon-possession, fighting for ultimate control of my consciousness. It wasn't supposed to be like this. Gonna be a shaky landing. I find the decrepit-looking, paint-peeling, old, wooden door of the hostel and push the button on the rusty intercom. It's quite an effort. Nervousness makes me so weak. No sound. Wait. No answer. Maybe it's a sign? Intrusive thoughts swarm into awareness like a plague of ravenous locusts. I'm getting a little breathless with nerves, half hoping no-one answers so I can just go home. No, that's ridiculous – it's a three hundred mile drive and I'm exhausted. Have to stay here tonight. I'm so fucked. Run. Just run away. Doesn't matter where – just go. Keep on moving.

"*200MPH.*"

"The mob is the other side of this door. Run now, while you still can. You're a vile sadist and they'll see it in your eyes."

I ignore the screaming-intrusions and sizzling anxiety as best I can, and press the buzzer again. Have to compose myself if I'm to appear calm and congenial, or someone might suspect…something. Still no answer. Shishitshit. By now, my mind is a scratchy, flickering cinema screen, terrifying images race across it: me harming others, them somehow sensing my intrusions, being outraged and thus attacking me for having said thoughts. Still no answer. For God's sake, just go home.

"260MPH."

Push. It. All. Down. I hate this feeling. Just go home. No. Yes. NoNoNoNo. Yes. It's the right thing to-NO! Should I ring the hostel in case the intercom is broken? I wish I knew what I want. Deep, deep down I do, but can't think about that. Thinking about *that* is the reason I'm here in the first place. Hot tar burns in my veins, my throat tight as I raise a shaking finger and press a third time. Don't think about *that*. Too dangerouschickenshitbuddhacalmsweingwasp.

"330MPH."

The sound barrier now in sight. Finally the old door creaks open to reveal a dishevelled young lad in jeans and t shirt, looking surprised, tired and a little stoned. I get a nonchalant, almost annoyed "Hi" from him but nothing more.

"410MPH."

…He knows. Soon everyone will know…

Bollocks, fuckoff, shit, cunt, poo. Shut it. Shut up. Trap, trap, trap door. Bollocks.

Sometimes repeating words and swearing at myself works. Most of the time it doesn't. It isn't now. I follow stoned-guy inside into one of the dreariest, gloomiest hostels in existence. The faded, watery-brown walls are covered in morose Emo posters, the lights are dim, windows grimy with old dirt, the air musty and the other guests decidedly cold. My polite smiles go unrequited. More despicable images flash through my head, along with a sense of the most terrible physical and psychological danger. One wrong move, that's all it'd take. I hope to God no words like "rapist" or "terrorist" come up in conversation. But why would they? I'm neither of those things. Because I thought it. Because I fear it. My thoughts might be able to make horrible things happen. Sometimes to me, sometimes to others, but always my fault.

"500MPH."

YestheydoNotheydon'tYestheydoshutthefuckup. Tits. Arse. Bottles. Bollocks. Ferrets on a train. That last one seemed to cut the bastard thoughts off. For a few seconds at least. I breathe deeply and try to look calm. It's all in my head. Definitely. Shutup. Attempts at conversation with my nonplussed host are stunted and awkward. I manage to get a name out of him – Pete – a traveller from New Zealand, working at the hostel to save on accommodation costs. We pop into the small, grotty kitchen. More lukewarm reactions from other guests, accompanied by gripping, electric pangs of danger:

"…What if they knew, these people? What would they do to you? Better hope you don't blush or meet anyone psychic…"

"590MPH."

Pulse quickening. Head throbbing. Just get through it. What am I doing this for? Shut up. Everything's trembling, hopelessly unstable, as the sound barrier approaches. Stop being so melodramatic. Get on with it. I've stayed in hostels before and found some folk quite friendly while others just politely keep to themselves. Here, everyone just appears cold. Not the best atmosphere for an insane twat like me.

I follow Pete up the narrow staircase and over grubby, threadbare grey-brown carpet to the third floor dorm. Something unexpected is going on inside me. Most of the time, but for those moments when the intrusions are really, really unbearable, I can keep a sense of distance between all the crap going on inside my head and the outside world at large. For all the strange internal drama of recent years, I've somehow managed to retain a certain superficial, outward confidence when it comes to polite small talk with just about anyone. Even when suicidal with anxiety, panic and intrusive thoughts, I can usually don a loose mask of amiability and muddle through. Keep it to myself. Act for England. This evening, for the first time in a long time, that's not the case. The boundaries of my internal terror are now pushing outwards to…something new, beyond the levels I can usually, shakily, control. Feels like it's expanding, leaking out; pushing to somehow burst through my skin and meet with the dangers of the outside world – burning my thin façade to a crisp.

"670MPH."

My face keeps accidentally drifting into a kind of pained, furrowed-repose, while my voice comes out taut and quivering. I can't quite get a grip on either of them. Instead of curative excitement at having finally arrived, it feels like all my demons have come along for the ride, and brought with them an unwelcome guest – a rising sensation of being dangerously exposed *right now* (instead of in the very near future, as is usually the case), of needing to hide my face, turn and run; that this is no longer just an internal battle. The mask is becoming dangerously loose and the consequences could be disastrous.

"700MPH. Brace yourself."

As Pete shows me into the dorm, he's now a little more talkative; mostly chatting about himself and his travels. I feign listening noises and expressions while trying to get the jump on this new, unsettling freak-out. Muscles starting to melt. Standing getting difficult. I'm shown to my bunk and assured that Pete will change the manky, old sheets before tonight. How kind of him. He finishes his talk with the following words, spoken with youthful admiration and awe:

"Oh, and this is the stabbing capital of Europe!"

The brittle mask falls to the floor, shattering into a thousand pieces.

"*750MPH.*"

Boom.

"*Ladies and Gentlemen, we've just broken the sound barrier.*"

Sink or Swim

An hour later and I'm walking into Glasgow city centre, through a barrage of mental chaos, my body on hyper alert. Pete's little sound-bite shorted a fuse. Something snapped. It's at times like this that some thoughts can *really* take hold. Like a red-hot knife sinking into warm clay, which quickly hardens around the blade, fixing it there forever. Some unpleasant thoughts tear clean past each and every defence and just settle, unhindered; a blinding beacon of pulsating shock, obscuring all other sensation. I flail and bargain with mind and nerves for all I'm worth, but I know it's ultimately useless. Some thoughts just set up camp. For good. Now, as I walk the streets towards the very centre of Glasgow, every breath, sensation and heartbeat screams the same phrase repeatedly: I'm going to get stabbed. The thought has internalised now, become as deep a part of me as my beating heart, my memories or the bacteria in my gut. It swims in my veins. There's just something about me that invites hostility. I look like a victim. A sitting duck, waiting to be picked off. A fish in a barrel. Now the mask has broken I'm frantically trying to create a new one in my mind: things to think about, say or do that'll distract me just enough, keep me one step ahead of the monsters. Fashion a new façade that won't arouse suspicion. But there's just so much more to conceal. Now that I'm completely freaking out, won't be able to hide it – the wolves will home in on my petrified scent. Only a matter of time. Consciously, I know this to be nothing more than another stray shard of nonsense in a messed up mind, but, at times like these, knowing it simply isn't enough: my manic, jittering brain can't, and won't be reasoned with. A restful nap was out of the question, so, I showered, changed and now I'm heading into town with a dizzying mixture of overtiredness and adrenaline-fuelled jitters. The plan is to get as drunk as possible, hope this was just a bad start and have a good night out to purge my mind of the deafening white noise.

I've never liked alcohol enough do develop a serious problem, the upside of which being that when I feel the need, I can get really wasted *really* quickly. After a few painfully awkward pints sitting alone in the middle of a busy Whetherspoon's, the rest of the night is something of a blur. I remember two things: One, getting absolutely hammered and chatting to an amiable young Glaswegian lesbian and her entourage in some small, generic, gay cellar-bar. And two, a sickening, sinking feeling that I was in over my head; my brain was going into meltdown. As though I'd swum into the powerful current of some huge whirlpool, now frantically splashing around in a vain attempt to escape its inexorable downward pull. Although, by this time I was pissed and stupefied enough to ignore some of the usual intrusive thoughts, the new, penetrating feeling of shock-and-awe had pierced everything, infecting all consciousness with an unavoidable and powerful sense that danger was now *incredibly* close. More so than ever before. A worried, almost tearful look kept creeping, unbidden, across my face, nigh impossible to control. Copious amounts of booze did nothing to purge it. Could I make this thing work without my game-face? There was now *so* much to hide. Plunging headlong into the deep end was supposed to be invigorating and life-affirming. It was meant to exorcise at least a *few* demons. It turned out to be more of a rude shock; an unmistakable feeling of drowning in my own inadequacies.

A Familiar Bolt Hole

I awake in the hostel dormitory the following morning, to the pungent smell of strangers' farts and booze-breath: a stale, stinky ambience filling the room. Despite returning completely plastered, I only managed about four hours of hollow sleep. I get dressed, head down to the kitchen for a cuppa, and drag myself outside to smoke and take stock. Last night's copious amounts of alcohol failed to purge the crash-landing sensation. It still courses through me: stomach like a clenched fist, nerves like old piano wires and muscles rigid with tension. Intrusive thoughts and feelings of nearby danger are now distinctly worse than they were back home. I practically feel them leaking out of my skin, darting around the ether like random electric shocks, burning the air…crackling, hissing, rogue psychic events that can and will make bad things happen. The worst things. I'm painfully hyper-alert. Everything is too loud. Head pounding like a pneumatic drill. I never imagined I could be so tired and yet so awake, all at once. This was a terrible idea. I'm clearly very mentally ill and the only realistic option now is to seek help. The very thought of it, though, and the paralysing, distortive fear creeps in again. The world shifts, morphs and contorts into ubiquitous danger. Trance-like, my mind's eye conjures those fearful and familiar scenarios of brutal lynching. However bad things are, getting help still seems the most dangerous option. Far too risky. But, I can't stay here. I know my mind and body well enough: when *this* freaked out, the intrusions and paranoia neither peak nor pass, making way for the next onslaught, no, when I'm this rigid they burrow in deep and take over everything, contaminating all perception and emotion, warping all to their chilling theme. It's happened before; their fatal sensation backlighting everything else, lingering on like a vomit-inducing stench, sometimes for years. The deafening notion that I'm little more than prey in this place, however ridiculous I know it to be, has already sunk, deep into my brain, and won't be letting up anytime soon. I feel it. I hate my brain. Hate my hypersensitive body. They've caused this whole sorry mess. I'm twenty four years old, have almost no money, can't hold down a full time job or cope with close friendships, have been single for over four years and now I can't even settle in this crappy little hostel for a few lousy days. But I'm not going home. As horrible as things are right now, the alternative is still mortally terrifying. No. Keep on moving. Keep running. From the problem. From myself. From the thing that can't be faced.

Tired, hungover and dosed up on caffeine and painkillers, I'm soon speeding along the M8, eastbound for Edinburgh. Save for the grumpy hostel inhabitants (most of whom probably weren't Glaswegian) everyone I encountered in Glasgow yesterday was friendly; I didn't get so much as a dirty look from a single person. I'd still love to try settling there, in the big, unknown city, but speeding towards Scotland's capital, the feeling of shock starts to lose just a little of its edge and I know that, sadly, my staying in Glasgow is unlikely. I visited Edinburgh once before, on an unplanned week away, in coldest February when I was struggling to cope with college, so I'll at least know my way around the centre.

I arrive in the middle of the world-famous festival. The centre of Edinburgh is sublime, utterly breathtaking. The centrepiece of so many modern city centres is, all too often, that depressingly familiar presence of the same old high street chains, languishing in weather-beaten modernist architecture that might've looked nice, once, in the 1960s, for about a week. In Edinburgh, however, the usual corporate promenade is dwarfed by an extinct volcano, rising majestically from the earth, proudly crowned with the elegant architecture of Edinburgh Castle. The lush, landscaped greenery of Prince's Street Gardens adorns the valley below with vibrant colour, and, across unfeasibly wide-pavements, shop fronts sit humbly in the grandiose Georgian architecture of The New Town. The powerful, resonant notes of a bagpiper, playing at the East entrance to the park, drift on the invigorating Firth of Forth air, busses glide up and down alongside bustling pavements, as the ancient, picturesque, green hills of Hollyrood Park rise in the near-distance. In my youth I was fortunate enough to visit Rome, Venice, Florence, Amsterdam, Bruges and Paris – Edinburgh is easily one of the most beautiful cities I've ever laid eyes upon. It's a feast for the senses, at least for a few seconds before feelings of awe and inspiration become either confusing or dangerous and get quickly absorbed into the concrete blocks in my gut, leaving only cold bewilderment. I think I'd actually prefer the confusion.

I spend the day taking in Edinburgh as best I can: seeing a few sights, glancing at the occasional recruitment agency window. I sit upstairs in the Mac Donald's at the west end of Prince's Street, considering my options while gazing out at the idyllic skyline. Beautiful, confusing, but perhaps not as scary as yesterday's scene. Edinburgh's leafy streets, elegant old buildings and changeable weather feel oddly reminiscent of home. In a general sense and obviously on a much larger scale, the resplendent castle and Holyrood Park remind me a little of Worcester with her grand, imposing cathedral set against the backdrop of the Malvern Hills. I feel a tad reassured by this vague sense of familiarity, and disappointed that I need such a balm. I remain keen on the tabula rasa offered by unexplored Glasgow, but my brain is in an even worse funk than usual. I don't have much money and a decision has to be made soon. Yesterday's freak-out remains potent, but is just a little less intense here.

The sun is setting up ahead as I drive back along the M8 to Glasgow. The internal drama of the last thirty six hours has been so tiring, I really can't face going out again this evening. So I sit in the communal TV room, watching a film with a group of despondent strangers, trying to ignore all the paranoia and white noise in my head. I'll drive back to Edinburgh tomorrow and look for somewhere to stay. It was an unbelievably bumpy start, but I won't be going home just yet.

A Beautiful Dead End

Pounding the Picturesque Pavements

The last of my funds are spent on five nights in an empty student room in Edinburgh's idiosyncratic, medieval Old Town. I still have a few nights booked back at the Glasgow hostel, but I'd rather not stay there. A dorm was a bad idea in any case. Ever since the evil circus of vile images, words and notions first gatecrashed into consciousness, sleeping in a room with other people became close to impossible. The idea I might sleep-talk about my problems, through some Freudian sense of a repressed need to seek help, is truly terrifying. No such calamity has ever happened, but any attempt to rationalise always evokes alarming images of being abruptly woken by other guests, righteous in anger, brandishing blunt instruments, ready to beat the living shit out of me. Ridiculous? Yes, but try telling that to a live-wired brain at four in the morning. I knew it would be a problem when I booked the dorm but with so little money, it seemed best to just suck it up and cope with the insomnia as best I could. I hadn't counted on my mental state deteriorating so rapidly on arrival. A clean break is the best option at this point.

The next few days are spent relentlessly walking the length and breadth of Edinburgh's ornate, Eighteenth Century New Town, visiting every employment agency in sight. Although picturesque Edinburgh has taken some of the edge off the initial blind panic, much of it lingers on. A new swarm of worries now dart among the more familiar doubts and anxieties. On arriving in Glasgow, unfamiliarity crashed headlong into familiar desperation, igniting shock instead of the much hoped-for exhilaration. It was so fast, total and uncontrollable: One banal throwaway comment by a guy who probably knew little more of the place than I, and my mind and nerves nosedived.

Still shaken by the experience, I can't help but wonder how much more fragile my state of mind now is: does another similar problem lurk in the shadows? Will I cope with it this time or finally implode? I try not to think about it but it looms up again and again like an elegant mental virus, making me feel physically sick with worry, day and night. Most importantly of all: do these newfound apprehensions, taken with the usual internal noise, make a fatal blushing incident more likely? If I'm struggling to keep a frantic brain under control, all the while trying to squeeze every last drop of energy from a fatigued body, just to get through the day, isn't it now even more likely that I'll panic and blush next time I hear anyone mention, say, a burglar, murderer or sex offender? What if it's the 'wrong kind of person'? The kind that would quickly jump to conclusions and gleefully round up a righteous posse to revel in a brutal lynching? This is the one fear that crowns them all. I don't even know why it's there. I hate it. It's so uncontrollable, so all consuming, like a deadly, venomous serpent living in my spine that could bite at any moment, bringing on the most agonising demise. It makes me suicidal. At times like these, such intrusions are like loud, obnoxious music blasting in the ears while trying to sleep or a blinding torch in the face while trying to converse with someone like, for example, a potential employer. Consciously, I fight to ignore it all, but those more animalistic areas of the brain *always* know when something's wrong; they stand alert, ready to fight or flee…mine don't seem to have an "off" switch. Thus my mental energies are continually pulled toward bizarre, futile ruminations when alone and, when in conversation with others, frantically repeating random words and visualisations in my head. None of this does much to allay the unease, but the alternative – to let scary thoughts just 'happen', feels like a death wish. For all of us. It's always fun walking around the big city, attending interviews with stuff like that going on your head…at least my newly-fashioned mask is working, if only just.

Four days into Project Pound the Pavements, the phone finally rings. The amiable voice on the other end belongs to Jenny, a recruitment consultant for the Edinburgh branch of an agency I worked for back home. She's spoken with the Worcester branch, has my details, several positions waiting and is calling to see if I can come into the office this afternoon. Bingo. Starting a new job will be stressful, and I still need somewhere to stay, but the moment the call ends I there's a momentary sense of relief. Finding a job and, hopefully, a surer footing, might just mean the extra mental chaos that began in Glasgow is finally settling. I can move forward. I walk back to the hotel and dig out the last clean shirt from my suitcase as the concrete blocks inside absorb the sense of relief, encasing it, beyond reach. And something else, deep, deep down in there is stirring. But I can't think about that.

Soon I'm back in the New Town, walking through a bracing wind, en route to Jenny's office. I find the address easily enough. My pulse skyrockets as I push the big, grandiose red door of the Georgian townhouse. Dizziness itself engulfs me. Inside, the agency occupies two floors of a huge, ornate, terrace; huge sash windows flood each room with light; illuminating original period features; large, regal doorways, a grand, sweeping staircase and thick red carpet throughout. Traditional elegance. I wish I was applying for a job in *this* building – its grandiose style feels somehow soothing…for a brief moment I feel almost pleasantly distracted. Dangerous. Concrete quickly absorbs it. It gets heavier. The left side of my brain throbs. And that worrying 'something else' is still flickering away down there…somewhere…I wish it would leave me alone.

I sit in reception, nerves hissing away like overheating water pipes. A toxic cocktail of deep dread, anxiety, desperation, exhaustion and an almost irresistible urge to bolt, has me shaky and close to throwing up. I'm beginning to sweat, muscles tense up. Jaw tightly closed. Everything painfully loud and vivid. I'm being pumped full of weapons-grade, industrial adrenaline, litre by litre. Jenny walks in. A tall, twenty-something woman of medium build with dyed-blond hair tied neatly into a bun, a warm, pleasant smile and huge, bright blue eyes peering keenly through dark-rimmed glasses; she's the picture of professional amiability. We shake hands and go through to her office.

Despite four years of incessant, spirit-crushing mental trauma, I nonetheless always *try* to approach such situations with a sense of optimism. Maybe today will be the day it all just stops? Perhaps I'll finally find the one magic word or idea that'll put it all into the right context and I'll finally be able to let it all go. Job done. Move on. Hallelujah. Thank God for that. Could our conversation be *so* engaging I'll manage to somehow rise above the usual internal storms? I *always* hope. Perhaps that's why the Glasgow shock was such a…well…shock. It was the exact opposite of what I was hoping for, what I still so desperately need.

We sit on comfy chairs facing each other – casual and informal – the office is spacious and looks out over a small well-maintained garden. We begin.

"So, what brings you all the way up here to Edinburgh?"

"This is my last chance. I don't know what else to do. I really, really need help but I'm terrified of what might happen, what people will think of me if I let anyone in. I'm running."

That's what I want to say, somewhere deep inside the heavy concrete. It's the thought that rudely obtrudes into consciousness as I nervously reply with some vague, noncommittal bullshit about needing a change, always having wanted to move here and so on. I hate this question. I can never answer it honestly.

"Tell me a little bit about your last job in Worcester…"

Jenny's manner is informal, direct and sincerely curious. I find her instantly likeable and, as such, this interview is a little less gruelling than all the others of recent days. A little. After a few sentences the conversation is increasingly drowned out by all the deafening white noise, in spite of all attempts to focus. Throughout our chat about Edinburgh, Worcester, my work history and a little about Jenny, the unwanted thoughts, and rogue-intuitions flood in. Snapping Jenny's neck. Poking her eyes out. Smashing her head on the desk. Offensive words. Bitch. Whore. Dickhead. Cunt. Half-formed pictures of her face turning in disgust and setting in motion a chain reaction that'll end it all. And, of course, the ever present, bone-terror that I'll blush at precisely the wrong moment. Or the right moment. Fighting to remain focused on the conversation and trying not to appear terrified takes everything I've got.

"Do you know anyone up here?"

Don'tsaythewordDon'tsaythewordDon'tsaytheword. Shut up. Speakerphones. Undergroundshoppingmallinspace. BackgroundDivaFarts. SlapShitPissNipples.

"No, not yet. A friend of mine was living here but he's ended up moving back just as I've moved up."

DeadDeadDeadDeadRabbitsOnTheToilet. GoThaneForthofFirthofFurofFithofSHUTUP.

I picture my brain exploding; grey matter, shards of blood-covered skull-fragments splattering onto Jenny's glasses and sliding down the wall - anything to shock myself out of the horrible thoughts and impossible feelings of imminent mortal danger, or at least counteract them. Punish myself for having them. But they keep on coming. If I did blush, might she politely dismiss me, thanking me for my time only to call the police the moment the door closes behind me? If the authorities wanted to speak to me I was sure to blush again. Would I be arrested? Wasn't this what I wanted? However awful it might be, at least the all-consuming, hellish anticipation would finally be over. I spend every waking moment afraid of it, so surely some macabre sense of relief would emerge amidst all the horror? After so many years of internal trauma it seems an almost inviting prospect. Images and visceral sensations of being lynched, condemned and abused follow. No. No, no, NO! NoNoNoNONNONO! I don't want it to happen; I want it all to just stop. Why is it even happening at all?

"And what sort of work would you like to try here?"

Leave me alone. My pulse thunders. The windows explode. I head-butt the wall until my cranium cracks open and noxious puss dribbles out. I grapple with my mad brain, with the overwhelming desire to run. I act my arse off while my mind throws up ideas of all of these horrifying thoughts somehow escaping, jumping out of my head, transmitting themselves through the air and into directly into Jenny's aghast mind. She knows. Shut up.

It doesn't matter. Shut up. BollocksBranFlakesFlapjacks. Crispyshits.

"Urm, anything really…"

Appear focused, polite and calm, whatever it takes, while silently panicking. Listen to Jenny and answer her questions. Flashes of anxiety spit out of my carefully controlled eyeballs, betraying my secret. I'm painfully, glaringly aware of the way I'm sat, every movement of my head, facial expressions, minute changes of facial muscles, my voice, the dryness of my mouth, the words I'm using. Every muscle, every inch of skin is being watched by an unseen ambush of tigers, ready to pounce, any microsecond. One wrong move, that's all it'd take. I momentarily lose control of an eyebrow or a painted-on expression. Does it look like I'm nervous? Going crazy? Does Jenny see through the dangerously thin veil?

She doesn't appear to notice. If she does, she doesn't seem to mind. Just let the thoughts happen.

NononononononoNO! ShitCuntBollocksArseFuckBitchSlapJack. NinetynineSeventyTwos.

"Okay, well, we'll give that one a try. I'll need to contact them first, of course."

Bad things will happen to all of us if I don't fight the horrible thoughts. Stupid fucking brain. Our session lasts about an hour, finishing with Jenny saying she'll be in touch. Did it go well? I can never tell. I didn't break down so I will assume so. I step outside into the fresh air, reeling from the whole experience, find somewhere to sit, roll a fag and decompress as best I can. I've got such a headache. And this was one of the easier interviews.

A New Start

My first weekend in Edinburgh I spend trawling lettings adverts online, in estate agents' windows and in any local papers I can find. Jenny and I settled on a data entry job, in the offices of a bank on the outskirts of the city, starting Monday. The thought of living with others, having to navigate, on a daily basis, the kind of internal drama endured during the interview with Jenny, is obviously out of the question. I need a place of my own. The trouble is, on a starting wage of six pounds an hour, almost all accommodation advertised is beyond my budget. All but one.

On viewing the *tiny*, grubby, third floor, broom-cupboard, advertised as a "self contained bedsit, seventy pounds a week", my initial thought is "I'm not *that* desperate. I'd rather go home than live here." Dead cats wouldn't swing. The following day I'm back signing the tenancy agreement. It's smaller than the room I'm renting at the University but, as the saying goes, beggars can't be choosers. Turns out I really *am* that desperate. It just adds to the feeling this is all a really bad idea, that I should just give up the ghost, go home and get some professional help. A feeling I doggedly fight to ignore. At least I have somewhere to live. I can stick around, for now.

Monday Madness

Work beings on Monday morning with the usual mix of misguided optimism and raging anxiety. Faced with the stimulation and excitement of a new job, does my psyche suddenly magically settle? No. Several scenes similar to the knife-edge interview with Jenny ensue as I meet my new manager and colleagues. Each encounter is navigated with nervous, vague, generic bullshit about why on earth I've moved three hundred miles north with no connections whatsoever, all for a spot of office temping. "I just wanted to try something new" and "I've always wanted to live in a city and Edinburgh is by far my favourite" and so on. I'm such a lying bastard. Everyone knows.

The morning is spent shadowing my new team leader, Christie. Drunk with panic and terror, but nonetheless craving the structure and distraction of a job, I fight tooth and nail to concentrate on everything I'm being taught. The work isn't especially complicated or demanding – entering finance proposals for small businesses and performing basic credit checks on company directors – but precious little of Christie's clear and careful instructions pierce the frantic, angry swarm in my head, made all the worse by the ever-present dizziness, dry mouth, tension headaches, sweating and much, much more besides. I feel constantly faint, yet primed for action. Imminent danger seems to skulk around the room like a lingering predator, biding its time, sharpening claws…licking ravenous lips. While I attempt to distract myself from the hailstones of intrusions pelting my head by repeating words internally –

"ShitFuckCuntCheeseGodSpainDieLiveBirthDeathCeilingBananas"

– I'm also *trying* to mentally repeat everything Christie's saying, in the vain hope that some morsel of information might just slip through the chaos and commit itself to memory. The interview with Jenny took place one-on-one, in congenial surroundings for about an hour; now, however, I'm sat painfully close to a complete stranger, all day long, in an open-plan office, buzzing with activity. Gruelling just isn't the word. My skull is a rattling pressure cooker. The left side of my brain feels like two tectonic plates grinding angrily against one another, crushing everything in between, including everything I'm supposed to be learning.

Lunchtime comes around and invitations to join others are politely declined with the excuse "I need petrol", which is true, but really I just need to be on my own, so I can drop this brittle mask and breathe normally. Stop this impossible game and just be a human being, or something thereabouts, for a good forty five minutes. I decide to go for a drive. Lacking a Sat-Nat or a map of this part of the city, I get completely and utterly lost in a matter of minutes. I drive anxiously around for what seems like hours, cursing myself, the roads, my near-empty fuel tank and dead phone battery as I turn and turn in an endless labyrinth of confusion. Following the brain-frying intensity of this morning, it's a pretty stressful afternoon. The sense that this is an ominous sign adds volume to a voice coming from somewhere deep inside the concrete saying "Just go home" and "Get help". After everything, I can't decide if getting lost on my first lunch break is frustrating, ironic or just downright funny, in an 'I'm-a-useless-moron' kind of way.

Eventually I find my way to the centre of Edinburgh and drop in to see Jenny to explain what's happened. She's very understanding and the Office are happy to have me back tomorrow. Tired and annoyed with myself, I head home via the charity shops to hunt for kitchenware. Food shopping goes on the credit card as my funds have dried up and I won't be getting paid for a good few weeks. Maybe I should just go home.

A Beautiful Dead End

This is it then; everything in place: an entry-level admin job and a crappy, cold little flat. I borrow from my parents to tide me over until payday; make the six hundred mile round trip home for the rest of my stuff and treat myself to a charity shop armchair, which just about slots in between the wobbly wardrobe and miniscule sink. Any hoped-for sense of renewal or distraction to be found in busying myself with a new life in the city is decidedly lacking. The elegant beauty of central Edinburgh provides a fleeting balm during the daily commute for the first few weeks, in those few precious seconds before the feeling becomes confusing and dangerous and sinks below the concrete. Feeling too much human emotion threatens to release into consciousness the chilling conclusion that I have to face up to this awful problem and confide in someone, which always engenders a curdling-terror, so, something inside me just shuts the humanity down, all of it, leaving little more than tiredness, anxiety and cold, sluggish sadness. That's about it.

At work, a low partition separates each desk, with colleagues on all sides. I tell myself it's a good thing: eventually I'll acclimatise to proximity with terrifying people – or "people" as I like to call them – and the macabre carnival of panic, paranoia and chaos will ease down. It doesn't. It gets worse. Every single day – in fact every time I enter the room – whispering, nagging paranoia rises to the surface, screaming that today will be the day it all goes horribly wrong. The façade of polite amiability, masking a desire to whack my head against the desk or rush outside into the oncoming traffic, is almost impossible to maintain. Attempts to suppress or conceal the turmoil inevitably fail from time to time, especially in conversation. Christie, sitting at the next desk, continually makes a touching effort to be welcoming, inviting me to work socials and bringing in some traditional Scottish tattie-scones and chippie sauce for me to try. Every time the mask slips a little, a glimpse of discomfort leaks out, and I worry I'm giving off the impression that I hate her. I can't cope with socialising. It triggers everything at once; the fear of blushing, intrusive thoughts, the sense of mortal danger, sadness, desperation…it all makes an unpleasant problem into an unbearable one. It's beyond exhausting. I just want to be by myself. All the time.

My flat has no internet or aerial, and the cheap plug-in one I buy that rests atop the combi-TV, that sits on the fridge at the foot of my bed, produces a signal so poor that I can only bear to watch a couple of programmes a week. All washing up is done in the tiny hand basin, which, given I'm not eating properly, isn't very much. The single shower and bath in the shared facilities are never more than lukewarm and, being so exhausted and zombified most of the time, I don't wash much either. I see very little of the other tenants, none of whom are particularly friendly. My first Saturday off, I curl up in the armchair and burst into floods of tears. I haven't cried in so long. This kind of outpouring of emotion used to feel cathartic. Not anymore. The flood threatens to become a tsunami. I have to force myself to stop and venture outside.

Most of my free time is spent hunkered down in endless rumination. I *have* to figure out how and why my mind has sunk into this awful quagmire of deplorable thoughts – how they could've appeared out of nowhere, poisoning everything; why it happened, what it says about me as a person and, most of all, how on earth I might overcome them. If I could somehow get past them, I really believe blushing wouldn't be a problem.

I don't want to be ruminating: if I keep busy and avoid it altogether, by the time I climb into bed, all the brainmageddon springs forth at once. A tightly-compressed coil cannot be held in perpetuity. Not if I want to sleep. The coil releases, everything erupts at once, a burgeoning sense of doom filling the room like a menacing night-spectre. I just end up lying awake all night, wide-eyed and catatonic, so, unfortunately, the rumination just has to be done. Sift through all the worrying mess in the hope of getting it right, figuring it all out, when all I'm really doing is keeping the monsters at bay. Barely. I ruminate incessantly, every second of every day, ever since that awful moment back at the factory, where this hell began. Watching TV, reading, listening to music, talking, going to the toilet, washing up, driving, trying to concentrate at work, listening to the radio, wasting time on the internet, you name it, there's nowhere the intrusions can't find me and thus nothing that can pull me from this endless need to think about everything. Without thinking about anything too specifically. Danger hides behind and beneath every thought, every emotion, every action. It creeps in unseen like a pernicious virus no matter what I do. When there was bullying at school, weekends and holidays allowed some respite; whenever my cannabis use got me down, I could always cut it back to the bare minimum; if I felt uncomfortable around someone, I could avoid them, but this problem stalks me wherever I go. It's the very air I breathe. Too much thinking makes it all the worse, especially that chilling notion that sooner or later someone will find out my terrible secret, raised voices and contorted faces ensue, and I'm slaughtered on the spot. A level of suffering I can't even begin to imagine, and yet, can somehow *feel* with visceral clarity nonetheless. Even worse is the thought that it's what I really want. An end to it all. Any end. This kind of fear can almost stop time. Make the world at large appear like someone else's confusing, faraway dream; a world where no frame of reference makes any sense at all; I've accidentally wandered into it, can't remember where I came in or how to get out and, increasingly, what the real world is really like.

So I have to think about the unspeakable thoughts, impulses and dark intuitions without directly thinking about them. Think of a safe to way to be thinking about thinking about things I can't bring myself to think about. Feel my way through it all with the scant puddle of emotion I have left. Everything else has solidified into cold, dead, heavy concrete. Everything except fear, that is. The notion that there's something inherently lemming-like, pathological and suicidal about my brain pushes at my thoughts like flames licking at a door. I push against it perpetually. It can't be true. I *know* it's all nonsense, that it's just my broken brain casting shadow puppets onto the world but, somehow, they scare me all the same. The horrible impulses to push someone down the stairs, to stab, to break bones, all penetrate scepticism with a horrifying clarity that *feels* so unavoidable, so real – as though they're things I really want to do, that I'm just repressing my true nature. It's the same with the distressing words that reach into my mind at the worst possible moment: Christie will try to make conversation with me and, as I'm flailing to muster the appearance of a calm amiability, words like "Bitch" and "Whore" invade my thoughts, igniting a storm of guilt, shame, anxiety, self-loathing and desperation. It's all just a trick of the mind, but it's *constant*; a shockingly compelling ghost train I've been trapped on for years, wearing me down, bit by bit by bit. I have a horrible feeling that it's only a matter of time until I lose this battle and then…

No. No, I have to get *around* the shitstorm of horrors. Somehow. The problem is, the stress of it all, coupled with the almost breathtaking fear of blushing and being lynched, mostly leaves me both exasperated and exhausted. Would you like a cup of tea, Rich? No, I'd like to die, right now. …I mean, um, yes please, no sugar.

Somewhere, somehow, there's an anomaly in all of this that'll be my salvation. A clear, comprehensive, earth-shattering insight that finally puts it all into some, innocuous context and everything will be okay. If only fear didn't have that strange, hallucinogenic effect on perception; contorting so much of thought. Of reality itself. I hate having to ruminate, to search for a way out of this never ending nightmare. I'd much rather be living life.

Day and night I wander the unending maze of unthinkable thoughts, mortified emotions and impossible choices. The walls themselves seem to shift, to whisper, to laugh as they recalibrate their deceptive layout to make it *seem* like there's an exit to be found. Sometimes, just when it seems I'm on the cusp of solving it, figuring it out once and for all, and maybe, just maybe, in a place where I can begin to move on, it's *exactly* then that a new, even more terrible intrusion or fearful scenario will pounce into consciousness, rendering all prior efforts null and void, as it's venomous claws dig into my flesh. Just when I think the scary mental apparitions can't get any worse, they do just that. A newer, even more vicious intrusion will erupt from nowhere; a comforting, imagined scenario in which I imagine being able to talk to someone about my problems suddenly bends itself into a fatal misunderstanding of epic proportions and I'm burnt to a cinder by unbridled rage and violence. I just can't shake this fear.

Then there's the eye of the storm: the thermonuclear tension between a desperate, howling, primal need to reach out for help; to break down like a weeping infant on the one hand, and on the other, the blood freezing, suffocating fear of just how much I'll be made to suffer if I do. I feel the latter with visceral, intuitive certainty, like the hand of Death resting on my shoulder. The suffering of recent years would be as *nothing* when compared with what they'll do to me. Just the tip of the iceberg; a mere warm up. It's the perfect storm. *So* much has to be repressed, just to function day to day – so many thoughts, terrors, questions and bewildering emotions – it starts to feel as though my unconscious is bursting at the seams. I rarely get a good night's sleep. When I do drift off, sleep is so poor, so shallow, that some mornings it feels as though I've just been trapped in a hollow, rigid, purgatorial-trance for hours – unsure if I've actually slept at all, and always awaken with a paranoid-jolt. Thus the situation deteriorates. And all the while I sense the looming spectre of The Thing. The Truth of The One Thing that I'll just *have* to do sooner or later. The Thing that's even worse than the risk of confiding in someone. No. NonononononononNO! I don't care how scared, tired and hopeless I am, I'll *never* do that. I'll find another way if it kills me. What choice do I have? My fight-or-flight response is continually primed for action – brain hyper alert, body rigid, all day, in all situations. With each spike in intrusions, in fear and desperation, I'm tiptoeing in wrought-iron shoes on razor-thin ice. I fight tooth-and-nail to act as nonchalant and calm as possible at work each day. It's truly exhausting.

The flat gets dizzyingly claustrophobic, so I take to the streets, endlessly arguing with my defective brain while shuffling around the picturesque city centre, miserable as hell. I miss my younger days when I could lose myself in a rich, fertile imagination; find insight and solace in elaborate, delightful, rejuvenating daydreams that went on for hours. There was nothing I couldn't find within myself back then, back when I enjoyed a spirituality so empowering, it felt like there was nothing I couldn't do. Now, any attempt to lose myself in sweet fantasy is quickly poisoned; every daydream infected by foul parasites; morphing into nightmares of catastrophe. Healing spirituality now seems like a cruel joke: it could provide just what I need if only I could let go. Fat chance. Letting go of all *this*? Of the dreadful thoughts and impulses? What would happen? Would I become a monster and have to kill myself to prevent me from eviscerating innocent people? Would others turn on me just for having the thoughts? Do I really want to find out if certain 'magical' intrusions can make bad, poisonous, deadly things happen to people? Make cars crash and pregnant women miscarry? Is that the price of letting go? No, the edifying release of Spirit is long, long gone. Fled in horror and disgust at the sickening apparitions of my vile brain. I'd flee from me too if I could.

As the fresh, Scottish air turns colder, I'm soon traipsing around half-closed shopping centres most evenings, looking and feeling like a wandering corpse. I glimpse my reflection in a shop window and feel completely estranged from the tired, thin, gaunt-looking stranger staring back at me. There's just no way around it; my consciousness is perpetually riddled with vileness. I try to think my way around it all but the insidious poison always, always, *always* seeps through. It's like watching a city being steadily swallowed up by a tide of toxic waste; the detritus of life floating around, broken beyond repair, lifelessly sliding around on the poisonous waves. The concrete's getting heavier. Left-brain headaches more prominent. I'm sure they'll turn into a tumour any day now. I sense a reckoning on the horizon. Cold dread drops a few more degrees each day.

Underneath all this hell, somewhere, right at the bottom of the visceral concrete, I'm an upbeat person. Always have been. The world is an incredible, beautiful place filled with miraculous wonders: music, forests, literature, science, mountains, feats of engineering, animals, oceans, people, inventions, all of it is breathtaking and wonderful – I know this with all my heart, but the evil, unfathomable horrors inside turn everything to ruinous danger and so it's all absorbed into the concrete like animals in quicksand. The wonders of the world now seem like a cruel joke; every pleasant feeling and thought is violated totally, completely, so they, like so much of life, must be assiduously avoided. Shut down. I'm scared, all the time, and nothing is working. No escape. I yearn to be free. Or at least be able to fully ignore all the crap this brain taunts me with. I no longer feel anything worth feeling. It's over. I can't live like this, it's so profoundly crushing. I want to die. There were several, awful moments of feeling like ending it all, back at the factory, where it all began. Over the years those moments grew more frequent until it I started to that that way most of the time. Now, it's all the time. Every second of every day. Continuing to live in this way demands more and more strength the worse things get. I have so little left. This problem has been slowly killing me from the inside for over four years now. The concrete mass in my gut gets heavier by the day, imbued with more and more of my dead humanity, as do the throbbing, worrying headaches and the painful knot in my stomach. Something's trying, pushing, to break free and I just can't allow it. Ever. There's only one way out of this nightmare: quickly, quietly and painlessly...maybe jump head first off a quiet, back street bridge somewhere with no-one around. Falling. Cold air rushing over skin. A hard surface racing up…impact. Then…quiet finality. Peace. A broken brain, broken open, leaking its useless, poisonous goo onto the cold, hard concrete. I'd rather it all ended like that than be killed by a baying, righteous mob. But I can't do it. However much I want it over, I could never, ever, in a million years, put my family through something like that. "I can't live with that…" becomes a morbid paraphrase: "I can't die with that." Can't leave knowing I'd break hearts. Mine broke into a thousand pieces a long time ago, but that's not the point. I can't inflict my misery on others. I have to go on living, but I really, honestly, don't want to.

'Life' continues in this way for about three months: fighting to keep a lid on the boiling cesspool while at work; to concentrate, speak with others, wear the brittle mask of affected composure, stay awake at my desk, force myself to sit and work instead of running at the nearest window; coming home exhausted but unable to sleep; not eating or washing properly; wandering the streets for hours lost in pointless rumination and getting absolutely nowhere. A profound, almost transcendent sadness burrows a little deeper each day until I start to loathe each and every breath. Every ray of sunlight. Each beat of my heart. I feel like a cursed man. I go to nightclubs to get wasted but often find them overwhelming and resume the endless urban zombie-shuffle. I discover a small relief in ice-skating: think too much and you fall over, hard. It feels dangerous to bring thinking down to such a minimal level but I decide that I feel a sense of danger whatever I'm doing anyway, so why not be thus in a slightly different way that effects something like a break? Despite the multiple cuts, bruises and blisters brought on by my bad skating, for a couple of hours a week, I'm able to be in the moment just long enough to relax, if only a little. I like ice skating. It's nice. I hate it when the session ends.

The medicine of a new life in Edinburgh clearly hasn't worked. It's just made it all the worse. For all my ruminating, running away and repressing of emotions, it nonetheless feels like I'm running out – out of time, of ideas, options…strength. But I still can't bring myself to face whatever might happen if I ask for help…or face The Thing.

Nonononononononononono.
Don'tgotheredon'tgotheredon'tgothereWednesdayCalendar.

It's now two years since I gave up cannabis – my initial assessment of the problem being 'cannabis psychosis' – but things haven't improved. Not one bit. I just don't know what else to do besides muddle along and try to ignore the worrying sense that sooner or later, *something* is going to give and The Thing will have to be faced. This is it, then. A new life in the centre of picturesque Edinburgh. My beautiful dead end.

An Important Visit

One Saturday afternoon, late in October, while wandering gloomily around the idiosyncratic, cobbled streets of the Old Town, I pass a little Wiccan shop, set in a small Tudor townhouse. There's a sign in the window: 'Tarot Card Readings £10'. I stop for a moment and stare at it, vaguely curious. I close my eyes, sigh and shake my head. No. I'm not going down that road again.

Much of 2004-5 was spent exploring the possibility that my situation could have some sort of spiritual or psychic origin and solution therein. The idea that all this terror was actually being caused by some sort of 'misalignment' or 'lack of grounding' at first seemed comforting, mostly because it suggested the problem might be solved entirely privately. Find the right spiritual practice, technique or idea and the whole situation might just be resolved without having to confide in anyone. A seductive and appealing notion.

At first, I simply read about zodiac signs and birth-charts; carried gemstones and burnt 'uplifting' incense sticks in my room. Some of the ideas behind these practices were interesting enough, but they didn't touch the anxiety, panic, sadness or, crucially, the intrusive thoughts. But the appeal of a psychic-fix remained reassuring, so I dug a little deeper, dived into a few rabbit holes here and there, intent on finding that much-needed holy grail. I built shrines in my bedroom, tried casting spells and read about angels, spirit guides, planes of existence and even conspiracy theories. This proved a wrong move. A person who's mind is beset on all sides by the most unspeakable intrusions, about which they're terrified to speak, will find little comfort in the notion of spirit guides, aliens and all manner of so-called 'psychic' phenomena. The idea of there being some unseen 'entities' that potentially had unrestricted access to my mind and, therefore, the horrible images and impulses I couldn't even bring *myself* to look at, only added fuel to the fire. It meant the paranoia around the risk of being misunderstood, that I usually associated with blushing in company, now also turned inward, as I feared offending 'spirits' and other-dimensional 'beings', all of whom potentially had obscure magic powers with which to punish me for said thoughts. Then there was the terrifying notion of telepathy. My paranoia levels went through the roof. And, of course, the intrusions remained immune as ever, simply feeding off this new, worrying twist.

The 'Psychic' approach had made things much, much worse. Eventually, I had to draw a line, get rid of all artefacts and add it all to the list of things I just couldn't think about. This extra concern of 'psychic paranoia' remained strong, but at least I'd stopped adding fuel to the fire. Nope, no tarot card reading for me today.

I wander the old town some more, pick at a sandwich outside a café and consider my options. Mum and Dad are visiting in a fortnight and I'm an absolute mess. How on earth can I maintain a calm veneer for an entire weekend? I wish they weren't coming. I don't want to disappoint or worry them. I don't want anyone to see my pathetic little existence.

Later, I pass the Wiccan shop again, deliberately, to see if I feel any different. Might I wrestle my mind into meagre submission just long enough to risk a reading? Could whoever is inside read my mind, glimpse the intrusions and recoil in horror? Maybe call the police? Would a tarot reading provide reassuring insight or yet another inflammable bad idea to fan the flames? I don't know, but given that I'd quite like to die, what have I got to lose? It doesn't feel like my mind can be controlled now anyway…or that it ever could. It might be a bad idea, but then so is everything else at this point. I'll give it a go.

Head pounding, stomach-knot tightening, I push the door and slip cautiously inside. The room is filled with the usual paraphernalia: colourful prints of voluptuous sorcerers, quartz-tipped wands, incense sticks and trays of gemstones like an rocky pick 'n' Mix. The sweet, exotic scent of gently-burning Nag Champa fills the air. A short, bespectacled, middle-aged lady with an English accent and incredibly long, jet black hair sits behind a desk, resplendent in a black velvet dress. She meets my weary smile with a sympathetic one as I say hello and ask about the readings. It'll take a few minutes to get things ready. After a nervous smoke outside, I browse the shop while waiting. Intrusions abound, threatening to transmit out into the ether and into the heads of the other customers. Angel spirits might be circling, judging my vile intrusions; gemstones and wands will heighten deadly telepathy. Any minute now, someone's going to whirl around, look straight at me and hurl incendiary accusations, full volume, for all the world to hear.

KeepcalmKeepcalmKeepcalmKeepcalmKeepcalmKEEPCALM.SpecialNosePrizeDeathCushion.

Soon I'm led to a little alcove, cordoned off with dark drapes, where we sit at a small table. I shuffle the cards and the reading begins. Some of what she says is a little off base: "You're going to meet a young woman soon, possibly a potential girlfriend." Hmm. If my homosexuality hasn't registered on this nice lady's psychic 'mojo', then perhaps the unpleasant thoughts will go undetected. Other assertions fair better: "You've travelled a long way. You'll receive an important visit soon." "You've left a lot of love behind. There's a lot of love for you back home." This notion is nice, but I can't help feeling the love of which she speaks, like all others, is just another part of life I've had to cut myself off from, for fear of calamity. Something that should be inspiring, but is in fact terrifying.

The last card from the pack is the death card. This was a bad idea. She tries to reassure me that in the context of this reading, it probably means "the death of a situation." Could it be the end of soul-destroying isolation? Or my freedom? My anonymity? I dread to think. I thank my host for her time, pay £10 for the reading and wander back to the flat. So my parents' impending visit could be important. I try to rationally convince myself that nothing is set in stone, all the while a chilling, foreboding sense of danger begins to buzz around my nervous system until it feels like an overheating set of old, frayed, overused fairy lights. I'd like their visit to be simple and straightforward; it's going to be so hard to keep a lid on things; I dread to think what might happen if I don't. The oblivion of trusting someone else with the facts of my mental illness? No.

Shitcuntbollocksnofuckoffshutupno.

Two weeks later, just before five o'clock on a Friday afternoon, the desk-phone rings. It's Mum. They've crossed the border and should be arriving in a few hours. I've been anxious about their visit ever since the tarot reading, but right now, at the end of another tiring week of work, it's nice to hear a familiar voice. Driving home I alternate between thinking this will be a simple, straightforward, pleasant visit and the terrifying notion that I just can't maintain the façade any longer – things have deteriorated so much up here and I'm finally running out of strength. I'm bone-tired, dead inside, beyond weary, the left side of my brain continually hurts and the knot in my stomach is so intense it's beginning to affect my posture. I'm going to have to confide in them and have no idea whether they'll be understanding or never want to see me again.

Later, in the cold, dark, autumnal air of early evening, I drive out to a suburban petrol station to meet Mum and Dad. Pulling into the forecourt, I spot their car. My heart pounds blood to the brain, turning my perpetual-headache into a rhythmic, cranial stabbing. I'm dizzy, jittery, manic…almost seeing double and feel I could pass out at any moment. Trying not to choke on the lump in my throat, we exchange greetings through wound-down windows. They're keen to keep moving and so follow me back into town.

Soon after, we pull into the Travelodge of The Old Town – a stone's throw from where I stayed back in August – and they get out of the car to say hello properly. They're had a long drive, so we haul the luggage up to their room and go straight out to eat. We're going to see my little hovel en route to wherever we're having dinner. All evening I'm painfully jittery and unsettled. However anxious I get at work, I can always be politely vague, keeping others at arms' length for some scant sense of safety. This is a lot harder around family. I run the gamut of every crazy strategy I've ever tried to keep myself calm, even for a moment, but nothing works. It takes everything I've got to hold onto the appearance of calm, while fighting the sense that, any second now, the words "I need to talk to you about something" could fight their way out of my throat, as if the sentence itself now has a life of its own I can't control; scrapping to escape, to force my hand, no matter what I do. I try and try and *try* to repress the feeling but this one won't go into the concrete where it belongs. It's like forcing a hand to hold down the handle of a boiling saucepan lid, no matter how much it burns. The scalding water must *not* be allowed to escape.

I find myself locked in the usual dance of dread: horrible intrusive thoughts, words and images about them, me and everyone around us; smashing plates over people's heads, pushing them through windows, chards of glass sliding into eyeballs; burning others with my lit cigarette, and all the while the fear that at any moment someone will utter a word like 'murderer' and I'll blush; the feeling that I want to jump out of the nearest window; the urge to howl and cry uncontrollably, to scream "help me!". I try not to notice the looks of confusion and concern on their faces. We return to the flat before they head back to the hotel. When they leave I go straight to the nearest shop to buy a six-pack of larger, which is frantically guzzled, while trying to watch a DVD. Maybe if I just get really drunk I can drown the free-falling feeling that this is the end of the road. But I can't keep this bullshit up all weekend. The booze isn't working. I turn the TV off and cry for a good long while. Why do I have to do this? Why won't it all just stop? I could be so happy in this world if all this awful crap would just leave me the fuck alone. It seems I'm so far beyond the pale, now. I feel like a feral animal, trapped outside in the cold, wind and rain, unable to find shelter, think straight or do anything other than howl.

I throw up into the toilet and climb into bed. Tomorrow, one way or another, it's all going to be over. Or maybe something will suddenly turn up? A pleasant distraction to wake me from…but I know it's pointless. Nothing else has worked, even a little. Everything up to this point has made it all so much worse. Nowhere left to run. I lie in bed, mind and body taut, exhausted, and frozen like a rabbit in the jaws of some vicious, salivating predator. Feels like my body is melting itself into a steaming puddle of poisonous anxiety and seething adrenaline. Eventually, a rigid slumber overcomes me. In the morning I wake before my alarm, electrified with fear, mouth dry as sandpaper, the knot in my stomach so tense I can barely move. The phone rings. It's Mum. This is it. She wants to know if I want to meet them somewhere or should they come and pick me up. Through shallow breaths I almost choke on my words: "No. Can you come over, please? I need to talk to you about something."

I spend the next hour in a trance-like stupor. Time turns to meaningless chaos as endless scenarios race through my mind. Too fast, too slow, not slow enough. Stop, go back, rush forward. Will this be the last time ever I sit alone in my flat? Will the police be called? Am I to be carted off to God-knows-where, publicly vilified; declared a monster; my freedom and anonymity lost for good? Why, why *why* do I have to do this? I've fought so hard to outrun this insane dilemma. I don't deserve it. I haven't harmed anyone. Every second of every moment since those first horrible intrusions back at the factory has been about avoiding this moment and, now it's finally here, there's not so much as a sniff of relief that at least it'll finally all be over. Just more and more and *more* pure fear and dread. I want to throw up again. Reflux burns the back of my throat. I'm hypnotised by foreboding itself coursing through every last inch of my being.

There's a knock at the door.

I let them in and put the kettle on. Mum can see I'm in a state so asks Dad to make the tea. It's abut to happen. I remember this feeling from years ago – the way I felt when I came out of the closet, that I'm about to jump and don't know if I have a parachute or just a useless, empty rucksack as the ground comes hurtling up. Only this time it's even worse.

"What did you want to tell us, then?"

The words stick in my throat. I don't know where to begin. I burst into floods of tears as Mum comes and sits next to me on the bed.

"Just take your time, there's no rush."

I sob uncontrollably for a while. Then, with red eyes and quivering voice I finally lift the suffocating lid, the sunlight and fresh air flooding in as I tell them. Tell them about my intrusive thoughts.

Ground Zero

A Timely Backwater

Throughout the summer of 2002, at the age of twenty, I worked as a general dogsbody in a local rivet factory. Having borrowed from the bank of Mum and Dad to buy an old car and clear debts accumulated during my whirlwind-coming-out-of-the-closet two years earlier, I'd ploughed through several similar temp placements and finally settled, early in June, at the rivet factory. Factories were never a favourite workplace but this one was more or less agreeable. After leaving a full time call centre job, I'd tried my hand at waiting tables (the only job from which I've ever been unceremoniously dismissed) worked in a handful of plant nurseries, offices and other factories before eventually landing there. Like all others factories I'd worked in, the daily grind was so eye-wateringly boring that time seemed to slow to a near standstill. But in this position I was at least left to my own devices and, crucially, allowed the use of my walkman. With the aid of a few rusty, ancient machines, easily older than myself, my job was to sort and pack rivets in a quiet corner of the dusty, grimy old factory. It was a sad time for the permanent staff as the company was relocating to China. Many had worked there for years, even decades. By contrast, however, after a turbulent eighteen months of fruitless soul searching, my time at the factory turned out to be just what I'd needed.

…At least, it began that way…

The conveyor belt was my favourite. About the size of a single bed, this rickety old machine looked like it belonged in a wartime factory. Dented metal trays filled with rivets were loaded onto a slope at one end, and motorised vibrations slowly shook them down through a funnel onto the squeaking, grey-green conveyor belt, with its frayed edges and innumerable ancient scratches. The task at hand was simply to sit at the conveyor and pick out the damaged rivets from each batch. That was all. Sometimes I'd listen to mix tapes on my old brick walkman but often, I'd just sit and think for hours on end, picking out the faulty shards of metal while tenaciously working to remove the broken, jagged thoughts from my mind. There were so many…

Searching for Answers

Two years earlier, aged eighteen, I came out of the closet, on a whim, for all the wrong reasons. It was a disaster. Until that point, I'd been easing out, bit by bit, as I grew in confidence. My Mother and most close friends had been told, each in turn, as and when I felt ready. I'd also had an earth shattering, life-affirming spiritual epiphany about a year beforehand that enabled a gentle, steady growth in confidence and self acceptance. All things considered, it was going really well. Then I met a guy, Tom, and came bursting out of the closet in the hope it would bring us together. It did, which, it turned out, wasn't the best outcome after all. Not everyone was pleased on that day. There were some heated arguments. In the long run, everyone was okay with it, but on that particular day, I was more than a little upset and flung myself at Tom's feet. It had gone badly but I'd gotten what I wanted. I'd soon come to regret it.

Our turbulent, abusive, four month relationship had a very strange effect on me. I'd allowed Tom almost total control of my mind and identity, accumulated a few thousand pounds of debt to get up to date with what I'd thought was the appropriate 'gay' lifestyle and, when we went our separate ways, I'd lost all traces of my spirituality, along with much of my identity. I could only superficially remember what and how things had been prior to meeting Tom, but now felt somehow 'locked out' from myself, and indeed, much else in the wider world. It became hard to understand or even remember how or why I used to think and feel all the things that made me who I was; they became painfully distant, even strangely…worrying. I was filled with a constant sadness that couldn't be explained: I was now nineteen, had everything going for me – on paper, at least – but despite my sincerest efforts, I could never quite seem to get my head above water enough to reengage with the world. The earlier spiritual epiphany had swept away swathes of a deep, dark depression I'd doubted could ever be moved, and facilitated so much personal growth to boot; without its subtle, empowering glow, I found it difficult to function much at all. Spirituality had vanished without a trace; a world of wondrous joys completely evaporated, leaving a mind haunted by a fragmented and confusing reality.

I'd experienced depression before but, determined not to let it get the better of me this time, I forced myself into amateur dramatics while working to pay off my debts. Still, I found myself forever drawn into infinitesimal ruminations about why I felt such sadness and disconnection; why it was so difficult to function, and, how and why things had ended up like this. I really had no idea. What was to be to be done about it? Suck it up? Pull my socks up and stop feeling sorry for myself? That was an approach I was familiar with and had used on several prior occasions, but this time it had no effect. This depression was just so hard to live with. And, crucially, once this problem was solved, how might such a calamity be avoided in the future? Life couldn't go on in this way, with me sinking into the depths every time things went a bit pear-shaped. I felt like such a dead weight, all the time. The riddle of my mind had to be solved – properly, and for good. Ruminating on this perplexing conundrum was soon interrupting everything from watching TV to listening to music: as though nothing could be engaged with without a safe and sustainable reason – one that wouldn't lead to sinking still deeper into the mire. But answers remained elusive as, most of the time, I was just so baffled, even alarmed at how profoundly sad I *always* felt. By the time I settled at the rivet factory, although the debts were steadily shrinking, these other concerns hadn't budged. Not one inch. It took so much energy just to engage with the world. Thank God I'd finally found somewhere to earn a wage while also getting *really* stuck into the soul searching I so desperately needed to do. Get it on with it and get it over with. Once and for all.

I secured a place on a local performing arts course, starting in September, so there was something to look forward to. I simply *had* to sort myself out in time for the start of term. Somehow, that edifying spirituality must be retrieved; there was just no way to envision ever being happy again without it, much less confident or well adjusted. I simply *needed* it, to provide the strength necessary to be myself around others. Without it, I was little more than a dysfunctional mess of emotional and mental chaos, but *with* it, I could be happy and joyous once more, and actually cope with both my weird brain and the world at large. It was time to find myself again, this time for good. And so I'd beaver away in the corner of the factory each and every day, patiently and meticulously sorting rivets, thoughts and emotions.

Countdown to Closure

By late August, the epic self-recalibration was at last starting to yield results. When not sat at the conveyor belt I'd load heavy trays of rivets onto a huge, old sorting machine that shook furiously as the metal pieces danced down through its rusty innards. Taken with my usual sleeping troubles and wholesale introversion-mission, it was all quite demanding, mentally and physically. So I was popping home at lunch for a cheeky little hit of marijuana. Weed was still very much a problem – I'd been getting stoned at some point, every day, for the best part of five years, through good times and bad. Although my use was now down to a bare minimum, there was still a pinning need for that little tonic every single day. The moment a way could be found to reconnect, permanently, with my spiritual side, I was sure cannabis could be left behind, once and for all. Right now, however, wasn't the best time to stop: the process of climbing out of the vast quarry of depression *yet again* and weathering the anxiety it increasingly engendered, was deeply demanding, so, for the time being, all strength had to be directed to the task at hand. Time was running out; college was starting in just a few short weeks. I envied those people that can just switch off when they need to. My brain had no such mechanism…so it was time for one final, big push.

Having made some progress – finally allowing myself to really feel the anger over all that happened with Tom; owning up to my own role in the whole debacle and then at last forgiving both him and myself – it seemed I was finally on the right track. As cathartic as the whole process had been, however, it was nonetheless far too slow. There were still so many heavy, self-loathing thoughts rattling around inside, threatening to hijack each moment, each emotion, idea or interaction. *"I'm no good"*. *"I'm a cringe-worthy eyesore"*. *"Positive emotion is dangerously, misleading"*, and so on. I didn't even understand why they were there, being so obviously erroneous. But there they were, all the time, dragging my mind down into dysfunction. Things just couldn't go on like this. Time to push even harder. With everything I had.

Despite my weed use now at its lowest ever level, I was still nonetheless obtaining the hits in some truly disgusting ways. I no longer got stoned recreationally, as had once been the case – to take the edge off the dull thudding of depression to just chill out, listen to music or sing – no, those days were well and truly in the past. But I was still struggling to function at the factory without at least a little daily dose. Nonetheless, all illusions of cannabis as something life affirming and enjoyable had long since passed – I was an addict and I knew it. Life without it was just unbearably tense, bright and deafening, inside and out. Spliffs and bongs, too, were now a thing of the past; I hated getting *really* stoned just as much as having none whatsoever. I simply bought the smallest amount possible, (usually just five pounds' worth) and smoked a tiny dose through a pipe. It was when the supply ran out that things got really disgusting: I hated buying cannabis because I didn't really want to get stoned and waste my time, but whenever the 'need' took me, and the proverbial cupboard was bare, I took to slowly and meticulously scanning the bedroom carpet with a reading lamp. Any stray crumbs or flakes went straight into the pipe, along with any dust particles or strands of carpet thread that couldn't be fully removed. Hard, dry, tiny lumps of mud scattered on the floor can easily be mistaken for solid resin, and all too often, if I couldn't be entirely sure, they'd go in too. Along with the odd stone. You can never be sure. Having often used my keyboard as a makeshift desk on which to prepare pipes, I'd also resort to regularly taking it apart with a screwdriver in search of any micro-morsels that might've fallen through the cracks. More dust-caked specks of 'I-hope-it's-hash' into the pipe and down into my lungs. Even if I'd recently dismantled the keyboard and knew there was nothing to be found, I still took another sweep, just in case. It was pathetic. *I* was pathetic, and I knew it. The compulsion of addiction is a strange, spirit-crushing force. Despite my better judgement, will power and ongoing attempts to distract myself or find another way to relax, the irrepressible feeling of a kind of manic, all-consuming emptiness would soon become so overwhelming that I'd be bent over every nook and cranny, hot lamp in hand, looking for a few crumbs of ganja to take the edge off. On more than one occasion, I roamed the streets inspecting the discarded ends of roll-ups, sniffing them in the hope they might contain some morsels of relief. There were a million and one other things I'd rather have been doing, but without just a tiny smidgen of that slight feeling of dopey-numbness, I was just too nervous, irritable and on edge to cope with much of anything. When all else failed I took a sewing needle to the inside of the old wooden weed-pipe, scraped off the oily residue of recent pulls and wiped the sticky, brown goo onto a cigarette paper. This would then be crumpled up into a tight little ball, put back into the gauze and smoked. Paper-hits always burnt far hotter than hash or weed; I'd exhale the disgusting, papery-resin smoke with burning throat and lungs and water streaming from throbbing eyes. Why was I doing this? I hated cannabis so much.

Nonetheless, the epic soul search was at last going somewhere, if only slowly, and at least the cannabis use was down to an absolute minimum. Soon I wouldn't need it at all…if things continued to improve. That was the problem: college was inching closer by the day and still I felt so weighed down as though wearing shoes of wrought iron. I'd made progress, yes, but it wasn't nearly enough. Time was running out. Anxiety started creeping in. All the amateur dramatics I'd so far engaged with had been small, ensemble roles and bit parts; doing them had allowed the confronting of some social anxiety, which was rewarding but ridiculously hard – a full time performing arts course was sure to be even more psychologically demanding. One of the many unfortunate side effects of my relationship with Tom had been the effect of his constant jibes about my taste in music and personal style. They'd left me with a kind of singer's-block. In much the same way that a frustrated writer can sit down to work and find their mind inexplicably jammed, so it had been with singing, my greatest passion at the time. Each time I opened my mouth to sing a note, I'd clam up, physically and mentally, even when alone. I couldn't make a sound without feeling utterly disgusted and ashamed of what came out, even confused by it. Almost all of us, singers included, hate to hear our own voices played back to us, but this strange block went deeper. I gradually got over the worst of it, but the thought that a similar neurotic mental block could happen again at college was a deep source of anxiety. My mind was too fragile. Only that long lost spirituality could fully exorcise all this crap, allowing me to finally move on with life. Depression be damned.

In the final few weeks of the factory's operation, the entire shop floor was dismantled, piece by piece. Soon the worktops, stations and machinery were all gone, leaving nothing but a few isles of industrial shelving and decades' worth of dust, grime and scatterings of innumerable metal shavings. My job now was to sweep away those last few remnants. Another fitting task, given all I was trying to achieve inside. But the clock was ticking: I was ruminating *hard*. How to uncover that spiritual well again? What did I have to do? What theoretical framework might bring it back to life, for good? How could I lift myself out of this perpetual stupor of gloom, properly and completely? Every last inch of the problem had to be meticulously analysed and addressed to the Nth degree and beyond. My identity, my future, my health; all seemed irrevocably tied to the desire and need for one more life-changing epiphany. There neither time nor room for uncertainty or mistakes. Day and night I pressed ahead, utterly bloody-minded. No more waiting. It was time.

Ground Zero

Sweep. Think.

Sweep, sweep, sweep. Think, think, think. Sweep, think. Think. <u>Think</u>.

 Progress thus far had cleared enough mental debris to allow a few rejuvenating glimmers of light through. But these were as nothing when compared the blinding epiphany of a few years back, that had empowered me to see off a previous bout of depression . So I carried on sweeping and thinking; thinking and sweeping, over and over and *over* again. Shifting dust around the vast, grainy factory floor, and thoughts around the ever-shifting corridors of my mind. I became so engrossed in the process that any interruptions or attempts to engage me in conversation felt deeply annoying. A breakthrough was close, I could smell it. I had little time, stomach or energy for anything else. Get rid of this depression and back to mental health. I wasn't seeing friends. Having not purchased any cannabis for several weeks by this point, more and more nasty shit was being scraped out of and recycled through the pipe. Splinters of wood got mixed in with the little, oily paper balls – it'd been scratched out so much. I'd drive home for lunch, smoke a negligible amount of re-recycled God-knows-what-it-was-by-this-point and return to work just a *tiny* bit stoned. Given the demands now being placed on my overheating brain, a little touch of doped-up-calm was nice – it enabled clarity of thought…sort of.

Sweep, sweep, sweep. Think, think, think.

As the days rolled into one another I found myself becoming increasingly nervous, even manic. I was getting there – finally forcing heart and mind to open up to…to…What? God? Transcendence? Spirituality? Life? Nature? I could never quite recall the elegant, idiosyncratic philosophy that had underpinned it all the last time around, however much I racked my frantic brain. Conventional religion was of no use, so the old philosophy, whatever it had been, was necessary. I just couldn't quite remember it. Whatever it was, that calm, centred-buoyancy I'd missed so terribly since breaking up with Tom was at last trickling through once more: a gentle, rejuvenating return to life. There were some truly golden moments of spirit-soaring joy as, quietly elated, still sweeping the old factory floor, I looked at last on that life-affirming hue. The world was coming alive again, colours and textures returning in momentary abundance, even the air itself seemed to tingle with light. I'd *made* it: reached the other side and defeated depression once again. And yet, it was still so fleeting and ambiguous. Piercing doubts would dart in unannounced, like a swarm of frantic, ravenous bats, and I'd come crashing down in a rush of panic and despair. What if I couldn't hold on to it this time? What if it was just a biochemical trick-of-the-light that had ultimately fostered my delusional idolisation of Tom? And why must it be chased? If only it would just linger, settle and reset the emotional thermostat so life could again resume. Having caught a glimpse of what I was so desperately searching for; what I'd dreaded was lost forever, I was elated, blessed, grateful, lucky, blissful, hopeful and in turn, shocked, worried, despairing and profoundly worried.

Think. Sweep. Sweepthink. Think, think, sweep.

Whenever the feeling peaked and soon after began to trail off, a hypnotic, bewildering and all-encompassing empty-sadness flooded back in like a resilient virus. It was like falling face first into a black hole, seeing it crush life, time and light itself as the sun shrinks in the distance. This wasn't supposed to happen. It's supposed to be a breathtaking tsunami of sweet rapture, sweeping all before it. *Sweep.* Think harder. *Sweep.* Concentrate. No distractions. *Think* .Get. It. *Sweep.* RIGHT.

Before long, the dizzying highs and troubling lows are infused, at both ends, with blind panic. My insides are alive again! Now they're dead. Now elated. Scared. Excited. Terrified. Calm. Up, down, up, down, *sweepthinksweep*. A runaway train. A rattling, out-of-control-rollercoaster with dodgy safety bars. I *have* to get on top of this: shut out completely the *sweep* dangerous negative thoughts and emotions and *sweep* hold the positives in a *think* vice-like grip.

UP! Thank God! *Sweep.* I'm Alive! I MADE IT! Glowing light and sweet elation. *Swink* Then down. *think* No. No,no,no! Draining despair and hopelessness. Unacceptable. *Thweep.* Solve this by any *think* means *sweep* necessary. Nothing else matters. UP AGAIN! Rapture! Hold it. Stay with it. *Sweepsweepsweep.* There's so much at stake. Down, AGAIN!? Crash. Panic. *ThinkSweepThinkSweepThinkSweepTHINK.* Come ON! Up again; then down again. Up. It's working! Down. No!! *Thweenk. Swapweep. Think, think, sweep.* All. Day. Long. It was giving me a terrible tension headache. My nerves were starting to stretch and recoil like bungee ropes.

Soon the vast factory floor is almost clean. Everyone's treading water now, waiting for it to close down completely in a few short days. I ask for something else to do and am told to just carry on sweeping. So I do. *Sweep…*JOY*…sweep, sweep…*the breath of life*…think, sweep, thunk,* *thweep*… Despair…bang! *Swalp, thank, swank, thw1nk. Sweep.* Tenuous joy again…I'm trying desperately to *think* control my *sweep* thoughts amidst this *sWeep* bewildering, *theeP* out-of-control-rollercoaster *WeepThiNkSwe3pth* feeling, and then, out of nowhere, it happens. Unbidden, an image appears in my mind's eye. Unlike any I've ever seen. A picture of disgusting sexual abuse.

"What the *fuck* was that!?"

I nearly said it aloud. I stop dead. Stare wide-eyed at the floor. A powerful lightning bolt of pure, unadulterated shock rips with quicksilver speed through mind and body. Every conceivable alarm screaming at once. Complete and total horror. Balls to bone. Shot through with nuclear terror, sickening disgust and a foreboding so strong I could pass out. Did the whole fucking world just turn upside down? Did that really just happen? Bewildered, distraught and in utter disbelief, I try to focus on something else. It comes again. More awful sexual abuse. This time in even more harrowing detail. Oh *God.*

"What the fuck *is* that?! Get the fuck out of my head!"

It keeps returning, each time more horrifying, vivid and detailed than the last. What in the world is going on?? I don't think things like *this.* Ever. It's just not *me.* What the fuck is happening?! It comes again, abuse so clear it's literally heartbreaking. Every attempt to dismiss or ignore it fails immediately and completely. I try to focus on external things — the distant sound of a radio from across the factory; on sweeping; on the people around me. Big mistake: a terrifying burst of further images, words, thoughts and alien urges explode into my head, all in the worst imaginable context. Sexual. Violent. Sacrilegious. Abusive. Racist. Homophobic. Sexist. Murderous. The worst of the worst; the kind of things I would never, *ever* consciously choose to think about anyone or anything. Bang, bang, bang, bang, BANG, like bullets plunging into grey matter. Out of the blue, for no discernible reason at all, in my mind's eye, I'm molesting, stabbing, tearing, denigrating, poisoning, murdering, raping and destroying everyone I either look at or think about. I'm not deliberately imagining these things, they just keep tearing in, uninvited, as though my mind has suddenly and rapidly been infected by the purest evil. What. The. FUCK?! Am I awake? Is this a nightmare? I physically pinch myself as hard as I can, in the hope of shocking myself out of it. More horrendous images flood in. I'm sweating. Short of breath. Now frantically, shakily sweeping in a terrified daze, body temperature spiking, I fight to keep an aghast-look of sheer horror from my face; force it into safe nonchalance while my brain is a hellish furnace. I fight the urge to burst into tears; to run screaming for cover. I flail around for answers: a busted neuron? A demon?! Too much recycled cannabis?? A government chip in my brain?? A misaligned chakra?? The unconscious mind?!? Why would it produce something like *this*?! The more I think, the worse it gets: more and more shocking, unimaginable horrors – images, words and thoughts, each one of me harming others for no reason at all, invading my mind's eye like a plague of raging wasps. It just keeps on coming. Soon I'm manically sweeping the floor in a state of private catatonia, trembling and sweating, every hair standing up, all the while desperately trying not to pass out or vomit from the inflammable, white hot adrenaline now screaming through my veins. I struggle to stay on my feet. I grip the broom handle for balance. Pulse is racing so fast I can feel my blood's thunderous, terrible rhythm. No matter where I look, what I think or do, these vile, unbidden thoughts flood in with devastating clarity. Knives penetrating flesh, skulls crushed with metal bars, hateful words shouted with ravenous disdain. It feels like being machine-gunned through from all directions; flesh hyper-taut from poison darts of concentrated, deadly stress; brain going supernova. I glance at an older lady walking across the other side of the factory-

"Kill her!"

Oh. Fuck. My bones feel as though they're about to shatter into a million pieces as the deepest, darkest, mortal shock strikes through my entire body and mind as I realise, for the first time in my life, I'm hearing voices.

It sounded somehow like my own voice, but disembodied, angry and definitely not speaking at my cue.

"Stab him."

"Oh my God!"

This exclamation is out loud. Mercifully there's no one within earshot. Suddenly it's as if my skull has cracked open like a nutshell; something very important is dissolving…boundaries of self disappearing, and each awful intrusion is on display; seen, felt and heard by everyone on the shop floor. It feels uncannily as though other people are now somehow causing the intrusions and voices; viciously manipulating my brain by some unconscious, hateful conspiracy.

"Fuck, fuck, fuck! Stop it! Pull yourself together."

I'm ready to run at the nearest wall or else collapse right here, in a puddle of terror on the floor. My entire body is afire with deadly tension. Nerves are electrified metal rods just seconds from vaporising in their own deadly heat. Toxic stress eats away at my very bones like sulphuric acid; I feel it, sizzling away, dissolving and disfiguring my flesh, mind and soul. No pain has ever struck this deep. It's my brain. It has to be. But it keeps on happening. I grit my teeth and, terrified of the world within and without, force myself to carry on sweeping as my mind falls apart before my very eyes, horrifying and open for all to see. It takes every last ounce of strength to just keep sweeping. I'm so scared. Not for others, but for myself. I'd sooner take a blade to my own flesh than act out any one of the mortifying swarm of horrors currently raping my mind; no question of that. No, I'm terrified that somehow, rogue fragments of this mental pandemonium might burst out of my skull and 'transmit' themselves into the minds of others – not the private emotional catatonia - just enough partial detail of the intrusions and voices to suggest I'm a twisted, deadly abomination that must be destroyed. I'll be dragged away, kicking and screaming, to be horribly tortured and killed by a baying, righteous mob. The mortifying open-brain sensation gets stronger. The very walls are ablaze, and closing in. I'm in an out of control race car, hurtling full-pelt at a stash of TNT. I feel violated by the intrusions – both physically and psychologically; and now, I fear for my life.

The last two hours of the shift are a timeless hell. I'm *desperate* to leave. To run. To hide. Is it something about the factory that's causing these awful apparitions? Will it ebb away at the end of the shift as I step out into the fresh air and head home? God, I hope so. Five thirty comes. It doesn't stop. Driving home, the sickening intrusions keep coming; their subject: absolutely everyone in sight. Every single person I glance at, think about or drive past instantly triggers mortifying images and tangible feelings of bodies being crushed under my wheels, going through the windscreen and much, much more besides. There's an aura of deadly danger around everyone. I glance at a family walking along the pavement and hear the voice again; barking out another murderous order. I tell it to fuck off and die. Why is this happening? Why, why, *why*?! What does it all mean? I desperately want to tell someone what's going on, that I'm in terrible trouble, but each time I think of doing so, a time-stopping, almost hallucinogenic feeling of mortal danger is as immediate and terrifying as the intrusions and voices themselves.

I arrive home and try to relax. Maybe I'm just overtired, in need of a good nap? I step into the bathroom to wash the day's grime from my hands. More hideous intrusions. A glance in the mirror and I notice a look of repulsion and hatred in my eyes; pupils small as pinholes. It feels as if my psyche is dividing in two: one half is, for god knows what reason, generating these horrible images, phantom urges, voices and intrusions; the other, outraged and appalled that such thoughts could enter my consciousness. Each half wants to tear the other to pieces. I'm starting to despair. Mum and Dad are home and the intrusions immediately direct themselves at them. The voices are trying to surface again but somehow I manage to push them from my mind. An intense frown is riveted to my face. At dinner, they notice my distracted look, so I tell them I've just been thinking a lot at the moment, nothing serious, all the while having intrusive thoughts of sticking them both with the cutlery. What the fuck is happening to me? I want to cry, scream, yell, knock myself unconscious, anything…but I don't say a word. Just sit and eat dinner in a state of silent pandemonium.

After dinner I lie on the sofa and try to get some sleep. It's no use: closing my eyes only makes the horrors more vivid. I'm rigid with fear, dread, horror, disgust and, transcending just about everything else is a deep, profound sensation like a deadly electric current coursing to every last inch of flesh. Each time an intrusion flashes into consciousness, I open my eyes in panic, only to find another following in quick succession. Soon I'm afraid to close my eyes for fear of what I'll see, and scared to open them for the exact same reason. Although the intrusions depict me harming others in all sorts of unspeakable ways, it feels like it's actually my own mind being stabbed, burned, raped, smashed and destroyed. Those intermittent feelings of buoyancy and calm from just a few hours ago have been abruptly and categorically usurped by a mortal terror. Unsurprisingly, I'm unable to drift off to sleep. Just lay on the sofa, rapt in painful awe, heart pumping Armageddon into every corner of my being.

That night, after hours of private catatonia, I eventually start to doze off. Nothing has stopped or even slowed the torrent of intrusions. In desperation, I consider explanations I'd never normally entertain: Alien experiments? Possession by evil spirits? Has someone put a…a…*spell* on me? Even in the midst of such mental and emotional trauma, questions like these seem ridiculous, but fan the flames nonetheless; along with the unmistakable sense that I'm completely losing my grip. Fast. As I finally start to sink into the drowsy, semi-conscious, intermediate stage between wakefulness and sleep, the intrusions at last begin to fade. But the fraught emotions and inflammable stress remain. Maybe it'll all be okay in the morning? My last half-baked thought before drifting off is: What if it really is a demon?

Grasping for Control

The disembodied thought whispers again: "What if it really *is* a demon??" Right on cue, my eyes catch sight of an emaciated, purpled-skinned, wrinkled and balding male…creature…with watery, pale yellow eyes. He looks back at me, caught off guard, surprised at being discovered. He's been feeding ravenously on my insecurities for some time now – some sort of underworld, psychic parasite. His cover's blown. I'm not supposed to know he's there. Wish I didn't. A penetrating jolt of dread shoots through my body as the piercing electronic buzz of the alarm clock snaps me awake. Oh God, what is happening to me?

I turn the alarm off and cautiously attempt to think about loved ones to see if the strange, unwelcome images from yesterday return. They do. With a heartbreaking clarity and force. All day long. Thankfully, the voices don't return but the appalling, terrible pictures, words, thoughts and strange, unnerving urges to harm others show no such sign of letting up. Stabbing, tearing, stamping, snapping, slicing, assaulting, violating, absolutely everyone and everything I love, and the world beyond. People in the factory, strangers on the street, even people on the television screen. Defiant through each heart-stopping moment, emotional thermostat through the roof, I start responding to the intrusions by deliberately countering bad images with frantically-crafted visualisations of 'good things'. I counter bad thoughts with benevolent ones and upsetting words by frantically repeating their antonyms in my head. It's all is very distracting. It doesn't stop the intrusions from coming, but reacting to them in this way brings some small amount of relief. All I'm doing is sweeping so right now it doesn't matter. They *have* to be stopped, or at least put right in some way. They're so heinous. The exact opposite of how I feel in every possible way. I have an intrusion of a knife flying at someone, feel its cold steel about to plunge their delicate flesh, rupturing organs and splintering bone, so, I intercept it, just in time, by imagining a bright green, luminescent force field around the target, protecting them from harm. It seems to work. But soon the intrusion comes again, laden with yet more anxiety, terror and panic. It penetrates the force field and injures its subject, sliding into the jelly of their eyeball, so I have to quickly imagine a healing light counteracting the damage; imbuing it with all the love and care that can be summoned through this hellish storm. The next time it doesn't heal quite so well, so the knife has to be intercepted with a powerful laser. This dance goes on, ad infinitum, all day long. Racist thoughts countered by politically correct ones; lit cigarettes doused with imagined water as they reach out to burn a passing colleague in the face; awful sexual images countered by visualisations of stabbing myself, slicing off my hand or setting myself on fire. On and on and on. Each counteracting visualisation or phrase works exactly *once* and must be more innovative and dynamic than the last. They don't stop the intrusions from coming – there's a rising sense of panic about half a second before each hideous invasion – but it at least evokes a fleeting, fragile sense of control. Very fragile. Whatever's causing these intrusions isn't going to win, I know that much. I may be beside myself with shock, disgust, paranoia and despair at what's happening, but I know who I am. I'd sooner drive my car off a cliff than act on any one of these vile mental apparitions. Simple as that. So fuck off.

The hours grind on in this baffling, traumatic, earth-shattering manner. The elaborate internal responses do absolutely nothing to stop further intrusions from materialising, and I have to be constantly on guard, ready to quickly concoct the next visualisation, word or counteracting idea. I *never* imagined I could ever feel *this* shocked, afraid and utterly appalled at anything, let alone my own mind. Something else starts to emerge from the poisonous stew; something that makes the whole thing that much worse. I'm suddenly afraid for my own life in a much clearer and less abstract way than yesterday afternoon.

Thin Ice

Stanley knives sliding into eyeballs. Bones snapping. Hands where they shouldn't be. Foul, offensive words, thoughts and alien urges towards everyone and everything. On and on and on and on, like the deafening beat of a hellish drum. Nowhere to turn, no way of escaping any of it. I feel in my bones that if this problem doesn't start to ebb soon, I'm in serious trouble. The pressure-cooker intensity is so profound that I feel I might snap any moment and stick my skull with something sharp just to make it all stop. I try desperately to snap out of it, but it just keeps coming. I've no idea why this is happening to me or even what it actually is. Mind and nerves becoming worryingly unstable. Constantly mortified. I've overcome my fair share of problems in the past, often with a good dose of stoicism, but if things don't change pronto, I'm going to need professional help. This is psychiatric territory, in the extreme. Is this what happens to murderers to send them over the edge and make them start harming others? I hope not. Professional help seems very much in order, right about now.

Violence, abuse and destruction continually penetrate consciousness, every moment is psychological Armageddon, but, as I consider seeking help, a small sense of relief mingles among the constant terror and dread. It's the best option. This problem is too immense to be solved alone. I'm not superman. The thought of getting help does nothing to halt the intrusions, but nonetheless brings a touch of relief to the burning emotional chaos… like a slight, soothing balm. A balm that attracts wasps.

In an attempt to defy, even placate this swirling tempest, I try imagining myself describing this strange problem to a doctor. The thought they might get the wrong idea inevitably, irresistibly, crosses my mind. The doctor's face turns in appalled disgust. Never, in all their years of practice have they heard something so debased, vile and inhuman. Almost shaking with indignation, they reach for the phone and call the police. As the scene unfolds in my mind, a feeling of imminent mortal danger creeps in like veil of death, quickening the blood, suffocating breath, obscuring every other thought, even the vile intrusions. Time momentarily slows down. Heart beats in my throat. Every nerve and muscle screams "danger!!", "Death!!", transfixed by the visceral certainty of fight-or-flight fear.

I *need* help, can't imagine how I'll ever deal with this problem without it, but every time the perpetual horror of the intrusions pushes me to consider potential confidants, I'm immediately standing on a mile high cliff edge in gale-force winds. This feeling rapidly absorbs all consciousness and everything around shrinks to total obscurity in its presence. I'm now doubly scared: of what's going on inside and petrified of what could happen on the *outside* if this problem 'gets out' and is misunderstood, even just a little, by any one person. Someone. Anyone. One crossed wire, that's all it would take. I'm hypnotised by the scenario. The fear consumes my every cell. It's just all too toxic. People wouldn't understand. A few short days ago, if someone else had told me they were having these kinds of thoughts, how would I have reacted? I don't know. I can't imagine I'd feel very comfortable around that person. The deathly emotions are starting to hijack every waking by thought now – I'm equally scared of thinking and of not thinking. Images of faces turning in outraged repulsion soon morph into the hateful screams of angry mobs, focused in their murderous rage; my fate sealed. Not for anything I've done, but because someone might misunderstand these awful intrusions as things I *want* to do. No, as much as I desperately need help, it's just far too big a risk. I'll have to find another way. Unless I…

"Oh no. Oh God, no. What if I blush?"

Code Red

Blushing was a huge source of anxiety at college. Mixing with others my own age was uncomfortable at the best of times, but whenever the subject of homosexuality came up, even in casual conversation, my face would burn a bright red beacon of shame. It was beyond embarrassing…it felt somehow traumatic, and so I was painfully anxious around my peers, always on edge, dreading the next inevitable trigger. I was hyper-vigilant in the extreme, to the point where a strange kind of contagion began to occur. At first it was just a few words, all the usual culprits: "gay", "queer", "homo" and so on. Soon, other, semi-related terms and phrases became a problem: "happy", "man", "sexuality", "male bonding", anything that seemed even vaguely close to that one dreaded subject felt palpably dangerous. It got really out of hand and quite debilitating. But I got over it. The spiritual epiphany of three years ago kicked the problem into touch. Now, however, as I sweep the dusty old factory floor in a state of private hell, that same strange, uncontrollable fear of risky-blushing rushes back to life with a vengeance. What if I go red the next time someone talks about a murderer? Or rapist? Oh *fuck*. I wish I hadn't thought about it. I try to forget but now…that feeling of deadly risk associated with trusting someone about my intrusions is merging terribly the old fear of blushing. A radioactive combination. Code Red. My mind is swimming in vile, perverse, violent and hateful intrusions. I'm bouncing off the walls in distress. I painfully need to ask someone for help, but I'm terrified of being misunderstood and assaulted so I *have* to keep this to myself and now, thanks to this sudden resurrection or Mr Red, I know I probably can't.

My veins are a particle accelerator in which some new, deadly, incendiary element has been forged in all this chaos. Now it courses through every part of me. Corrosive, inflammable, deadly. The rabbit-in-the-headlights feeling goes up several notches – almost physically painful. My head throbs and nerves creak from the stress of it all. Oh God, why is this happening to me? Why now? Just when I was so close to solving my problems. I was up there. I'd found it again, made it to the other side. It was going to be okay.

Now, there's suddenly so much to hide; so much I need help with and no idea what on earth is going on. I'm a strong enough person but this is beyond anything I could've ever imagined. There's an awful feeling that I can't do this alone and an even worse one that doing so is the *only* safe option. There's too much at risk. What will happen if I blush at the worst possible moment? "Why is he blushing *now*, when we're talking about *that*?", "No smoke without fire." "Y'know, I always wondered about him…" What do I do then? Explain my intrusive thoughts? Some people might be compassionate, but that can't exactly be counted on. I'm fucked. Totally fucked. I'll have to keep all this hell inside and find a way to solve it alone. Be stronger than I've ever been in my life. Somehow. I'd better stop smoking weed.

Holding Pattern

College soon starts and absolutely nothing changes. Despite two weeks of abstinence from cannabis, the intrusions show no sign of letting up. I meet new people at college and continually have unwanted thoughts of stabbing them, groping them, burning their eyeballs with my cigarette, and that these horrors are being telepathically transmitted into their unsuspecting heads. The continual shock of each and every intrusion is like being stabbed in the heart a thousand times a day. I become pathologically consumed with how I'm coming across, and scorched every second by the thought of a fatal blushing incident. My heart implores me to get help, as my mind conjures up scenarios of the tortures I'll have to endure if this problem is misunderstood. I can't risk it, under any circumstances, so I perform, like I never have before. Affect a calm and collected veneer while going to pieces inside. All day, every day, wherever I am, whatever I'm doing, it doesn't stop, or ease down, even a little. I can barely think straight, so I have to enact a version of myself based on memory – on such a knife edge all the time that I have only a scant grip on reality.

The emotional and psychological turmoil of this perfect storm has a strange, worrying effect. My insides were at first redraw with the trauma of it all. Soon, rawness turns to soreness. My heart, my gut, every part of me that's capable of feeling something, anything, reels and aches a little more each day. After a couple of months, I feel my insides beginning to shut down, as though the very ability to feel isitself giving up the ghost, sinking, toughening up beyond anything natural, compounding itself in cold, dead, concrete. It's like watching myself die from the inside out. Soon, I feel very little of anything at all, save for anxiety, dread and paralysing fear.

Somehow I make it through the first term, but nothing changes. I get the feeling it's all over for me now. I can't see how I'll solve this without help and feel certain of what will happen if I do. Game over. There's a horrible fear that, as long as this problem persists, I can never again be emotionally close to another human being – never again be honest about my life or how I'm feeling. Closeness means someone might figure it out – not all of it, just enough to get the wrong idea and call the police. Every day and night I'm coldly-terrified and *deeply* ashamed of each and every single intrusion. I occasionally allow myself a little hit of cannabis with the lads at college, in the hope it might bring some relief. It doesn't.

I catch a documentary on TV over Christmas about cannabis psychosis and, although my experience doesn't quite match those described, I sit watching in silence, still as a statue. The weed has got to stop – completely and for good. Maybe things will improve if I get off it permanently? God knows I have the motivation now. I can't live the rest of my life like this scared, tired and alone all the time. All I can do is wait…and hope for the best. For all this hell, somewhere inside, I've still got oodles of strength left in me. So I'll wait it out. For as long as it takes. It feels like the real answer might be down there in the concrete somewhere, solidified in the vanishing darkness, deep, deep down, dangerous and out of reach. There is a way to get to it – a thing I *know* I have to do – but I can't. For the sake of all that's good in the world, I just can't.

The Final Rush Hour, Part II

The car glides down the gently-sloping back street that leads to the main road. The blazing brilliance of the morning sun hits me in the face. It's breathtaking. Soaring in the eastern sky, shining exquisite, golden rays down onto the town below, the sunlight glimmers on the still-wet tarmac: a shimmering strip of blinding silver. Sublime. I can *feel* it. Not just know it mentally or remember a vague, sketchy outline of how it used to feel, but actually tangibly sense its radiant beauty, right here, right now, completely unhindered. In my *heart*. I rev the engine and run over a family on the pavement. Only, I don't. The inner-concrete is gone. Shattered into a million tiny pieces, carried away on a carefree breeze. The capacity to feel has returned at long last, with a vengeance. I'm human again. But rediscovered humanity has no impact whatsoever on the usual cacophony of horrors. Intrusive thoughts and screaming paranoia still rage within; a deep, primal howling that knows a brutal end is inevitable and very, very close. Closer than it's ever been. Inches away. Inflammable danger flanks each and every moment of newly remembered joy; every last inch of regained humanity and sensation are stalked by imminent, pulsating death. But I fight none of it. I smash the windscreen with my fist and hurl a glass dagger at a passerby. No, actually, I don't. It's a weird image in my head. I'm in the eye of a sunlit storm about which I can do absolutely nothing. It's far too late to resist any of it now and, frankly, if all it really achieves is the hell of the last four and a half years, I'd rather just let the intrusions stab and the anxiety burn. And the brightness shine. Burn and shine; terrified and uplifted. Resign myself to this insane ambivalence. No more fighting, let it All. Just. Be. Even if it kills me. If I die today, at least I'm not dead *inside* anymore. Better late than never. I can at last face the music knowing the truth of who I am. Not the scathing, whispering 'truths' of the intrusions, but pure heart-and-soul clarity. I know I'm not a monster. Mum and Dad know. That's all that matters. I wouldn't turn back now even if I could…would I?

The end of the little back street borders the main road down to the river. A brief gap in the morning traffic opens up, and I pull out into a convoy of steadily-crawling commuters. I wind down a window for some fresh air and the light, spraying sound of tyres rolling over wet tarmac rushes in. We're heading downhill, towards the river. A couple of miles to go yet. As the River Severn comes into view, and my heart delights at the sight, I can't help but wish, on some level, that it hadn't come to this – that I was having only joy for breakfast, not this strange end-of-the-road platter of terror, horror *and* eleventh-hour rejuvenation. I begin to wonder…was the factory really the start of it all? There were all kinds of weird mental problems in my youth, some oddly similar to recent troubles, at least in terms of their irrational, penetrating distress, but none ever got this out of hand. Was it all just a warm up for what was to come? For what's happening now?

Something in the Shadows

Merry Christmas

Christmas time, nineteen eighty six. A four-foot plastic tree stands in the corner of the living room, resplendent with stringy-tinsel, a mishmash of home-made and shop-bought decorations and multicoloured fairy lights. Mum's homemade shoebox-nativity scene sits atop the old, wall-mounted gas fire. The cork-covered chimney breast is adorned with greeting cards and tinsel, fastened to the panelling with dressmaker pins. A leaf-shaped wicker-tray of assorted nuts sits on the carpet before the fire, a stocking either side. The air crackles with a warm, electric grow. Buoyant, tantalizing excitement. I can barely contain myself. I'm four years old. I love Christmas.

Christmas was my favourite time of year: the presents, decorations, food, the visiting of family, the story of Jesus, the festive songs, everyone exchanging pleasantries and all the great Christmas TV. Most of my earliest memories are of around this time – the sound of Band Aid's 'Do They Know It's Christmas?' over and again on the radio (released two years earlier but in heavy rotation every December since), Europe's 'The Final Countdown' and Berlin's 'Take My Breath Away'. An evening journey into town to marvel at the colourful lights; seeing Father Christmas in whatever department store he was visiting and, of course, festive cartoons: the entire season was a blissful-high.

Walking in the Air

That year, I was treated to my first ever viewing of the evocative animated tale 'The Snowman', by this time already a festive staple on British TV. I vaguely recall someone saying something like, "You'll like this, Richard" as, with a loud click, they pushed in the plastic button on the big colour TV in the living room. I nestled down next the glass screen as the picture warmed up, and was soon whisked away by beautiful moving pictures and haunting music. The boy in the story was about my age, and even wore the same coloured dressing gown. The absence of dialogue in this silent piece had a truly hypnotic effect; I was transported by the music and pictures, as though there with him: building the snowman, my nose turning red in the cold air, basking in the warmth of the house afterwards; on tender-hooks as he snuck outside in the dead of night to see the snowman and sharing in the awe as he magically came to life. Set to the beautiful 'Walking in the Air' song, their hand-in-hand flight over snow dusted towns and countryside was enthralling - the perfect Christmas adventure. The boy rushes downstairs the following morning, to bright, brisk music, a gushing smile on his face, dashing past his parents and out the back door to greet his magical friend, only to find he's melted into a pile of slush and snow, his hat, scarf and coal-buttons resting atop watery remains.

As far as I can recall, that was the first cartoon I'd seen without dialogue or, crucially, a happy ending. After such an uplifting, magical tale, the sight of that poor, sad boy finding his new friend melted into nothing, to the sound of mournful strings and piano, was *really* unsettling. I didn't cry or complain; just felt shocked, saddened, even scared, without really understanding why. After all, it was just a story. Mum would've probably offered reassurance by saying The Snowman had gone to heaven or to work for Father Christmas, or words to that effect. I shrugged it off as best I could and went on with the other, more pressing and enjoyable activities a four year old boy must attend to. Still, there was something about that strange, evocative and unsettling ending that was hard to shake…something deep…jarring…lingering.

Something in the Shadows

Sometime later – perhaps that day, week or month, I really have no idea – I found myself suddenly and inexplicably scared of the little boy and his giant snowman friend. Each time I stood or walked in an unlit area – like, for example, passing through the small, unlit hallway from the kitchen to the living room – big, bright, evocative images of the two characters filled my head. They stood, holding hands, at the foot of the garden, basking in the eerie darkness, taking *tiny,* almost imperceptible steps towards the house, to come and 'get' me. The scenario flooded in, vividly, over and over again. Whenever I found myself in shadow, even for a second, I could see it all. All except their faces – I couldn't bring myself to look on those. But I their monstrous intent was clear as day. The chilling scenario developed: the huge, towering snowman and his young accomplice trying to gain entry to the kitchen through the back door. That's what would happen if their tiny steps eventually brought them up to the house. What would they do to me once inside? Just thinking about it was horrible, even confusing, but the transfixing fear it engendered was unmistakable. There was a horrible ambiguity to what the actual outcome might be; I just knew that they were after me – precisely *because* I feared them. Fear was their food, their sustenance: breakfast, lunch and dinner. As was I. If I was able to feel calm and unaffected by this idea they'd remain stuck at the bottom of the garden, frozen to the spot, whether I was in light or shadow. Perhaps they'd lose interest and go in search of another child's terror to feed upon. But that just wasn't the case: I *was* scared. Really scared. Every single time any part of my body was in any dark space - so much as a hand or foot in the shadow of an object, even in a well lit room - I could *feel* their tiny steps slowly but surely edging toward the house. Once back in the light, if I was able to calm down enough, they'd be 'reset', back to the bottom of the garden; fixed to the spot. But still out there, waiting, one thing on their mind. So I'd run through the unlit downstairs hallway every single time. How close had they come? Halfway up the garden? They couldn't have advanced that far in so short a time…could they? Every time so much as a vague thought of them entered consciousness, I felt in terrible danger. I was diligently careful; sat as far from shadows as possible, as just looking at darkness filled me with a sense of panic. Thinking about them was so horrible, but not thinking about them was worse. It was dangerous.

Some evenings, when it wasn't so intense, it was almost a game: I could run through any dark space with a speed far superior to that of their little, shuffling steps. I was safe enough, for now. But I absolutely never deliberately set foot in darkness and *always* ran, just in case. Standing in a shadow to taunt them with my superior speed was out of the question. It all went up several gears, however, when lying in bed. The bedroom door was always propped open, light from the upstairs hallway flooding into the room. That was the bedtime rule. But the light *inside* my room wasn't on, and the bed was behind the door, in the shadows. So every night I'd lie awake, beset by a crescendo of worry. Sooner or later their tiny steps would bring them right up to the back door. They knew exactly where I was, what I was thinking and just how much I feared them. Fear fuelled their ravenous desire like a blood-scent to hounds. How close were they now? Had they made it into the house? I'd climb out of bed and walk across the landing into my parents' room to complain about "monsters in the garden". They'd reassure me and I'd return to bed, but really, I just wanted to walk through the lit upstairs landing to 'reset' my shuffling adversaries back to the foot of the garden.

Strangely, even at so young an age, I felt embarrassed to fully explain these bizarre fears to anyone. They were nonsense and I knew it. The idea that these two characters were present outside simply because I feared seemed downright odd. The ultimate fear wasn't that they definitely *were* there, but that they *might* be and so to think of and fear their presence was dangerous. If they really were out there, they'd never get through the locked back door and into the house. If, perchance, they did gain entry, screaming would soon summon my parents who would promptly deal with them. I was as safe as I could be – Mum and Dad couldn't control the darkness outside and I was okay where I was. In theory. Nonetheless, the very fact that I feared them so much fuelled a toxic mixture of emotion and imagination that would cut clean through all rationalisations, allowing the vivid, near-tangible images to flood in, unhindered. The more I feared them, the more real and powerful they might become; able to walk through walls, give my parents the slip and catch me unawares. It was somehow my fault for being so scared in the first place. Running across the hall or lying in bed was so blindingly scary; I was barely able to think. Somehow, it seemed like I'd not watched the cartoon 'properly' or come to the 'right' emotional conclusion. It was all my own stupid fault. Even back then I knew that reassurance from Mum and Dad would provide only the scantest morsel of relief – soon, a new, undiscovered corner of fear would open up and the relentless predatory shuffle of The Faceless Snowman and his little accomplice would begin anew. Tiny, *tiny*, step, step, step…step…step…step…   …step…

The Monster Café

Irrational fears of phantom threats are common in the vivid imaginations of small children. Most kids go through the Monster-Under-The-Bed-Phase at some point and outgrow it sooner or later. Not so in my case. The Snowman and his little chum were a recurring source of dread for several years. Each autumn, the nights drew in, bringing with them a deep sinking feeling; a dread so much larger than myself. I knew that soon, I'd be pathologically avoiding the shadows for months on end. As the years progressed, the slowly-shuffling-duo were joined by a host of other imagined antagonists, all derived from an ever-swelling blacklist of TV programs, films and adverts I'd found too intense. A group of salivating Gremlins, straight from the 1984 film, inhabited the small space at the foot of my cabin bed – similarly fed and sustained by human fear – ready to tear me to pieces the very second said fear reached a critical peak. A cliff-hanger ending to an episode of the soap opera 'Home & Away' had featured an old, brain damaged former headmaster listing shakily around an abandoned house. In later episodes his story panned out well, and my older sister tried to explain that he was harmless, as per his rehabilitation, but the eerie, ambiguous drama of his debut had already done the damage. I was too young to really understand his condition. The spooky montage of his shaky form ambling around a dark, abandoned house, camera shots cutting to his feet, hands and the back of his head, burned itself into my mind. He now lived in the small space between the side of my bed and the wall, but also threatened to emerge from every dark corner at any given moment. Subsequently, I went through a phase of terror at being left alone and drove the rest of the family to distraction, following them in and out of every room. This one eventually settled down as the character caused no trouble in the soap opera, but he still lived behind the bed, still a threat. Just like the Snowman and Gremlins, he knew my every thought and fed ravenously on terror. There were multiple others, too. The slightest thought of any of them, or doubt about my safety, however small, would spread in my mind like wildfire. Often it was like being completely hollowed out inside, fear consuming all other psychological functions. Checking the phantoms' hiding places provided little relief. They weren't there anyway, but they *might* be, and yours truly was too weak and pathetic to face them if they were. This was just something I somehow deserved for being scared in the first place. Should've known better. I *did* know better, but it made no difference. Countless nights, I'd wander into my parents' room in tears but their reassurances always proved fruitless. As soon as I settled back into bed, the threats were present once more, a foul and lingering stench with no discernible source. The bedroom was an open house for lingering maybe-monsters that gorged themselves on human fear, and I the only one stupid enough to feed them my delicious foreboding. There was even a phase of reading comics aloud to the ghosts and monsters I knew weren't there, just in case. My mind was such an embarrassing basket case. I was beside myself almost every night. Finally, one evening, around the age of nine, my parents got so tired of the impossible problem that I got a good, loud telling off. I got back into bed, pulled the duvet over my head, gritted my teeth and shut tight my eyes, refusing to open them under any circumstances. Eventually it worked. Each night I went to bed in this way – still very much afraid but also knowing it was best to just grit my teeth – literally - glue my eyelids shut, refuse to open them until morning under any circumstances. Eventually I'd fall asleep. By the age of around ten, the in-house ghouls and monsters had receded to join the Snowman and the little boy in garden, where they remained in resentful banishment. I was still afraid they *might* be there; that my mind's annoying tendency to conjure the worst might somehow call them, or a similar malaise into existence and into the house, if I wasn't careful. But at least the bedroom seemed a little safer now.

A Safe Distance

Away from the nocturnal unpleasantness, I was more often than not a joyful, if lonely child, forever lost in the lighter side of a fertile imagination. I often had trouble mixing with other kids; I was always the annoying hanger-on you went to for a spell when you fell out with your real friends, and then ditched upon reconciliation. I had a tendency to annoy other kids, to be hypersensitive, excitable, bossy and argumentative. I had no interest whatsoever in sports and wasn't the owner of a games console, and so was very much a spare part. But I had God. We weren't a religious family there were no regular church visits or even a bible lying around the house – a few members of the extended family were religious but the majority weren't, so there was very much a 'take it or leave it as you'd like' attitude in the immediate family. But I had my own, entirely private spiritual life that I dearly loved.

Sometimes, in morning assembly at our Church of England school, whichever teacher was leading the morning's proceedings would close by leading us in a kind of verbatim-echo-prayer wherein they'd say a line, and we'd all repeat. I rarely repeated every single word; just those that chimed with my own private sense of God. Sentences or phrases that evoked ideas of a distant, angry or brooding deity were duly ignored. Whatever they were talking about, it wasn't the God I knew and loved. God was a presence, a force; an evocative light and tangible feeling that lit up the world. It was sublime. In the darkness of the night time shadows, however, it was of little use. Then my mind would race headlong into frightful conjurations, no matter what I did. If I could relax enough to pray, things might be okay, but that was rarely the case and wasn't much help. It was an odd contrast. Bright, expansive joy illuminating the world by day; mind-bending fears of harrowing phantoms by night. I just assumed it was my own stupid fault and kept a safe distance from anything that might add to the problem.

A Little Safety

I deliberately avoided watching anything on TV or VHS that looked even remotely scary: not so much as an innocuous children's ghost story – it just wasn't worth the repercussions. After seeing Michael Jackson's Thriller for the first time at the age of eight, the ensuing freak-out meant I wouldn't watch anything described in the TV Guide as a "Thriller, starring so and so…" Dad gave endless reassurances that most thrillers contained no monsters or ghosts but, most of the time, I wouldn't even finish reading the descriptive paragraph, let alone watch the bloody thing. The same applied to 'scary' adverts. Remember those 'Scotch Head-cleaning' adverts with the dancing, bespectacled skeleton? They were a definite no-no. Even so much as a hint of sinister music and I would either change the channel or leave the room. It seemed to work. Things certainly didn't get any worse. My older sister often bemoaned the fact that we weren't allowed to watch many of the "Grown-up films" our peers' parents permitted, but I was secretly very glad of the fact. All such films would cause more night time paranoia, and there had already been more than enough of that. If I visited a friend's house and they suggested watching some or other horror flick with an eighteen certificate, I'd simply refuse, even threaten to leave. The years went slowly by and I found that as long as scary stimuli were fastidiously avoided, the problem was prevented from getting too out of hand again.

As I grew older I began tenuously trying the odd, *slightly* scary film or TV show here and there, but rarely anything with a fifteen or eighteen certificate. The comfort zone slowly, incrementally expanded, until I made the mistake of watching Stephen King's 'IT' at friend's house at the age of twelve. This one caused more than a few problems, and I was forced to revisit the practice of shutting my eyes *very* tight in bed, afraid of the weird tricks my brain would inevitably play, often not falling asleep for hours. But, gladly, the duration of these residual horrors was starting to shrink from years to months. One day, while in conversation with a few other kids in the early days of high school, the subject of 'IT' came up. A few of our group admitted to being terrified of going into the bathroom alone or to bed after seeing the film; just one person said they were unaffected. Being cautiously vague about the extent and duration of my own post-film freak-outs, I asked others how long theirs lasted. The answers ranged from a few nights to a couple of weeks. I was too embarrassed to confess that at that time, my own would usually stretch from, on average, three to six months, only to be replaced by new spectres if I wasn't careful. So that little detail I kept to myself. I really was getting too old for this sort of nonsense.

In the latter part of 1994, just barely into the second year of high school, I took on a morning paper round. I already had an evening one, but liked having my own money, and the increasing demands of burgeoning adolescence – CDs, fashionable clothes, trips to the cinema and the like – weren't cheap. My parents could afford to buy such things, but believed it better that I work for such luxuries, especially since I insisted on their necessity beyond the biannual indulgences of Christmas and birthdays. So I took on the morning round.

The evening round had already brought a little contact with a few darkened nooks and crannies, but they were few and far between, in sociable hours and usually adjacent to well lit areas. Cycling past a dark alley or driveway brought on a momentary dread as my erratic mind imbued it with all manner of otherworldly dangers. Ironically, on the odd occasion that a rough-looking drunk or intimidating older teenager emerged from the darkness, their presence was oddly reassuring – humans were far less distressing than any of the terrors my mind could concoct. The morning round, however, brought new problems and, surprisingly, new solutions.

Enough is Enough

The early morning round began in mid September, while the mornings were still light and relatively warm. The early start meant it was finally time to reign in bad bedtime habits: I had a tendency to dither over going to bed at a reasonable time, drink too much tea and consume too many snacks late in the evening. Once in bed, providing the monsters remained at bay, I'd toss and turn for hours, frustrated and bored, and *really* struggle to wake up the next morning, often half asleep throughout the school day. If I was to hold down an early morning paper round, such habits had to be broken. A strict bedtime routine was in order: a newer, healthier version of the old eyes-tight-shut method. After abstaining from tea for a few hours, avoiding late night TV and having a not-too-hot bath followed by a mug of warm milk, I'd say my prayers, climb into bed and listen to a couple of slow, soothing songs, at a minimal volume. The new routine helped a little, but still wasn't enough to calm my ever-whirring brain, so, I'd simply lie there with my eyes shut and mindfully focus on 'sleepy' thoughts, feelings and sensations, in the most single-minded way possible. It took several weeks, but I eventually became adept at gently 'concentrating' myself to sleep, nice and early. Also, drifting off while everyone else was still awake meant the maybe-monsters could, frankly, piss off.

Each morning, cycling around the idyllic suburbs, delivering the national papers, there was already a steadily growing foreboding at the back of my mind: the spectre of those dark winter mornings, looming on the horizon, engendered a sense of dread that swelled at the very thought of it. How was I going to cope? Surely mornings, however dark, wouldn't be *that* bad, would they? After all, I was thirteen now: I knew ghouls and monsters didn't exist…what was there to be scared of? The first few indigo mornings in October weren't too bad, but soon, after a few short weeks, I was outside, cycling through the cold, echoing-darkness at six thirty in the morning.

Our house was situated in a quiet crescent, on the edge of town. Along the foot of the garden ran a little brook, beyond which was a small farm. Thousands of years of water erosion had carved out a little valley along the banks of the stream, and our end of the street was close to the bottom, about twenty meters from the water's edge. An array of huge, lush trees lined the far bank which, along with the steep, sloping hill of the farm opposite, bordering the countryside, meant there was zero residual light beyond the garden. Only a vast, empty blackness where The Snowman and his little friend had first materialised. This made getting my bike out of the shed in the early morning darkness quite scary; *if* Mum was in the kitchen having breakfast. If she was still in bed, it was a blood-chilling ordeal, as all manner of dangers threatened to lunge from the darkness.

The road outside our house wound around the corner and straight up the hill, first passing a row of huge, old conifers that swallowed up the light of a solitary lamppost; their flailing, jagged fingers casting menacing shadows all around, even in the slightest of breezes. Behind them lay the brook and more empty fields. Adjacent to the conifers was a backwater of decrepit old garages, unlit and, mostly, unused. Passing this scene in the cold, blustery darkness, I'd pump the pedals *hard*, fighting to ascend the hill with as much speed as possible, trying desperately to think about something, *anything* other than the plague of phantasms my brain insisted lurked just out of sight. Those fear-hungry, predatory threats – ambiguous in definition but crystal clear in their menacing immediacy – that same old feeling of inexplicable danger, drawn ever closer by my own pathetic inadequacies. I dared not look. One or two imagined spectres followed me up the hill in hot pursuit; feeding on ripe fear. I never actually saw them, but that meant nothing. The rest of the journey to the newsagents, to collect the morning papers, was punctuated by several similar, dark corners and worrying trigger-points, but none as bad as the conifers and garages by our house.

Despite a typical, adolescent awkwardness around others, made all the worse by having recently realised my homosexuality, I was nonetheless glad to escape into the safety of the little newsagents, and stand for a moment among reassuring electric lights and the presence of the living. I'd collect the large, fluorescent shoulder-bag of neatly ordered papers and cycle another half-mile to the designated area: A picturesque, leafy, suburban idyll a little further along the brook. Here, the waters flowed through the middle of a large, sloping, open field, encircled by an estate of detached bungalows and sandy-bricked semis; the grassy verge descending down on either side to another tree-lined waterfront. By day it was a lush scene; in darkness the unlit field was swallowed up by ominous blackness. This part of the round was exactly like the conifers: scared to look; scared not to. Furtive glances down into the blackness revealed no discernible dangers, but paranoia still insisted that a lurking, sinister 'something' down there had noticed me, aroused to the hunt by my enticing fear-filled stench. If I refused to look, the horrors would skulk ever closer, palpable, poised to pounce.

As the end of the round approached, the sun struggled over the eastern horizon, turning the sky dark blue, bringing with it the welcome relief of puffy-eyed, dressing-gown-clad residents, stirring, switching on lights and opening curtains. But this salvation came later and later each day. This was getting ridiculous. I was thirteen now, for God's sake – far too old for this silliness. I *knew* it was all nonsense, but my mind just kept on finding new and innovative ways to make it all so terrifying nonetheless.

Sweet, Sweet Defiance

I'd always known, in varying degrees, that these weird phantoms existed largely in my head. Checking behind the bed or in some dark corner, I knew, even before looking, there was nothing to be found. Tricks of the mind. Age and education had brought greater lucidity than was the case back in the days of 'The Snowman' but, oddly enough, this did absolutely nothing to stop my brain from turning cartwheels in such situations, conjuring up every imaginable monster.

Fear is a strange, intoxicating, distorting broth. However: the goal of having my own money, coupled with the need to be wide awake and able to concentrate at school felt absolutely crucial; the prospect of giving up the morning round for a childish fear of phantoms was beyond ridiculous, so I decided the best thing to do was pray. As mentioned earlier, praying was never a boring chore; more a life affirming private ritual that, nonetheless, required immense effort when alone in the darkness. Being now somewhat older, wiser and perhaps a *little* less scared than the four year old boy who'd so feared 'The Snowman' and so many other monsters, it seemed some hardcore praying might at last be a possibility.

Each morning, on leaving the house, I mindfully and diligently recited my way through various generic prayers, adding a few of my own. It wasn't the frantic, fearful chanting of guilt-ridden Hail Marys or the intense supplication of pious begging; nor was it praying for protection. Just a mindful focus on those uplifting, positive thoughts and feelings I'd always associated with God, channelling them into the payers themselves, *despite* the fiend-inhabited dark corners, rather than as a nervous or reactionary chant. The latter never worked anyway. Any attempt to fight scary thoughts would always render them the worse; I knew it was all in my head, so, I worked on finding and cultivating positive, empowering thoughts and feelings, despite the alarming and downright annoying conjurations of my erratic mind. Although unaware at the time, I was essentially training myself to ignore the internal fears *and* their external triggers. It was very much a form of mindfulness, enacted solely to cope in the darkness. Continuing with the strict bedtime routine, I'd meditate myself to sleep nice and early every night and begin each day cycling around the neighbourhood, delivering the papers, all the while in mindful-prayer. Day after day, week after week, month after month. The leaves turned a crisp brown; I pedalled and prayed in the darkness. Winter winds blew the branches bare; I prayed and pedalled. Rain and snow came down, and I prayed and pedalled and pedalled and prayed and prayed and prayed. The mental-demons salivated in outrage as I defiantly refused to acknowledge them. I was hyper-focused throughout. Through autumn, into winter, over Christmas and well into the New Year. By the time spring was stretching and yawning its way onto the scene, old leaves blown away, colourful buds blooming into life, winds easing down and mornings gradually brightening, all the physical exercise, dedicated mental focus and strict night time routine had finally paid off. Something in my brain and nerves had stabilized. I no longer feared the dark. At all. There were no more spectres in the garden or ravenous phantoms lurking around dark corners. What was behind the conifers? Mud. Water. Maybe the odd fox. Nothing more. I'd done it. Spring was in the air and, at long last, I had control of my mind. The Snowman really had melted.

The Final Rush Hour, Part III

The commuter-crawl trickles along the western banks of the River Severn, slowly inching towards the bridge, and abruptly stops. Up ahead is a set of temporary lights, ushering the traffic around some road-works. I'd forgotten about them, until now.

So…a slight delay en route to Armageddon. Okay. One part of me is glad; the probably-fatal confrontation delayed just a tiny bit more. I take a moment to bask in newly-awakened senses; the delicate rippling of the Severn's gentle current, the ubiquitous radiance of morning sunlight; even the sterile glow of the red traffic light up ahead has a deep, sensual texture. Incredible. Maybe I'll be okay?

Another part of me is annoyed. Reality-bending fear still pervades everything. The air itself throngs with imminent danger. It's not going anywhere. All attempts to wait-out, or else avoid my mental troubles have done no more than foster a false hope, drawing out the whole gruelling process. But the survival instinct is as natural as breathing. Fight or flight. I know which one I prefer. Nonetheless, there's no outrunning this problem. The epic levels of resistance brought on by my own survival instincts have only delayed this inevitable day. They certainly didn't prevent the eerie and harrowing events of the past few days, as my mind finally began to collapse in on itself in an epic swirl of underworld symbols and hypnotic ciphers. The whole world fell away and I could see only the haunted realm of the unconscious. Weird shit. The Snowman and all his maybe-monster friends pale in comparison. But I *did* defeat him. All of them. I put the hours in and brought my weird brain to heel, just in time for adolescence. It was over. I could cope. Any yet, there's a sense that mindful-prayers won't help me today, just as they proved useless in the events that followed at high school. There were some real-world monsters coming down the tracks, not unlike those that probably wait with baited breath at work…

Thirteen…Unlucky for Some

Thirteen…Unlucky for Some

A typical school morning, just after eight o'clock; all morning papers delivered, all prayers mindfully recited and I'm back home, in my room, burning my scalp with Mum's hairdryer in a vain attempt straighten an unruly fringe. It's the mid-90s, long bangs are all the rage but I can never seem to get mine straight enough. The popular boys, with their trendy coats and confident swagger, all have beautifully straight hair. I don't wear a coat to school; there's a no logos policy that absolutely no one follows, but Mum insists I do. I don't want to provide anyone with any more ammunition than they already have by wearing a sensible, plain coat, so, I just wear my PE kit under my uniform to keep warm. It also means not having to expose any flesh in the changing rooms. Two birds: one stone. I'm painfully shy and hopelessly self conscious. Today we have PE, second period, so the nerves are already heating up.

The last "Bye" echoes up the stairs as Mum leaves for work – Dad and my sister left a little earlier. I reply in kind. Most other kids living a good mile from the school gates would probably have left home by now, but I can't. Can't afford to spend a second longer on that awful playground than is absolutely necessary. Also, I'm starting to enjoy these brief spells in the empty house, just before and after school. I recently realised I'm gay and decided *straight* away (pardon the pun) that my sexuality is not a subject I'll be discussing with anyone while still at school. No one. Under any circumstances. Too risky. I'm absolutely fine with this newfound discovery – Mum explained homosexuality a few years ago, in a fairly brief and balanced way, but the comments, jokes and casual homophobia are so ubiquitous that I've quickly learnt the importance of keeping a neutral façade. I've no desire to act like something I'm not and don't see that it's anyone else's business, but the stories of people being beaten up, ostracised and even hospitalised for coming out of the closet, are enough to elicit a prey-like hyper-vigilance in the presence of others. Even my family are prone to the occasional comment. Everyone is. I was before I knew myself – so, whenever in company, the mask must be worn. At all times. It's nice to have a break in the empty house and set it down for twenty minutes or so before the day of hiding begins. Besides, it's *far* too early for a safe landing on the vast, perilous plain of the high school playground.

Timing is Everything

8:20. In the living room, watching breakfast television, keeping a watchful eye on the little clock in the corner of the screen. School starts at 8:40, but it's still too early to set off. Try to focus on the TV program. Distract from the simmering worry, the utter helplessness. Interesting segment. A different presenter. God, I can't wait for the holidays.

8:21. Muscles melting into a steady quiver as the moment approaches. Stay calm. Focused. I *must* appear as indifferent as humanly possible – can't appear vulnerable or upset before, during or after the daily jibes and shoves. Deep breaths. Focus. You can do this. Look calm while feeling the exact opposite, all day long. It's quite a feat. Nerves humming with frenetic activity like an old telephone exchange. Mentally and emotionally, the bullying is a challenge to cope with. But the intense physical reactions that are on another scale. My body always seems to betray me by shaking, tensing up, or making my voice quivering and taut. Any sign of weakness invites more trouble.

8:22. A plummeting feeling creeps in. I try to focus on something Mum said one morning, when I'd been explaining the situation at school: "Don't worry about these silly kids, just get on with your education". The look of bewilderment and concern on her face was reassuring – she clearly wished there was more she could do, but just knowing she was aware of the situation and so obviously concerned was a little comforting. Getting teachers involved is a bad idea. Their interventions rarely work and tend to make the situation that much worse.

8:23. Count the seconds. 1…the first few seconds are comparatively safe…2…still a small window of…3…certainty and…4…safety before…5…time's almost…6…up. I wish I…7…could just…8…stay here…9…all day…10…in the…11… empty house…12…away from all the…13…worrying prejudice and…14…having to cope…15…on my own…16…don't think like that…17…breathe calmly and…18…get ready to…19…focus…you'll be…19.5…okay…**20**. Okay. Here we go. Frantic butterflies and wobbling limbs as I step gingerly out of the front door. Reflux flushing upwards as I retrieve the bike from the shed for the second time this morning, mount it and start cycling once again towards the war zone.

Leaving *exactly* twenty seconds after the clock hits 8:23 provides just enough time to cycle up towards school, past the newsagents where I collected the day's papers just two hours ago, stop at the library to lock my bike up, then walk at a steady pace to the school gates, crossing the threshold *just* as the bell rings. I even know the exact mid-level speed at which to cycle; a touch too fast means arriving early and standing out like a sore thumb; a touch too slow means arriving late, having to walk into the classroom while everyone else is already seated. No, thank you.

I used to lock my bike up in the bike-sheds at the top of the playground, like everybody else, but at the end of the school day, the unsupervised adolescent exodus across concreted no-man's-land was just too intense, too scary. It allowed more opportunities for hostility, for shouts, shoves, missiles, and people kicking at my heels. I hate being so bloody sensitive. For all the newfound mental prowess that melted the evil Snowman, my body nonetheless goes into a nervous-meltdown in such situations, making the all-important, nonplussed façade that much harder to maintain. I'd love to just turn around and punch any one of those obnoxious pricks but I know what'll happen; I'll shake, burst into tears and never hear the end of it. I've been told countless times by countless adults over the years to "try to be less sensitive", to accept that obnoxious behaviour is "just the way boys are" but, not for a lack of trying, I just can't seem to master it. The comments, taunts, glares and shoves, still go straight through me, like flaming arrows. I don't know why. I don't really care what any of these dickheads think of me, it's more what they can *do*, how hard they can make the school day, if they see fit. And their wolf-like predatory glee is often chilling.

I shore myself up as best I can, but the ammunition gets through, and I turn to jelly. I feel so out of place these days, especially since discovering, or rather, admitting to, my homosexuality. All mental and emotional strength must be spent on not giving anyone the pleasure of seeing how hurt, scared and alone I am. Thus, crossing the playground to the bike sheds at the end of the day became too much. Also, more often than not, I'd get to my bike and find it pulled over, the tyres let down or the chain pulled off. I tried locking it up at the sports centre just outside the school gates but enough people clearly knew it was mine as I'd often find it in a similar state, the bikes next to it untouched. Dad even fitted solid tyres after they'd been let down or slashed for the umpteenth time, but still the gears or chain were routinely interfered with. Or the spokes kicked in. Just what one needs at the end of another shitty school day, when there's still the evening papers to deliver. There's a small library that occupies an old Victorian school house just a couple of minutes walk from the school gates, that has a few inconspicuous bike ports – a safe little backwater. The staff don't seem to mind my bike being left there all day and my trusty steed, although unsheltered, is at least left alone and still in working order at the end of the school day.

Bike secured, I cross the main road, walk through an open churchyard and up the cobbled-alleyway that leads up to the sports centre car park, adjacent to the school gates. By the time I reach them and cross the threshold, there's a cold sweat on the back of my neck, my pulse picks up, breathing becomes shallow, skin prickly-taut, and the lump in my throat so bulbous it feels like I've swallowed a grenade. I brace myself as I walk through the gate and onto the playground. At this point, there's always a feeling of stepping onto a vast minefield, populated by unseen marksmen and salivating predators. Stupid, hypersensitive body. Stay calm. Don't make eye contact. The bell usually rings somewhere between this first step onto No Man's Land and the moment I reach the doors to our section of the Arts Block. Everyone has their own group, and each loiters on their respective territorial spot of dusty concrete, before the bell. Well, almost everyone. I could stand alone on the spot and look like a frightened rodent, ripe for blood-sport, or wander around by myself, fastidiously and meticulously avoiding proximity to anyone in particular, also looking and feeling like a frightened rodent, ripe for blood-sport. There are rarely any teachers outside this early, before the first bell, so it's always best to arrive at *just* the right time. I revel in a smug sense of self satisfaction at this meticulously-timed arrival, exerting a small amount of control over my school day. Once that bell rings, however, such calculated luxuries are nowhere to be seen.

Swift and Sudden Fall from Grace

For the first twenty minutes of the school day we sit in registration. Most of the class sit and chat, while Mrs Howell counts heads. It's pretty informal. Which I hate. I sit alone, second desk from the front, in the line nearest the door. Occasionally, little broken off bits of rubber or screwed up bits of paper are hurled in my direction, along with the occasional shouts of "Loner!" and "Queer!" Mrs Howell doesn't seem to notice. Try not to flinch. Sit perfectly still. Look straight ahead. Show no signs of a reaction. Given that my back's perpetually turned, the mornings when nothing's thrown or shouted are just as excruciating – I never know if the hushed whispers and giggles are about me or something else entirely. Paranoia consumes mind and body like a virus, rendering every noise, giggle, whisper, squeak of a chair leg, *everything* almost unbearably loud and dangerous.

High school started reasonably well, but then, about a third of the way into our second academic year, it all went south. There'd been some bullying problems at primary school, but an intervention by teachers and parents helped put an end to it. The bullies and I eventually became friends. Until we started high school, that is. Then they shunned me from day one. It didn't matter. We shared no classes and my older sister knew the siblings of the new popular clique. Socialising with other boys through the intensity of burgeoning hormones was tricky – not least because I still had no interest in football, computer games or porn (the latest craze) – but, towards the end of the first year, I'd made some new friends among the in-crowd, so things were going reasonably well. The only problem was, I remained as hypersensitive, excitable and literal as ever. I never really 'got' banter or sarcasm and tended to either take everything to heart or misunderstand where the unspoken 'line' was and just piss people off, more often than not. All of which soon added up to a series of crossed wires, falling-outs and a couple of fights that soon landed my social stock right at the bottom of the pile. Being estranged from the all-important popular boys, I was now little more than a fair game whipping boy for the one remaining group of lads who just about tolerated my presence. In break time they sat in the Arts Block Hall, eating snacks in a circle of chairs as I sat, quite literally, on the outside, enduring more verbal abuse by the day. I began to wonder if the problem really was me, and not the other lads. It seemed that every time I tried to befriend other boys, my attempts to impress would just alienate or annoy them. Eventually I stopped orbiting the last-ditch-group of obnoxious arseholes, and opted instead for the of dusty, red corduroy-carpeted wooden benches of the small 'Social Area' adjacent to the girls' toilets, frequented by many of the geekier girls in our year. I wasn't exactly an insider there either, but could at least have civilised conversations without being insulted too much or accidentally pissing anyone off. Girls were easier. Of course, this newfound association with them finally cemented my reputation as an outsider. I decided it best to follow Mum's advice, bury myself in my education and try not to worry too much…

Love Thy Enemies

When things first started to deteriorate at school, although upset and annoyed, with both myself and the other lads, I remained defiant. The disciplined structure of the bedtime routine and mindful morning prayers were paying dividends: my mind was now a strong ally. I wasn't exactly happy with the situation, but felt able to rise above it and just get on with life as best I could. Once I realised I was gay, however, all that began to change. I knew how bigoted and cruel people could be, how commonplace and acceptable homophobia was among teenagers and adults alike…now, I suddenly had this deeply personal, socially-toxic secret. I became jumpy and afraid more often than not. There was now *so* much more to guard against.

Isolated and scared, but determined not to let it get me down, I turned once more to my spirituality. I perused my standard-issue Gideon Bible for inspiration and came across the line "Love your enemies and pray for those that persecute you." This seemed to fit nicely with my idea of God, in-keeping with the mindful-positivity practiced each morning during the paper round. So I did. I prayed even more diligently, endeavouring each night to forgive the day's taunts, repent my own frustration, and vividly imagined a perfect love enveloping everyone at school. While the bullying didn't stop, opening up my heart so completely in this way proved an enormous source of strength, precisely when most needed. There was a wonderful side effect, too. Away from school, countless moments of deep, profound peace were gleaned from the simplest of things. Sitting in the back of the family car, gazing out at the world rushing by with barely a thought in mind, I was often filled with a gently-glowing elation I could never quite explain. Riding through the fresh, spring air in the tantalising quiet of the early morning was similarly ecstatic. Even something as simple as getting lost in a film or listening to music was a profound, unspeakable delight; this sense of openheartedness and ubiquitous love filled life outside of school with an edifying-fullness so wonderful, warm and uplifting. At school, I was still very much on edge, but this new, deeper level of spiritual strength invigorated and shored me up, for a time at least.

But something soon changed…As I sit through another endless, uncomfortable registration period, my skin is uncomfortably hot and prickly, as usual. The more I try to look, think and act calm and unaffected, the more I quietly panic. I frantically read the posters on the wall, over and over again, in an attempt to distract and calm myself but, having already done so a hundred times each morning for several months now, the effect proves less distracting and more like a flailing, futile ritual. Escape into sweet daydreams would help if only they didn't render me that much more startled whenever one of the small missiles connects and, naturally, my uneasy jolts amuse and further encourage the gunners. I've tried resorting to the steadfast, mindful prayers practiced in bed and on the paper round, but, in *this* environment…it's difficult…too difficult…tooficult…difftooficult…to, to, two, too, 2, totototopotatotototo…to concentrate, to *c-o-n-c-e-n-t-r-a-t-e* much on anything, ANYTHING thinganything, least of all something so deeply private and personal as my spirituality. Anxiety just boils over like a slowly erupting volcano. Also, I can't quite seem to muster enough love right here and now, in the thick of it, to rise above, to calm down. Emotions and paranoia are running far too high today, so instead, I try to distract myself as best I can by strategising the day ahead. Who can I sit by in Science? What's the best route and time to cross the playground after Maths? Will I have to hide in the toilets again? Some lessons are harder than others, depending on the demographic. Maths, Science and French are bearable; English, DT and Geography, less so. PE is absolute torture. Today is a PE day – second period after Geography. The bell finally rings for the end of registration. I don't know which is more uncomfortable; sitting here for twenty excruciating minutes with nothing to do, or sitting in Geography, struggling to concentrate on the lesson, while shitting myself about PE. The bell rings and the rabble rise from their desks. I try to avoid being noticed as we filter through the classroom door, into the danger zone of the hallway, and sheepishly approach the girls I sit with in Geography. Won't be long now.

The steadily-boiling dread at the thought of another PE lesson – boys only, and usually run by a single teacher, either unaware of, or else uninterested in, the realpolitik of his class – usually begins to rear its ugly head on a Sunday evening. At this point, I know there's a whole day of other lessons, paper rounds and an early night before being thrown to the lions, so the feeling is unpleasant but mercifully distant. Manageable. But it's *there*: a quietly-congealing toxic soup in the stomach; a coppery taste in the mouth, and a quivering of the nerves…all slowly gathering pace, whatever else I may be doing. A whistling-kettle, slowly simmering on a hob that can't be switched off. As the hours pass and the anxiety builds, I savour each and every non-PE-moment. However bad I feel, at least I'm not *in* PE right now. But, by the end of Geography, my ability to concentrate has all but gone, there's a medieval mace in my throat, its spikes interfering with breath. Thoughts race out of control and I try not to shake. Steady my face and voice. My jaw goes tight. Saliva dries up. Everything inside quickens – blood cascades through veins; nerves an overheating mess of smoking wires. It's like this. Every. Single. Week. More than once I've felt a powerful desire to just jump out of the window and run. It's an almost reassuring sensation. I don't want the attention or for anyone to come after me or try to help in any way, I just need to get far away from this place. Fast. I imagine the intoxicating, cathartic taste of fresh air and the daring of sudden liberation. But I can't do it. I'd get caught, and brought back with an even greater air of weirdness than already attends me. The bell rings, cruelly sounding the end of the lesson. It's so loud. It's shrill, pulsating rhythm pierces to the bone. I get up from my desk and walk as if on a threadbare tightrope towards the classroom door, down the steps, and along the hallway towards the changing rooms. Feet so unsteady beneath me I feel like a drunken jellyfish.

About an hour and a half later, following the morning break, I'm sat with the girls in a quiet corner of our English class, still reeling from PE. Nothing particularly bad happened. It rarely does. Nonetheless, I still feel like I've just stepped from a 500 MPH downhill train. Something is very wrong. Either with me, the situation, or both. Somewhere along the line, school stopped being an unpleasant experience and became an unbearable one. These days there's an alarming jolt within me every time a door opens; a shudder at every noise, shot through with the paranoia of hunted-prey, and every time a teacher leaves the room, I go into a private state of blind panic. It's all beginning to look like something beyond my ability to cope. That steely-mindfulness that helped melt The Snowman once and for all is nowhere to be found at school, and I've no idea why. It would be damn useful, that's for sure, but the threats here are that much more alarming than any spectres or phantoms ever were. Something about this place has the ability to short circuit everything else, to reduce my consciousness to an unintelligible mess of fear, white noise and all-consuming anxiety. It probably has something to do with that one music lesson when Mrs Curfey was off sick...

Thirteen...Unlucky for Some

The strange thing about my memory of that particular music lesson is the way in which any attempt to recall it is so unmistakably messy. I have quite a good memory; can usually pin down most events the exact month, with an impressive amount of detail to boot. *This* memory, however, is so saturated with such intense, confusing emotion that it exists like some bizarre, unfinished surrealist painting. All attempts to excavate it from such distorted depths are incredibly difficult. I know it was a sunny day, but can't pin it down to spring, summer or autumn...it was either Year Eight or Nine on the school calendar...It would've been a Wednesday because Music was always on Wednesdays, year in, year out...but I can't link it to much else. All I know is, it was a sunny afternoon on a fairly typical day...and I was thirteen...

Paper round. Prayers. Polished shoes and studious learning. Getting on with my education. Loving my enemies. Avoiding them as much as humanly possible. Rise above it all. Today is music, fourth period, just before lunch; usually quite anarchic in terms of behaviour but Mrs Curfey manages to keep a loose lid on things and I don't have to sit near anyone too obnoxious. Just get through it as best I can, like any other day. My parents sometimes try to reassure me with reminders that there're "only a couple of years left". They mean well, but to me, it feels like an unimaginably long prison sentence stretching out across endless shitty days.

The Music Block was an archetypal backwater. The huge, modernist Arts Block building had a long wing of language classrooms. One side faced the vast, chaotic playground; the other, was a rarely used path, right on the edge of school grounds. The path led away from a quiet corner of the playground to a small, little-used field near the main road. It quite literally led from nowhere special to somewhere utterly unimportant. Sitting in any of the language classrooms along the ground floor of the Arts Block, the only time you ever saw anyone traversing this route was if they were arriving late, running up to the main entrance, or traipsing lazily over its middle to the Music Block for their once-weekly lesson. Across the backwater path, up a short ramp, the music building itself looked out of place: a two-storey, flat-roofed structure no bigger than a detached suburban house; bricks and mortar covered in dark planks of painted-brown wood that probably saw a fresh coat sometime in the seventies. White paint cracked and peeled from the single glazed window frames. Hidden away beneath a row of indifferent conifers, in this tiny, irrelevant corner of school grounds, dwarfed by the mighty Arts Block with its innumerable high windows, was the pitiful, dust-encased music department. The two teachers that inhabited this glorified shed make up the entire staff. Downstairs are two classrooms, and no one really knows, or cares what's upstairs. Broken instruments? Stacks of old sheet music that are more dust than paper? An undiscovered Shakespearean sonnet could be hiding up there, and that's where it'd stay, forever, under the lock-and-key of school-wide indifference to the building it inhabited. Suffice to say, music lessons aren't taken very seriously.

I hide myself amongst the girls as we shuffle up the ramp and into the hallway outside the classroom. I cross my fingers, wishing Mrs Curfey is in a bad mood today; this will make for a more disciplined, less rowdy and, crucially, safer lesson.

She's late. No adult-in-charge awaits us as we stand outside the classroom, about twenty five of us squashed into the tiny, musty, faded-magnolia hallway. A small, enclosed space without windows or adult supervision – my absolute *favourite*. Seeing their opportunity, different groups of boys begin to focus attention on Yours Truly. Many of them don't usually associate with one another; their varying social status being so disparate. But today, my presence is bringing them together, uniting in gleeful disdain. Some whisper to each other while fixing me with smirking eyes; others attempt impressions, others openly taunt. I try to ignore it. The charge is led by Adrian Watson, the 'hardest' kid in our year. Shaved head, a sleazy demeanour and a penchant for rarely keeping his hands to himself, Adrian makes many people's skin crawl. But he's good friends with every member of the popular crowd and, it's said, he'll get into a fight with absolutely anyone, even adults, as even if he loses, he has a large family of hard-nuts who'll settle the score. Not someone you mess with.

The girls with whom I associate don't join in with the taunts, but don't exactly take my side either, save for the occasional, half-hearted, cautious, "Leave him alone". They let me tag along most days, but have no desire to rock the fragile social-boat, so I'm basically alone in such situations. I try my level-best to rise above the tirade and wear a look of indifference, but I feel trapped, exposed, scared. At least half of the lads joining in don't bother me in the slightest, but we all know what Adrian Watson is capable of. Hopefully Mrs Curfcy will arrive soon.

She's clearly not coming today as, after about ten minutes, Mr Farron – the school's only IT teacher – rocks up with an annoyed look on his face. Farron is regarded by most with even more hilarity and contempt than the music teachers; a stuttering, twitchy, bespectacled little man in his late forties, with an anarchic swirl of thinning, greying hair; he commands about as much respect from teenagers as a senile librarian. As the adolescent mass pours noisily into the empty classroom, we discover the tables have been rearranged. Not the usual four, straight rows facing the piano that sits in the far corner by the window, the blackboard to the left of the class; no, today, someone's had the bright idea of arranging them in the shape of an inverse, capital 'E' – one long line facing the blackboard with two, shorter, perpendicular lines at each end and one in the middle. The piano hasn't been moved, but looks now like more of an afterthought, adjacent to this new arrangement, not the lectern-like centrepiece that it usually is. Farron's opinion of musical education is instantly clear, as he sits himself down behind the piano, completely out of sight and says nothing for the next ten minutes.

We're usually expected to sit in our designated spots but, with Curfey missing, the tables rearranged and Farron hiding away, seating is suddenly a free-for-all. The girls I normally sit with find a spot in the far corner, next to the piano, leaving no extra space or chairs for their usual hanger-on to slot into. Soon the only seat available is smack-bang in the middle of the long line, facing the middle prong of the 'E'. Right on the edge of where the rest of the boys have seated themselves. My so-called allies are on the other side of the room and I'm sitting right next to Adrian Watson. Great.

Ten uncomfortable minutes later, Farron stands up and asks, "Do you know what you're supposed to be doing for this lesson?" His question is met with a unanimous chorus of dry, sarcastic affirmations: "Oh yeah, Sir, she told us last week", "Yeah, we know what we're doing, Sir, don't worry" and so on. Every answer is unmistakably tongue-in-cheek, but twitching Farron seems satisfied and sits back down behind the piano (presumably to do some paperwork, read a book or just twiddle his stubby thumbs). Out of sight, and, in his utter indifference, out of mind. This is going to be a long hour. PE with desks and chairs. Hopefully the Pack to my left will distract itself with something, or someone else. A few minutes pass and it's soon clear that, today, that's not going to be the case. Some excited whispering, murmuring and sniggering, and soon the first wave of questions comes, with Adrian as the mouthpiece:

"Why aren't you sat with your girly mates, Rich? Don't they like you?"

I don't respond.

"Why d'you hang around with the girls? Is it 'cuz you're gay?"

The interrogation comes down the line, initially from the two popular boys with whom I was briefly friends in year seven. Adrian turns to his left for material, then back to me for delivery. I hear most of it being muttered in his ear before it's officially and publicly said, which serves only to ferment a mixture of dread and annoyance. They begin with the subject of my sexuality, which, by now, I'm used to:

"Does your Mom know you're a bender?"

"D'you fancy Steve?"

"Have you ever bummed a bloke? Do you bum your Dad? Does he bum you?"

And so on…and so on…and so on, ad nauseam. Tap, tap, tap…drip, drip, drip. If this went on for any great length of time it'd surely wear me down. But it won't. It's just one lesson. One shitty hour. I'll be okay.

Most questions I don't dignify with a response. I'd normally just bury my attention in the work, try to appear as nondescript as possible and wait for the lesson to end. The problem today is, there's no work to speak of and I'm sat right next to the very dickheads I strive so fastidiously to avoid. Still, as unpleasant as this is, it's really just the same old jibes and insults, just in closer-than-usual proximity. They seem to have more impact this close-up, though; less space and time for me to work with, to focus, to ignore. Oh well. Suck it up. Take it on the chin. Time marshal all the powers of epic concentration I've honed so well during the morning paper round. I ignored the Snowman and his ravenous entourage; this is no different. Ignore them long enough, they'll get bored, stop and move on to some other amusement. What else can be done? You don't stand up to Adrian Watson: I heard talk of him having fourteen brothers and sisters, every one as tough as him, and a father who used to beat him before he moved in with his Mum. I've only been in a couple of fights in high school and could handle myself well enough, but the problem was always that I always ended up walking away as I simply didn't care enough about winning. I lacked the adversarial grit necessary to see it through to the end; I'd find myself thinking: why am I doing this? What is this proving? I could be at home watching TV. I'm just not a fighter. So I'm not scared of most of the popular boys individually, but they've closed ranks before, and Adrian is another matter entirely. Single-minded focus on ignoring these morons is the only way to go.

But the line of assault takes a sudden detour and, sensing things beginning to deteriorate, I feel compelled to respond:

"D'you wanna fight Simon after school?"

"No."

"Why not?"

"'Cause I don't."

"What about Martin?"

"Nope."

"Chris? You should fight Chris."

"No, thanks."

"Well he wants a fight with you. He's gonna start on you. You'll have to fight him or you'll just get beat up."

More murmuring from down the line…

"If you don't fight one of them, then they'll all start on ya at once and you'll get yer head kicked in. So who's is gonna be, Rich?"

I sigh and shake my head in disbelief. This has gone beyond obnoxious insults now. I'm being threatened. What's going to happen to me after school? All of them, together? A double bind I can't escape? And all for their amusement. What a bunch of sad dickheads. I'll forgive and love my enemies tonight when I say my prayers but, right now, I want to punch every single one of them.

The crowd now warming up, others chime in. People I rarely even look at seem to want to join the fun:

"He won't fight anyone – he's a right pussy. Just beat him up anyway."

"He always runs away. You'll have to corner him. I'll help you."
"Me too."

Adrian again, "Do you wanna fight me?"

"No."

"I'll beat you up if you don't fight Simon."

"I'm not doing it."

"I'll have to beat you up, then."

"Still not doing it."

I know they're just out to wind me up, to plant ideas in my head to scare me shitless but, the problem is, it's working. And trying to appear calm, unaffected and indifferent while actually scared, angry and upset is exhausting. I get the feeling I'm not doing it very well. My face is probably a picture of anger and distress. This is what they want. Just don't bite. I dig deeper for as much mental resolve as humanly possible. I *have* to ride this out. Seeing I won't take the bait, the subject returns to my sexuality:

"Have you ever fingered a girl?"

"Nah, he's queer. Everyone knows he is."

"Are you? Are you a queer, Rich?"

"No."

I can feel my body tensing up now. Head starting to throb.

"Have you got a boyfriend?"

Through gritted teeth: "No."

 "Can I be your boyfriend?"

"No."

I close my eyes, sigh and shake my head again. I'm so tense and angry now, there's just no chance or appearing calm or indifferent. But I *have* to keep a lid on things, somehow, so I stop answering, as the probing, loaded questions continue. What the *fuck* is Farron doing behind that piano? Why can't he just run *some* kind of class and put an end to this torture? Stupid fucking excuse for a teacher.

More people join in, including some nearby girls. The group of geeky girls in which I normally hide myself remain on the other side of the room, chatting, joking, laughing – having a great time and apparently oblivious to the occasional weary glances I shoot in their direction, looking for an escape. Kara, another hanger-on, like me, is sat nearby and, seeing her opportunity to impress the boys, chimes in:

"He loves Michael Jackson. He's got loads of posters of him all over his wall."

Kara's never been to my house. Another girl nearby reprimands her but it's too late now. It's open season.

"Do you like little boys, Rich? Like Michael Jackson?"

"No."

"Nah, he's more like Michael Barrymore."

There are lads I knew at primary school, we've not spoken with years; now even they join in. I don't like where this is going…beyond their usual 'fun' and mutating into something altogether more callous. I'm *really* starting to get pissed off, ready to lash out. That must be what they want – for me to explode at Adrian so he can kick the shit out of me for the afternoon's entertainment. Even more join in. It's spreading around the room now, a contagion. Comments, jokes, impressions, coming from everywhere like a game of dodge-ball. My female 'allies' also join in from across the room, thinking we're just having a joke about Michael Jackson. So now it's almost everyone. I'm close to snapping. I'm not going to lash out at anyone but I've definitely had enough. This is turning into a really, *really* shit day. It's going to take a lot to forgive my enemies in prayer tonight. Bastards. I wish I knew what time it was – how much longer I've got to put up with this shit. I consider getting up and just walking out. I've done it in the past and am inches from it now. Farron probably wouldn't even notice. But no, that's a bad idea. It'd only create more material for future taunts. I *have* to ride this out. Besides, the anger is actually marshalling my powers of concentration now. Watch me ignore these fuckers until they all disappear.

I'm reaching within, refocusing my mind anew when I feel something beneath the table touching the side of my leg. It's Adrian's hand. How pathetic. What's he going to do? Tickle me? Dickhead. No. No, he's not doing that. His hand starts to creep across the top of my leg. A jolt of tension shoots through me, head to toe, and I push his hand away. It creeps quickly back, finds my genitals, jiggles them around. I'm suddenly shot through with an onslaught thunderbolts: embarrassment, shock, fear, rage, shame, exposure, desperation, all tear through every muscle and bone in a microsecond. Aghast, in utter disbelief, I push his hand back once more.

"Fuck off."

"Don't tell me to fuck off. I'll kick yer 'ead in."

The hand comes back yet again. I push it away. He pushes it back, this time with more force; now he knows where he's going. He's molesting me. I can't quite believe this is happening – now there are a thousand deadly thunderbolts of emotion, colliding, crashing, coalescing into something else…something I don't understand…can't describe…something dark and infinite in its…its…I don't know. I'm frozen

Down the line, the two lads that began this circus with Adrian realise what's happening, and start to giggle with delight. Others catch on and grin with gleeful gratification. Still others just stare at me, stony faced. I keep pushing his hand away. It keeps returning and touching my penis and testicles. I'm on fire inside. Half of me is a volcano, ready to erupt and burn to a crisp Adrian and everyone else around me. The other half is paralysed: chained to the floor with the suffocating, wrought-iron bonds of immeasurable, unspeakable shock and awe. This second half is far stronger, and wins the battle. Or does it?

As I stare at the blackboard, my genitals still being accosted; mind and body frozen in shame and disbelief, something else emerges. Something beyond scary. A swelling tide of certainty momentarily bursts through everything else I'm experiencing, sweeping all before it, consuming every thought, sensation and emotion. It's beyond anger or rage. For a second I'm entirely consumed with pure, violent force. I'm ready to pick Adrian up by the throat, smash his head hard against the desk, throw him through the window, jump out after him, land on his skull and stamp on it until there's nothing left. A force within me has arisen and I'm ready to kill him, to destroy every last inch. I am death itself, about to consume. It's so unmistakably clear, so powerful and deadly, I briefly forget where I am or what's going on and recoil in horror. It's the scariest thing I've encountered and it's going inside *me*. Terrified, I shudder at this murderous rage, refuse to engage it and consciousness returns to the room. Adrian carries on.

He puts on a 'girly' voice and asks again if I want to be his boyfriend. I ignore him. Some other girls nearby ask what's going on:

"Richard, is he touching your privates?"

My stomach whirls like a rattling tumble dryer. I feel sick. I'm sweating, dizzy, my skin drum-tight and crawling all over; every muscle hard as wood, nerves a blazing hellish inferno of rage, shame and disgust. Eyes raw with held-back tears. Everything around is bright, vivid, a million miles away and simultaneously painfully, dangerously close. My insides, emotions and mind now belong to Adrian, his gleeful audience and this infinite, awful moment. I have no agency. Utterly in their hands. Literally. Disgustingly. Something about this moment is scorching me...my entire psyche...my mind itself. I manage a slight nod. This small, open acknowledgement of what's happing makes it worse…it adds to the shame, to a sense of personal failure. He does it again, just as one of the girls calls Farron. How far is this going to go? I can't believe what's happening. I can barely speak or move. I'm a statue, cast in stone, baking in the heat as the birds shit on me. Head and heart are thundering with a thousand emotions. My gut is a swirling, bubbling swamp of pure poison. I have to get out of this room.

A blasé "Just a second…" comes from behind the piano.

One of the girls gets up and goes over to Farron. Finally, he stands up and looks in our direction.

"What's happening, Richard?"

He's asking *me*?? Why is he asking *me*!? Why not that bastard Adrian? I don't know what to say. Now every pair of eyes in the class is on me. Why have I got to say it? It's horrendous that it's even happening, now I've got to *announce* it!? My voice breaks and quivers as I force the words out through the shame, disbelief and a tension-fastened jaw:

"He's feeling me."

The class erupts in riotous laughter. My face burns bright red. Farron twitches, blinks rapidly and raises his bushy eyebrows in comic incredulity.

"I *beg* your pardon?"

My mouth's dry. No, it's watery, ready for vomit. No, I'm going to pass out. No, I want to but can't. I'm cold and hot and dead and raging inside and I want to run and wish I'd never woken up this morning. I force the words out again:

"He's feeling me."

Another chorus of rapturous laughter explodes as my face again glows like a red sun. I'm angry beyond words, desperate, humiliated, scared and utterly bewildered. A piece of meat for the baying, ravenous pack. I can't believe this is happening – not just that it's okay for me to be repeatedly molested like this, but that it's actually, apparently, hilariously funny. Like something out of a Carry On film. 'Carry On Being A Bunch Of Inhuman Fucking Arseholes'. Farron pulls an annoyed face and half-heartedly mutters:

"Stop it, Adrian."

He sits back down behind the piano.

Excited whispers of "Do it again!" come down the line, leading to more molestations, but a warning from the girls nearby puts a stop to it. Instead, Adrian takes out his pen and starts drawing on my shirt-sleeve. More laughter and praise for the master of ceremonies. More taunts and pointed questions. I've completely stopped talking or responding; now using everything I've got to stop myself from bursting into tears. I can't. Believe. This. Is. Happening. I'm a toy; a rag-doll to be pulled apart like cotton wool. At least he's stopped interfering with me. Now he draws on my face. Again, I push his hand away but, clearly enjoying himself, he comes back for more. Nuclear explosions of toxic rage, desperate self-loathing and shame collide within me. I'm almost out of my body. Why am I letting him do this? I want to grab that pen and stick it in his smug face, then go over Farron and knock him out. But fear of playing into Adrian's disgusting hands checks that impulse with fiery terror. Enough is enough. I'm leaving. I don't care anymore. I stand up, and some of the boys let out an excited "Oooooooh!" as if there's about to be a fight. Adrian stays in his seat – he actually looks taken aback, even scared. Has he pushed me too far? I hesitate for a moment. Stare at him. The scary, violent rage is safely at arm's length now, burning me instead of him. I have to get out of this room.

Farron notices I've stood up:

"Where are you going, Richard?"

"To the toilet."

Surprised, a little indignant: "You haven't asked permission."

"I'm going to wash my face. Adrian's drawn on it."

Everyone can see what's going on and yet once again I have to explain my abuse to this pathetic excuse for a teacher. He gives a slow, disappointed, disapproving nod and tells me not to be long, before returning to his seat behind the piano. I walk behind the row of lads and along towards the classroom door, in a haze of bewilderment and shame.

Tipping Point

The music room door closes behind me with a loud, harsh click. Its sound echoes and reverberates through the dusty indifference of the empty hallway. I pause for a moment, close my eyes, release a long sigh, shake my head. I should be relieved to be out of there, but there are now too many feelings to identify a single one. Outside, the sun beats down, baking the greyed-tarmac of the path to the Arts Block. I can't believe that just happened. I consider walking off site. My bag's still in the class, but who cares? I push the main entrance door, step into the fresh air and try to ignore the surging adrenaline and nausea. I descend the ramp to the main path in a strange trance. Shock. Reeling. The burning sensation of a scalding hob or light bulb…skin throbbing as fingers snatched away. My whole body…my mind too. Soul-incinerating stress. Something deep inside has numbed as, blinking in the sunlight, I cross the path, fighting back tears, shame and an overwhelming urge to smash the entire school to pieces, brick by brick. And, of course, still striving to appear calm for fear of being seen in such a state and attracting even more ridicule.

I reach the wooden door to the Arts Block building, despondently pull it open and enter. No one in sight. I'm in a different building to them, for now; I should feel just a tiny bit safer. I don't. These are the micro-moments of momentary solitude in which I can let the mask slip, take a break of a few seconds from this horrible, soul-destroying game, and just be myself. Just like those twenty minutes before school when everyone else has left…only more like twenty seconds. And my guard can never drop too far: you never know who's about to come around the corner. But these little moments help clear my head, momentarily…get me through the day. But not today. The tempestuous aftershock of what just happened is still ricocheting within, obscuring all other thought and feeling in a swirling firestorm of rage, disgust, terror and abject shame.

I trudge along the long corridor toward the toilets at the end. I don't have the strength to muster any kind of speed. I'm not deliberately stalling – who wants to return to more loaded, bigoted questions about what I was doing in the toilets – but I just can't go any faster. Fuck Farron. He's probably forgotten I've even left the room. Still no one out here. I glance in through the windows of classroom doors as I pass: some buzz with activity as teachers stand at the front, engaging their students; others sit at their desks while the class work in silence. I feel even more removed from all this now than ever before. I can't believe what just happened, but then, why am I surprised? I don't want to be in this place anymore. I've had so much more than enough. I'm going to have to go back in there and rouse what little strength I have left to keep a lid on things and get through the rest of the lesson. I'm still so angry, so shocked. At what happened and how much I wanted to kill Adrian. I can feel the harm that keeping this nightmare to myself is doing; that it's burning some important part of my psyche, but there's nothing to be done. I can't risk confiding in *anyone* about my sexuality, lest every subsequent encounter turns into a re-enactment of what just happened. I'll just have to suck it up and sort this internal mess out when I finally leave this shithole.

I pass a few rows of disused, dented, pale-grey lockers near the end of the unfeasibly long corridor and enter the boy's toilets. No one in here either, thank god. Yes, thank *god*, so much that I get to be alone in this moment when all I really want is to break down in the arms of someone who cares and won't judge me for my sexuality or sensitivity. But there's no one. Thank you, *god*. You're suck a fucking help. Such a source of edifying love and strength and…you can fuck off. Mustn't think like that. God is all I have to lean on. I wander in through the smell of stale tobacco smoke and humid-piss, past the old, green stalls, their doors covered in scratchy graffiti, arrive at the hand basins. I can't believe that just happened. I'm going to have to dig really, *really* deep tonight to forgive this one; rise above all the hatred and cruel bigotry, somehow get past the rage, despair and shame to find some way to love my…my…I can't believe I'm expected to go back in there for more abuse. Why does it have to be this way? Why are people so *vile*. And why should I give a shit about anything, if this is the end result? No, no, *no*. If I think that way I'll never get any peace of mind. I have the rest of the school day to get through, and the evening paper round to do. I run the tap and inspect my face in the mirror. The blue ink still scrawled on my left cheek, vandalised like the toilet doors reflected behind me. I glimpse a look of disappointment and hatred in my eyes – with the school and the students, yes, but also with *myself*. Why didn't I just unleash? Punch his face in? He was touching my fucking privates. Why does this kind of shit happen to me? Why can't I be more like the other boys and not so meek and socially backward? As I wash the ink from my face, I try to plunge my spirituality for the strength to love Adrian and his audience, if only as a means to empower and console myself and rise above. I can't do it. Especially as I have to go back in there and, frankly, I'm sick of it. Forgive it all, wipe the slate clean, ready for the next round of abuse. Yeah, great. God be praised. The spiritual-fullness that shores me up is *not* on the menu today. Instead, the trickling, splashing sound of the running tap reverberates around the empty toilets, illuminating just how cold and lonely this situation really is. I can't help thinking it. I say my prayers, go to bed early, get up at six, deliver umpteen papers, do all homework on time, polish my shoes and even read ahead in the textbooks. Get on with my education. Focus. Forgive. I try for all I'm worth to love my enemies and *this* happens?? I've been trying my best not to notice a worrying, sneaking suspicion at the back of my mind for some time now…the now obvious intuition that I just *can't* quite manage to be as loving and forgiving as these circumstances demand. Today it's stopped being a suspicion. It's a truth. Fuck this shit. I'm sick of this crappy school, these vile kids and useless teachers; sick of being good all the time; sick of being gay, of being different; sick of being young and stuck in this shithole; sick of god's passive benevolence and definitely, completely sick of my meek, awkward, pathetic little self. I don't know how much longer I can cope with this.

I dab my stupid face dry with toilet paper, wander out into the corridor and drag myself back towards the music block, a shuffle to the gallows. What'll happen next? Will they have done something to my bag? Put something on my chair? Who knows? I exit the Arts Block, cross the backwater path, walk back up the ramp, take a deep breath, force what just happened to the back of my mind and push the classroom door. Here we go again. Don the mask yet again. Hide the fear, anger, resentment and bewilderment from my face, whatever it takes. I go in and sit down. The class seems quieter. No one says anything to me and nothing else happens. I spend the remainder of the lesson staring at the wall. Afterwards, few of the girls ask about what happened. I don't want to discuss it. Or think about it. It was horrible, but it's over now. That's all that matters. I don't want to risk drawing any more attention to my sexuality by discussing any aspect of what transpired in that classroom. I cycle home at lunchtime in a distracted, despondent trance, still reeling. The anger, disbelief, shame, and all the rest still swirls away beneath the surface, but since there's not a lot that can be done with it, I decide it best to just try not to think about it and get on with the day. Forget about it. They're arseholes. I always thought so and today just confirms it. One day I won't ever have to be around any of them ever again. By the end of the school day I'm cold, numb and tired. It's easier to manage, doesn't require masking, forgiveness or any great feats of concentration. It's a strange relief.

The "ADHD" Days

Bursting Out

Fourth period, just before lunch, on a warm July afternoon. I loiter alone outside Mrs Brown's chemistry class, my tie loosened, shirt un-tucked, sleeves rolled up; a stereotypically dishevelled teenager. I lean nervously, impatiently, against a wall at the far end of the long, dusty, first floor corridor of The Science Block. It's an old, 1930s building — a relic of the days of gender segregation, with ridiculously high ceilings and single-paned windows, long corridors and a row of thick, cold, brown tiles where the wall meets the hard, scuffed floor. Housing just two subjects — maths and science — this old building is older and indeed, much quieter than the bustling Arts Block. With no one else in sight, the echoing-silence of the corridor is deafening — a stark contrast to the storm of exciting, electrified emotion dancing through my every cell. A jittering, erratic, sugary-rush fills me from head to toe; giddy excitement and restlessness. On the other side of the classroom door, the lesson continues in my absence. I've been sent out of class as punishment for disruptive behaviour.

Stupefying anxiety around other male peers remains very much a problem. I'm as guarded and on edge as ever I was; the glowing coals of ubiquitous bigotry & obnoxiousness in that particular fire remain in plentiful supply. As we crawl wearily through the final few weeks of Year Nine, however, the bright beacon of the summer holidays finally in sight, something has changed. I don't pray very much anymore, or have much 'love' for enemies; I've stopped polishing my shoes every Sunday night, going to bed early and burying my head in textbooks. I've given up all but one of the four paper rounds I had and have almost completely lost interest in *every* aspect of school. I hate it here as much as ever but, in recent months, I've finally stopped *caring*. I still enjoy learning, very much, but in *this* environment? Meh. Throughout the troubles here and at primary school, I was repeatedly told by adults to "grow a thicker skin" and "learn to be less sensitive". Is this what they had in mind? I've no tolerance for this place anymore. None. What. So. Ever. If it burned to the ground overnight I'd be truly elated. I might even do a little dance on the still-warm ashes. That's how thick my skin is now: a tough, dense hide, made of alternating, leathery-layers of indifference and contempt for everything in this place. Except, of course, for the other lads. Whenever they're together, which they invariably are, they're still able to rouse a blinding fear, on a daily basis.

Glancing through the small window of the classroom door, in among a collage of bored faces, I notice Lauren Powell lift her head. She clocks me peering in, smirking, and tries to suppress a laugh. Not the usual, unpleasant, mocking laughter of mean spirited mind games, no, Lauren is actually laughing *with* me. It feels exciting, weird…a giddy, scary intoxication. It makes a change from the usual, nerve-wrecking fear.

The real animosity was always with the boys. I've been anxious around absolutely everyone over the last few years, but there was never really any particular ill-feeling with the girls. I get girls. I have an older sister. She and her friends used to babysit me on a Friday night when Mum and Dad went out. They liked my chattiness and sense of humour, and I theirs. I don't fancy girls at all, so their presence doesn't set the hormones racing or brain into a nervous nose dive. Recently, while caring less and less about most things, I've been gaining a little in confidence and occasionally chatting with girls beyond the usual group that tolerates my presence.

Mrs Brown had reprimanded Lauren for talking and laughing too much in class. She then briefly left the room and Lauren was quite vocal in her dislike for "that stupid old cow". Lauren is easily one of the most popular girls in our year, but, as we both attended the same primary school, we've been at least acquainted since before either of us could write our names. I'm fine around the popular girls these days and hate this place as much as everyone else *and* I'm finding this lesson torturously boring, so I begin to make fun of Mrs Brown's speech impediment. Today, we've been learning about *"Bwomine"* and *"Borwon"*, so there's plenty of material to play with.

Lauren *loves* it, as do her entire clique. Their joyous laughter, the uplifting sound of resoundingly positive approval, is like a shaft of light opening up in a long-darkened dungeon, an intoxicating rush of crisp, fresh air flooding in. Brownie returns soon enough, and I worry the show is over, but repressed snickers abound. The life-giving oxygen still flows, the shaft still illuminates the stale dungeon dust. Soon it's time to break off into groups for practical lab-tasks. The fresh air and light were wonderful, even invigorating, if only for a moment. Now the fun's over.

The prospect of having to find others charitable or desperate enough to partner up with a loser like me has become a form of ritual torture. Sticking out like a sore thumb always feels very, well, sore. I hate having to work in groups, with all the skin-crawling social awkwardness it entails. Not today. Today the usual group that permit me to lurk on their periphery are suddenly quite keen to have me on side. We settle down to work but, but each time Mrs *Bwown* mentions *"Bwomine"*, *"Borwon"* or the *"Bunsen Bwurners"*, Lauren and her friends shoot amused looks in my direction. I feel strange. Something reactive stirs in my gut, thousands of tiny, heated bubbles race to the surface, whispering, *"You can break out of this. You know how. Now's your chance. You might not get another!"* I'm suddenly impossibly restless, uneasy about what's going on inside me. The usual, worrisome-guardedness and preoccupation with what's going on around me is mixing with something else. Giddy, tingling excitement escalates by the second, skyrocketing, flooding my head with a drunken, sugary, adrenaline-glaze that mingles with, the usual, fish-out-of-water feeling. There's foreboding, too. I know what I'm doing, what I'm about to do, is wrong. Mrs Brown is a perfectly nice human being, just trying to get through another day at work. She doesn't deserve ridicule or disruptive behaviour. This incendiary cocktail makes the task of settling down to work akin to doing origami on a rollercoaster. I imagine. I don't know. Can't think straight. I've been injected with the amphetamine-rush of positive interaction. Breathing is fast. Feet and fingers drum out restless, erratic rhythms. Jitteriness abounds. I need some more of that oxygen. More light.

Concentrating means keeping my head down and being the same old loser; I do it because it has to be done; because it's the only way to at least try and ride out this weird, cruel world of high school I can never quite fathom. Now, suddenly, unexpectedly, there's an alternative. Lauren laughed *with* me, not *at* me. As did her friends. For a few ecstatic seconds I didn't feel like a walking abomination, my thoughts briefly distracted from the daily war. I felt...like...something else. Some of the other lads who so often leer with gleeful contempt in my direction had actually looked taken aback by my entertaining of the popular girls, even jealous. There might be a way to change it all. I'm always, *always* afraid in this place; each and every day is a feat on endurance. A constant feeling of an intense, invisible, deadly pressure on every inch of skin, a sense that danger could come at me at any moment, from any direction; muscles forever taut and primed, head always pounding. Is there now a chance to change things? It's a stupid idea, but maybe just a small, controlled amount of mischief could do the trick? Let in just a little more of that oxygen and light? Keep the momentum going just a little more, without things getting out of hand? These thoughts race through my mind at breakneck speed. The dizzy-elation, restlessness, excitement, dread and confusion dance around mind and body. A festival of ambivalence. Concentration has evaporated. I'm possessed by the intensity. I have to do *something*. My parents' usual attempts at reassurance echo in my mind: "You only got two years left." I try to focus on it to calm myself down. Instead the clarity of the prison sentence spurs me on. Two more years. *Two*. I've got to do it. I *have* to. Burst out of this terrifying dungeon, breathe the fresh air and bask in the light of…of…whatever the alternative to all this shit may be.

Brownie's back is turned. Her yellow-rinse, perm-mullet wobbles furiously amidst a cloud of chalk dust as she frantically scrawls important information on the blackboard. I really should be paying attention to this, but I can't. I want to. I can't.

We're using plastic syringes to measure liquids. I avail myself of an empty one, walk quietly over to the nearest sink and fill it with water.

This is a terrible idea. I don't want to do it. But even the slightest possibility things could change…god, I hate it here.

Two more years. Two more years of feeling like an outcast-whipping-boy-freak in this place. Two more years of daily intimidation and unchecked homophobia. I can't take it anymore. I might not have to. Something tantalizing is pulling me on, an irresistible magnet.

I take a detour on my way back to my seat, and empty the syringe into Lauren's face. She shrieks with laughter. More cracks in the dungeon walls. Brilliant light bursts though. Brownie turns around and shoots a stern scowl at Lauren:

"Lauren, why is your hair wet?!"

"Um… I had an accident. Sorry, Miss!"

A disapproving nod at both of us, an annoyed sigh and she returns turns to her frenetic blackboard-scribbles. Repressed giggles abound. A jet of water from an unseen assailant suddenly connects with my face. Friendly fire. It's working! Oh my god, it's actually *working*!

A clandestine water fight begins. Syringes spray water in every direction – faces, clothes, bags, work, displays on the wall, all caught in the crossfire, all heightening the hilarity. More aghast looks from the boys. Stone and dust crumble and fall from the dungeon roof as the brilliant light of connection floods in. I'm high. Giddy with freedom. The prospect of settling down to work is now out of the question. Two more years. I hate this place. I'm scared of what the other boys can do. I hate the way their scathing looks, digs, shoves and mocking laughter can tear me to shreds – make me feel I'm something that belongs in the sewer. But right now, for once, I actually feel someway normal. *We're* having fun. We. Us. Plural. I'm participating *in* something. Something *fun*! My head is a million dazzling fireworks of joy – erupting with erratic, anarchic excitement. I'm almost out of my mind. Water shoots across the room with less and less stealth. The dungeon roof opens up into a gaping, skyward hole. The sunlight blazes in. The chains are loose. The sound of pressurised water splattering against the back wall, and the sight of me frantically wiping it with my shirt sleeve were the last straw for Mrs Brown. I was sent outside. Buzzing. As though a silent-yet-rapturous applause had followed me out.

I look away from the door window. Don't want to get Lauren into any more trouble. I'm overwhelmed with elation and liberty while also nervous, shocked and deeply embarrassed. What on earth just came over me? This is the end of Year Nine. In a few months time our all-important GCSEs begin apace. This is no time to be dicking about. My future's at stake, for goodness sake. Whatever happened to embracing that empowering and unconditional love? To being defiantly good and rising above it all? I feel guilty. Such an idiot. But the insane rush of liberation at having broken, however briefly, from the impossible, crushing weight of social exile is powerful, intense…and frightening. I've been here before…

When in Danger, When in Doubt, Run in Circles, Scream and Shout

Back in primary school, I'd experienced some bullying along similar lines. Attempts to join in with other boys by playfully interrupting their football games had backfired: their annoyed response soon escalated into full-blown, daily taunting. I became the daily, lunch break game. I was hypersensitive, took *everything* to heart and in tears on a daily basis. It all came to a head the day I attempted to walk off site in floods of tears, aged nine, after an unsympathetic teacher asked the class: "What shall we do with him?" to which the ringleader gleefully replied: "Make him lose all his morning and lunch breaks for the rest of the year." Miss Ashton just looked at me and nodded in contemptuous disbelief – in much the same exasperated, disinterested way Farron had done in that awful music lesson. So I walked out, but was intercepted by different, more humane member of staff.

Mum and Dad got involved and, with the help of concerned adults, the situation was resolved. I hadn't made the connection between kicking their football away, their annoyance and subsequent prolonged hostility. The boys had taken it too far, for sure, but I was told that the real root of the problem was that I was "too sensitive". Happily, my adversaries and I eventually became friends.

When I was finally invited into the inner circle, outside of school hours, I was happy, ablaze with excitement and constantly on guard. As usual, I had no interest in 'boy' things like football or Wrestlemania and didn't own a games console. I was into Thunderbirds and little else, and was never much good at feigning interests to curry favour, however much I'd have liked to. As ever, I struggled to 'get' their world. There seemed almost no common ground. I could never quite grasp the way they communicated with each other much of the time either. I understood the words they'd use, but always felt as though I was listening to dialogue from another culture. But I *had* to keep them on side. Stay in their good books. I found myself constantly in the clutches of a nagging worry that at any given moment, my 'strange' behaviour, sensitivity and annoying sense of 'otherness' could land me once again on the outside, regarded with contempt and ripe for ridicule. I knew I was still too sensitive to cope with another bout of bullying, so the swirling storms of nervous energy were channelled into making them laugh. Make fun of myself. My interests. Authority figures. People they didn't like. Anything. It worked insofar as getting me into their good books, but as soon as the laughter died down, the visceral fears of being outcast and unable to cope, immediately flooded back in, bright and loud as ever. In those moments it was as though I could almost literally feel myself standing back on the playground, crying in a corner as a hoard of hostile boys came running over, chanting fresh taunts. Keeping that scenario at bay felt like skating nervously around the edge of a black hole. I could feel the gravity of it pulling on me at all times. I could get sucked in and crushed at any moment.

Thus the laughter I garnered with my frantically assembled jokes and impressions was a fast-acting drug. Elation, release and momentary peace at the sound of their delighted roars and giggles, a brief sense of safety and ease, soon followed by a crushing emptiness, mania and alarm as the insecurities crept back in. I was in their good books *while* they were laughing, I knew that much, but what about when they *weren't*. Sooner or later I'd put my foot in it or get left behind in some way. So I worked harder and harder at making them laugh. The more it worked; the higher the stakes seemed to be; the more inventive I had to be to keep coming up with material. Improvise. Push the envelope. Keep them laughing and the danger at bay. That was all that mattered.

The feeling that this was an all-too-fragile peace never really went away. Jokes and impersonations escalated to ill-conceived stunts and disruptive behaviour in class, resulting in being ejected from lessons almost daily. It seemed underneath it all, I was still that scared, tearful little boy, the dangers of a heightened sensitivity barely concealed beneath a woefully thin veil of affected 'bad' behaviour. I just *knew* that if the mask should slip, that sensitivity I could neither change nor control would invite more gleeful hostility. Burn my hard-won, tenuous position in a heartbeat. Underneath the comedy and bravado, there was just something about me that seemed to invite hostility. So I just had to stay in the boys' good books, for the sake of my own sanity. The attention and apparent kudos brought on by my strategic clowning engendered a chaotic mix of hyper-exhilaration and inward anarchy I didn't much like. I knew all the obnoxious behaviour wasn't really 'me', but any attempts by well-meaning adults to reprimand or coax me back to good behaviour felt like an inhumane conspiracy to snatch away a hard-won, thin-ice sense of safety.

Standing outside the classroom door, sucking up my punishment, alone in the corridor, I felt like a complete idiot. I hated myself for behaving this way and, much of the time, didn't even understand why I was doing it. All I knew was how on edge I felt around the other boys and that, as had been pronounced by literally every adult, my natural sensitivity wasn't an option. So I kept getting into trouble. In the end, though, it was all for nothing, as during the last few weeks of primary school, the bullying resumed. Perhaps I was a liability that couldn't be tolerated into the high-stakes world of high school. My bad behaviour stopped overnight.

A New Strategy

So, as I stand outside Chemistry, awaiting Mrs Brown's pleasure, the shit-storm of extreme ambivalence is somewhat familiar. High-octane emotions: elation, joy, excitement and relief; deep foreboding that I haven't done enough and will soon be back in the dungeon;

bewilderment, guilt and downright shame at the way I've acted. And now, all this laced with the transfixing hormones of adolescence, this incendiary cocktail is far, *far* stronger than it ever was in primary school. Mind-bending. Almost blinding. I can barely stand. I'm scared of it, and of my ability to act like an obnoxious little bastard when intoxicated with the hope of currying favour with peers. But still nowhere near as frightened as I am in this place, every single day. Two. More Years.

Conversation and kudos followed the idiotic behaviour in Mrs Brown's class – a brief and welcome hiatus from my status as the hanger-on, always trying to hide among the geeky girls. Such moments of sudden social change were like stepping from an Antarctic midnight storm straight onto a sun-baked paradise beach. A few more similar incidents brought more of the same, among the popular girls at least. They began singing my praises among one another, welcoming me into the fold in a way that was totally unexpected and quite touching. I still couldn't interact with *any* of the boys – popular or otherwise – many of whom appeared irritated by my newfound status among the girls. Nonetheless, for the first time in <u>several</u> years, I was waking up in the morning and actually looking forward to going to school; the downside being, I soon had almost no tolerance for the old strategy of keeping my head down and hoping to be left alone. It rarely worked and I felt constantly exposed: hyper-aware of every single facial expression and physical posture – every muscle and position from eyebrows to fingers – and my voice; everything that might come across as 'gay' or vulnerable in any way had to be micromanaged with military focus and constant acting. Even then it didn't guarantee safety. The last few years of school were like being a poorly prepared secret agent, abandoned behind enemy lines. Enough was enough. And then some. Time for a change.

The final school bell of Year Nine soon rang out and the holidays were at last upon us. That summer a truly clichéd adolescent transformation ensued. All the popular boys at school were dyeing their hair blond, so mine went black. I started listening to hip hop CDs with 'Explicit Lyrics' warning stickers on the cover. I took up smoking. Truly the stupidest thing I've ever done. I returned in September with an affected bad attitude and a master plan: to deliberately play the obnoxious-bad-boy-clown for a few short weeks – just long enough to well and truly burn my old social status and hopefully cement a new, safer, less isolated place among the perilous social schemes. That was how the whole horrible situation at school would be turned around. Then straight back to work. As sick as I was of that awful place, my education still mattered.

The "ADHD" Days

And so it began: smoking in the bushes at break time; back-chatting teachers with everything from clever arguments and funny quips to shouting and swearing; random outbursts of clownish behaviour, playing truant and much, much more besides.

Misbehaving and *not* getting caught was one of those magical skills other people seemed to possess. It ingratiated me with the popular female clique, but I never knew quite when or how to stop and was *always* the one who got caught…

Mrs Taylor, our history teacher and form tutor, was a bright and pleasant, if somewhat prudish older woman whom I'd always respected. Unlike other teachers, she made the entire class stand every time the Headmaster, or any similarly prestigious member of staff, entered the room. She was strict but engaging; her history-tangents, whether on or off topic, were always fascinating, informative and wise. She spoke with a crisp, high-pitched, public school accent, not unlike those old wartime BBC voiceovers. By comical contrast, however, she sang along to hymns during morning assemblies with one of the lowest voices ever to issue forth from a human being. Her angry "How DARE you" admonitions were also similarly deep and booming.

She was running late for our history lesson one morning, when in the absence of anything to do, the subject of her voice came up, so I began performing a few impressions, both of her high-pitched, Queen-like conversational tones and her glass-shaking low range. They were an instant hit. Lucy, my new best friend at the time, and one of the most popular girls in school, literally fell off her chair in fits of laughter. So I went over to Mrs Taylor's desk, donned her cardigan, glasses and handbag and developed the act further, to great fanfare. It was at that precise moment she walked in, demanding an explanation. Still wearing her effects, her bag in my hand, I managed the unconvincing reply:

"Um…I was looking for a rubber, miss. Someone threw it over here."

Caught red handed. I was immediately kicked out of her form group and moved to a lower history set.

The hourly music session prior to year ten had been mandatory, but the GCSE Music course was optional. This affected the demographic of the class enormously; while the frivolous atmosphere remained, folk like Adrian Watson were elsewhere. In GCSE PE.

During one slow-starting lesson, Lucy and I were messing around while waiting for Mrs Ranger, the school's other music teacher, to pull her finger out and start the class. Lucy stole a few items from my pencil case and threw them across the room, so I grabbed her entire pencil case and did the same, without first zipping it shut. She then threw my book, so I lobbed her bag, and so on. Next, she started to advance on my position from across the table, so I gathered my coat up into a ball, tucked it into the hood and pulled tight the strings to make a kind of cushion-on-a-string. As I swung it around in anticipation of the onslaught, another teacher emerged from the storage cupboard just behind where I was sat. I didn't see what happened; just suddenly felt the coat stop swinging. I was told that the second she emerged, the cushion-coat-weapon hit her full pelt, square in the face, wrapped twice around her arm and promptly bounced off once of her breasts. The whole time, I remained sat in my chair, facing the other way, completely unaware of what had happened and, crucially, still holding onto the strings.

"You stupid boy!! What are you doing!?"

Wide-eyed, strings still in hand, I slowly turned my head to find a comically-enraged middle aged teacher glowering at me. She ordered me out of the room as I half-heartedly apologised while trying to repress a smirk. The girls were laughing helplessly. I'd done it again.

All too often, it was the laughter that was the problem. Their belly-laughs had a strange effect; the sense of lingering danger remained, but the sound of joyful shrieks at a latest stunt elicited a sense of relief and momentary safety, a brief second with my head above the water, before sinking again as the laughter died down. The moments before any given joke or ill-advised act were a discombobulating melange of emptiness and panic; those immediately afterwards comprised a sense of bewilderment and annoyance at my antics, a sinking fear that it wasn't going to be enough and, of course, the rapid return of that gripping danger. It was a toxic mix. High school alliances were tenuous at the best of times, so I had to keep coming up with new material. I routinely took things too far, spurred on by a gleeful audience. Getting caught was never the plan, but at least the kudos of being 'bad' would help create further distance from my frail, rabbit-like former self. Or true self. After a while, though, many of the girls came to expect the bad behaviour, even encourage it, as though my purpose was simply to alleviate adolescent boredom. The antics themselves did nothing whatsoever to stave off hostility from other boys, quite the opposite in fact, so disappointing my audience was a risk I wasn't prepared to take. The girls often stood up for me, which was wholly embarrassing, but better, indeed safer, than the previous situation. Standing up to the boys wasn't going to work, and the adults on site couldn't or wouldn't keep me safe, so the act simply *had* to continue.

Increasingly, I felt I had no control over this monster I'd created. Why was I doing this? This was my education, for God's sake. I'd worked *so* hard up to this point. Why throw it all away? Certainly, nobody *made* me behave like an idiot. I felt like an absolute dickhead much of the time, deeply ashamed at what was so obviously terrible behaviour. Attempts to return, as planned, to academic devotion after a few short weeks were always hindered by a profound unease; a hazy, dizzying and chilling flashback to how things used to be, with the panicked thought: "I can't go back to that!" ringing out like a police siren. Returning to a life where I dreaded to turn the corner of every corridor, when just walking across the playground was a dangerous foray into No Man's Land. And I, a sitting duck, waiting helplessly to be picked off. I could barely bring myself to think of it, and yet the sense of it pushed itself into my mind with every single attempt at sitting down to work, behaving and getting back on track.

My school work deteriorated rapidly. Detentions and letters home became almost as frequent as weather forecasts. Each was worn, outwardly, like a badge of honour, but experienced inwardly with a quiet sense of despair at just how much I was throwing away. Sabotaging myself to the Nth degree. But I couldn't go back. At least now I had allies.

My changed status among the girls invited even more hostility and ridicule from certain boys. I'd managed to gain friends and now, new enemies. A handful grew more hostile than ever. Lads who'd barely noticed me before. Many of them fancied the pants off of Lucy and often seemed incensed at how close we now were. The more vulnerable I felt, the more of an idiot I was in class, just to keep the allies I had on side, and those manic worries at bay.

Concerned teachers tried a number of interventions. The heads of Science and English both sat me down individually, for a chat about why I'd fallen so spectacularly from grace. I was frequently hauled into the office of Mr Williamson, our new head of year, who'd shout a repertoire of choice lines:

"There's nothing special about you, boyo! I've seen a hundred lads like you before - that think they're above it all and they're ALL wrong! You're not going off the rails on my watch!"

And my own personal favourite:

"It's your prerogative, lad! I still get paid at the end of the month whether you pull your socks up or not. It's your education, not mine!"

This one always baffled me. I often felt like saying: "Well, if it's all the same to you, then, I'll just piss off home." But I never did. By this point he was usually red with rage and growling like a wolf.

He later changed tact and became chattier, even friendly, using the odd bit of teenage slang. Still fairly young himself, he seemed to have a desire to be 'down with the kids'. It was somewhat endearing. I enjoyed our little chats, in his broom-cupboard office under the stairs, in a quiet corner of the Arts Block, but they didn't make the slightest difference to my behaviour. I felt bad for him; for all the teachers I so routinely pissed off. I knew I didn't want to be in that school and knew exactly why, but *that* wasn't something that could be discussed with anyone under any circumstances. There wasn't a great deal they could say or do to change that. I was just clinging onto what little safety I had.

After countless letters home, detentions and ticking-offs in his office, Mr Williamson eventually decided I was on drugs. After all, my parents weren't divorced or poor, so what possible reason could there be for all the bad behaviour? I must just be a lower middle class brat on narcotics. In his history lessons, he'd often attempt to joke with me in front of the class:

"So, Rich, have you been popping pills at lunchtime?"

"Have I what?"

"Been popping pills? Dropping tabs? You go home for lunch, don't you?"

"Yes."

"So what have you been up to?"

"I had my lunch."

Friends had to explain such turns of phrase to me. I had no idea what he was talking about. On one occasion, while being escorted across the playground following a latest misdemeanour, one wet and windy morning, while nursing a sore throat, he 'caught' me taking a throat lozenge and demanded to see the packet. Yes, it really was a Strepsil. A gateway lozenge. I wasn't on drugs.

As the chaotic months of Year Ten rolled on, several ill-fated attempts were made to reset the situation, knuckle down to work and put it all behind me. But I was finding it increasingly harder than ever to settle down to anything at all. As we'd sit in lessons, in relative quiet, everyone else getting on with their work, I find myself increasingly anxious, restless, even paranoid; gripped by a blinding cocktail of dread and panic that I was on borrowed time; that at any moment it would all go south again. Something would happen. It felt horrifyingly inevitable. Whispers could start, gathering fiendish pace like scurrying rodents. Those nerve-melting knowing looks would return; harbingers of impending disaster. Faces would turn in joyous contempt as, once again, I'd have done something to unwittingly oust myself. Or maybe people would get bored and see through the act; see the pathetic, scared little queer beneath the façade and cast me out yet again. I didn't know if my new allies really liked me or just enjoyed the stupid antics. I could still be pretty socially clueless much of the time. Everything always seemed to be hanging by the thinnest of threads. I could feel it…the slightest push…one foot wrong, and…*snap*.

I tried to ignore it and focus on school work in hope of catching up, but just sitting there, trying to read and write now brought on a profound fatigue and weariness, topped off with a dull headache. Back in those outcast days, my academic achievements had been among the highest in our entire year-group, but now…this jittering brain of mine was glazing over, refusing to play ball, wanting nothing whatsoever to do with anything even vaguely associated with those horrible, dangerous days. The exact same thing would happen when trying to catch up with schoolwork at home. The old tensions of late primary school were back with a vengeance: barter, beg, steal or borrow to fit in with others in the hope of keeping the social schemes on side, or concentrate on work. It seemed impossible to do both. Socialising was always so offbeat, so unpredictable and took so much energy. Settling down to work, behaving and just being my sensitive self always attracted the wolves. Consciously, I knew what mattered: schoolwork, my future. But something primal inside knew there was much, *much* more at stake.

This Can't Continue

As Year Ten drew on, the summer break fast approaching, almost a year since that seminal water-fight in the chemistry lab, relations with teachers, my parents and the other boys continued to deteriorate. The fresh air of liberation had turned decidedly stale. Fighting to control my bewildering emotions and behaviour while navigating the social jungle was an uphill struggle so, some days, it seemed the only way to stay out of trouble was to just stay out of school altogether.

Truancy was, for the most part, painfully boring. A handful of arbitrary days off with friends had been planned, even fun, but, most of the time, each day would begin with the intention of going into school and at least trying to make it all work. I'd cycle past idiots shouting homophobic abuse for the umpteenth time, remember that I'd neglected to do my homework yet again, all the while feeling increasingly alienated from the world at large by the worrisome burden of my secret sexuality. Tired, overwhelmed, and ever more socially awkward, certain I was going to mess up again, I'd double back. I was still getting on the wrong side of the other lads, and now the teachers too. There was so much missed work to catch up on. I just wasn't in the mood to be shoulder-barged and taunted left, right and centre, all the while acting like a dick and pretending not to care. Sod it. I could write my own sick notes easily enough. So I'd cycle to meet the girls at our usual pre-school smoking-rendezvous behind the library, and then ride away again.

Mr Williamson and others probably thought I was off living it up, taking drugs and having oodles of tearaway fun; in fact most of those truant days were spent sitting alone on the field at the end of our road. Mum was working part time, so I could pop into the house for a few hours now and then, but it was always safest on the field. There was a six foot high bush, down by the quiet, babbling backwaters of the old brook. It was largely hollow inside, with a two foot high entrance-tunnel carved out by other of its patrons. Squatting right down, waddling like a duck, it was easy enough to get inside. Once there, you were hidden from the world in a quiet, litter-strewn den of mud and ivy. During the summer months it was bearable: those unplanned flights from obligation usually meant there was nothing to read or no music to listen to so I'd just sit there and smoke, bored out of my mind. But at least I was calm and not pissing anyone off. Sometimes I'd walk the suburban backstreets or sit on the swings at the racecourse, but most of the time I just sat in the bush by the brook. At least I wasn't on edge, in the presence of obnoxious arseholes, or getting into trouble. Whenever in school, I was ever more disruptive, rude to teachers who tried to keep me in line and utterly disillusioned both with myself and the whole sorry mess. Clown-like behaviour had now descended into resentful disruption. I felt left behind and was envious, even resentful of those who could have a social life *and* concentrate at the same time. And I hated myself for the whole messed up debacle. If only I wasn't gay…or at least not so meek, none of these problems would exist. When the summer holidays at last arrived, I couldn't have been more relieved.

Year Eleven, in those days the final year of mandatory education, began as badly as Year Ten had ended. Less than a fortnight after school started up again, I was suspended for the first time ever, for singing and talking during a mock exam and pulling old bits of plaster from the wall of one of the decrepit old music classrooms. Upon return, I was put on report and made to sign a Behaviour Contract in the sobering officialdom of the headmaster's office. Things were getting a little too real.

During the suspension, Mum and Dad removed the TV from the living room and all but the basic foodstuffs from the kitchen. Temporary exclusion from school was *not* going to be a holiday. It was incredibly boring. Bad behaviour when at school was now being punished by placing me in isolation, which meant spending the entire school day in an office in the presence of any available member of staff - also mind-bendingly tedious. Sitting on a plastic bag down in the bush one cold, wet September morning, the rain beginning to soak through my coat, I decided enough was enough. Squatting here, hiding away from my problems among the litter, the smell of damp mud and cigarette butts in my nostrils, was now so boring and uncomfortable that school, shithole though it was, actually seemed the better option. Official isolation at school and removal of privileges at home was working. Effective punishments had finally been found. I actually felt glad. I didn't like acting like such an idiot – just didn't know how to stop. But, in my final year, did I really want to throw it all away because of a bunch of ignorant homophobes? No, definitely not. I pulled my bag from its spot among the damp ivy, assumed the duck-position and waddled out past the discarded crisp packets, cigarette papers and broken lighters and out into the daylight. I could sneak into school unnoticed. Somehow, I had to make this work.

The Last Straw

The final week of September was going really, really well. I attended every lesson, on time and in full, behaved, paid attention, completed and handed in all homework and had my report-card signed by each teacher with accompanying comments of "No problems", "Behaved well" and "Well done – keep it up!" Even some friends were supportive. Everyone was surprised, including me.

On the Thursday morning we were told that, after our first lesson, there was to be a special assembly, lasting all of second period. No one knew what it was for and it seemed no members of staff were prepared to tell us, either. Very unusual, especially given that assemblies were almost always held during registration period, before the day's lessons began.

First period was history with Mr Williamson, the Head of Year. He refused to comment on the upcoming assembly, but did say to me:

"I spoke to the Head this morning, Richard. You're doing really well."

This was said in front of the class. Several people smiled. I felt like a Labrador that'd just done a back flip and been rewarded with a delicious treat. At last my behaviour was under control. The lesson passed without incident and Mr Williamson joked as he signed my report-card:

"I don't know why I'm signing it – I'm the one who has to check it at the end of the day! Well done, Rich."

We then filed down the two flights of stairs from the history department and into the lobby to find the entire school quietly converging on the Arts Block Hall, any and all chatter being sternly shushed by a united front of teachers. It was an almost eerie atmosphere as we shuffled into the hall.

A thousand kids squashed together onto a thousand plastic seats, cheek-by-jowl, chair-leg to chair-leg. The entire teaching staff had squashed themselves into the aisles along either side of the hall and the Headmaster, Mr Williamson and other heads of year all sat on the stage in stoic sobriety. As we squeezed into our seats, we were again told in no uncertain terms to keep quiet – this was to be truly a sombre assembly. No one was quite sure what the occasion was. Ordinarily, the entire school was only ever assembled like this once a year, for the last morning of summer term. Whatever it was, it was clearly a very serious matter. An announcement, perhaps? Was the school closing? Had a pupil died? Some voices whispered that it was a special tribute-assembly to commemorate Princess Diana's recent and tragic death. I doubted it: many famous people died in the four years I'd spent at this school; none had prompted an assembly before, so why would we be having one now? The funeral was over a week ago and watched by half the world. I dismissed the idea as probably just another sensational school rumour. Chinese whispers. How wrong I was.

Solemnity and ceremony abounded. There were readings and poems from all the senior members of staff. Then some more. And more still. They weren't going to devote the entire hour to this matter, were they? Yes. All of it.

The reactions of nearby students varied: some seemed to think the assembly timely and appropriate; some were quietly incredulous; others simply wore the usual bored-in-assembly look. Like my mate, Mel, next to whom I was sat, and a handful of others around us, I was a little surprised at the pomp and scale of the whole thing but agreed with just about everyone on the planet at the time that Diana's tragic, untimely death was a great tragedy that warranted a little solemn reflection. However, after about twenty minutes of readings from members of staff while their colleagues looked on, many visibly crying, it started to seem a bit much. Mel and I exchanged a few bemused whispers, as others around grew restless and also began quietly muttering to each other. Then came Candle in the Wind. The sight of Mrs Nevis, the formidable head of Pastoral Care – she who could freeze even the most delinquent teen with a single, icy glare – crying along with her colleagues made a few of us smirk in disbelief. It wasn't long before I noticed, and indeed *felt* the burning glare of Mr Williamson as he glowered furiously in our direction. Pure rage. If looks could kill, he'd have ended us both there and then. Mel and I were made to stand for the rest of the ceremony, fixed in his wrathful, almost predatory glare. Afterwards, as everyone else dispersed for morning break, we were escorted upstairs to an empty classroom on the top floor. Williamson came thundering in, glowing red, almost foaming at the mouth and delivered a full-volume tirade, inches from my face:

"Right, that's it! I've had enough of you, Sunshine! I'm going to do everything in my power to get you out of this school as soon as humanly possible! Your days in this school are over! I don't care what happens to you after the way you just behaved!"

Like a red rag to a bull. A heated, high-decibel argument ensued. I protested that others had been whispering and smirking; we were being singled out. This was flat out denied. Mel quickly apologised, I argued the point. Williamson showered me with a barrage of booming insults, character assassinations and even the odd profanity, all delivered so close I could feel the heat of his engaged-red face and the air-blasting eruptions of his voice on my skin. Incensed, I gave it all back. I was later told our yelling could be heard from the ground floor. The verbal dust-up ended with Williamson storming off in much the same manner he'd come in. I was placed in isolation for the rest of the afternoon, sent home at lunchtime and told not to return. The next day my parents received a letter explaining that I'd been "temporarily excluded until further notice". The TV was removed once again and I was instructed to write a letter to the school governors, explaining my side of the story. The letter was indignant and unrepentant, missing entirely both the point of the exercise and seriousness of the situation, so it wasn't sent. Instead, Mum and Dad wrote a surprisingly insightful letter touching on the influence of bullying on my behaviour. I had no idea they'd made the link. I remained convinced the school wouldn't expel a former high-achiever like me, especially after I'd finally gotten back on track. A few days later, while out accompanying a friend playing truant, Lucy and another girl tracked us down. They'd called at the house to see how I was, only to find my tearful mother at the door with a letter in hand. They'd come straight down to the riverside where Dan – my first male friend in years – and I had said we'd be. I was greeted with four words: "You've been expelled, Rich."

I was gobsmacked. What would happen now? I was dumbfounded. It was like being punched in the stomach. A bomb had just exploded inside. The future never more uncertain. And yet, at one and the same time, as the girls head back to school and Dan and I decide to walk further up the riverside, away from the city centre, something is different. As I gaze over the shimmering waters of The Severn to the fields opposite – the sight of so many gruelling PE lessons and Sports Days – and up to the adjacent grazing fields that served as one of many hiding places and escape routes, I realise…it's finally over. My parents will be furious and God only knows where I'll be sent for the remainder of the academic year, but my time in that awful place, my ties to it, its hold over me, it's all over as of this very moment. It's not how I'd ever envisaged it all ending but at last, suddenly, it has. The sun shines gloriously down as a gentle breeze rustles the riverbank foliage and ripples the water below. The distant, muffled sound of city centre traffic is somehow soothing. The fields opposite are now, to me, just fields. I never have to set foot in that awful place ever again. I'm free.

What have I done?

The Final Rush Hour, Part IV

The dazzling morning sun burns brightly in the clear blue sky, its fiery brilliance dancing in all directions. A few rays catch the gently-rolling waters of the sepia-coloured Severn, as it sweeps majestically before the grandiose Cathedral. They reflect back, a thousand shimmering jewels, winking up at the old bridge. How many people have passed over this bridge of a morning and beheld this unspeakable beauty over the centuries? Thousands, I imagine. How many times have I seen it and felt nothing? Something worse than nothing…I don't know. Now, I feel *everything*…

This morning my insides are alive once more, in ways I never thought they could be again. Every scintilla of poetry of the exquisite picture before my eyes dances inside me, to the most profound depths; my heart leaping for joy as my soul breathes it all in. Alive at last. All the while, my brain boils in incendiary, industrial-grade adrenaline; stomach a critical, rattling inferno as deadly danger stalks every square inch of observable reality and beyond. I'm free. They're going to kill me.

Beautiful as it is, the river feels unmistakably like an ominous threshold, crossed for the final time on a one way trip to unavoidable death. It seems that neither the events of the last few years, nor those turbulent school days contain any clear answer as to what on earth is going on; how it's come to this. However bad the situation at school became, those disciplined days of mindful-prayers, meditative early nights and active mornings on the paper round meant that, away from the insane jungle of high school, I still had reasonable control of my mind. I was okay within myself, just not within that shithole. Once I was free it was all supposed to go away…get easier. But after getting kicked out, something crucial about my mind began to change…around the time I first began smoking weed…

My Little Green Friend

My Little Green Friend

A billowing cloud of ivory-white smoke swirls lazily up into the haze of a late-summer afternoon. A spliff is being passed around the group, as we sit on the kerb outside Dan's house. It has a sweet, spicy smell and an oily-woodbine taste. A gentle, burgeoning feeling of settled-tranquillity creeps gently into consciousness as the world beyond the cul-de-sac fades to the farthest reaches of insignificance. Do all other cares. We're here. We're now. And little else. Who knew concrete could be *so* comfortable?

Everything's messed up. The rebel phase had been about surviving, by any means necessary, those constant threats and the manic-nervousness of school. Life outside the school gates had been a different story. Those days of strict routine, mindful prayers on the morning paper round and meditating myself to sleep every night had melted the Snowman once and for all, and paid dividends beyond. While I was beside myself with fear and anxiety *within* school grounds, I was always able to leave most of it at the gate and enjoy a fairly robust mental health away from that awful place. The day I found out I'd been expelled, all that changed; the drama came with me.

I'd fantasised daily about the sweet moment when I could leave that hellhole. There were so many iterations, all bathed in the bright light of liberation, the torture finally over. When Lucy had tracked me down and told me I'd been kicked out, that moment had come. In the worst possible way. The relief I'd felt was profound, and I was glad to not have to cross that threshold ever again, but the mushroom-cloud and reverberating shock following explosive news turned out to be far, far more impactful and long lasting than any sense of relief.

I was deeply ashamed with and disappointed in myself, drowning in a near speechless-disbelief at what had happened, stuck day and night in a perpetual, aghast daze. Throughout those wayward days, getting back on track had never left my mind, it *had* to be done, and when it finally *was*...one stupid mistake and...boom. The mental problems of school were no longer something awful to be endured, almost ritually, at a certain place and time, no, now they were with me morning, noon and night, wherever I went, whatever I did. My whole body was constantly heavy with a saturating, grim realisation that never seemed to reach its peak; the sense of catastrophe, guilt and unrelenting judgement swelling each day as I'd wake up at home, late morning in an empty house (everyone else out at work) to a bottomless and immeasurable regret. There was a strange, ever-present, adrenaline-flavoured-heat to the whole cocktail. I was drowning in it. I no longer liked or trusted myself much at all. I used to feel like an outcast, but now, as far as my education was concerned, I really *was* one. There were rumours that everyone hated me for disrespecting Diana. Things were unbelievably tense at home. Almost everyone I encountered was keen to remind me what an unthinking idiot I've been, as if I wasn't already thinking the same thing every second of every day. Well...almost everyone. There was one group: Dan Matthews and his mates.

A New Group of Friends

Interacting with anyone at that time – relatives, neighbours, the nice lady behind the counter at the local shop – absolutely anyone – a toxic melange of guilt, anger and deep embarrassment engulfed me. Being around most people was than a little stressful, even disorienting. But I'd recently made friends with Dan, a nice lad from school, at a time when his best mate, Martin, and my closest friend, Lucy, had fallen head-over-heels in love. They were seeing more and more of each other, and less of everyone else, so I was cycling up to Dan's little inner-city cul-de-sac daily to shoot the breeze with him and his other mates. And this afternoon we're getting stoned.

Mike had been a student in the year above us before leaving at the end of the academic year. Tall, built like a brick shithouse and decidedly rough around the edges, he'd been one of the hardest kids in his year group. He made it to the bitter end of school life, despite getting into fights, throwing a few chairs and swearing at teachers. At school, I'd always averted my gaze whenever he passed, even during my own tearaway days. Another scary lad, although in this case we'd never really interacted at all. Getting to know him now, he's actually quite friendly and hilariously funny. He made the spliff and so has the honour of 'Builder's Right's – lighting up and smoking a lion's share before passing it around the group. Next, it goes to his girlfriend, Naomi, who can be quiet and sweet but always nice to chat with. After that it's passed to Karl, who comes from a big family and went to several different schools for reasons I've yet to glean. Martin and Lucy rock up and also partake. Martin, also a year older, was expelled from several schools, banned from driving before the age of seventeen and has been arrested with Dan countless times over the years. All of them are mostly reformed now, keeping out of trouble, but nonetheless totally sympathetic and non-judgemental about my own recent troubles. They weigh continuously on my mind like an iron hat, but, at least with these guys I don't feel like a complete pariah.

Now it's Dan's turn. He hogs it for a few minutes. A little too long for my liking, but I say nothing. He's blond, quite short, bespectacled, potty-mouthed, sporty, thoughtful and funny. We barely spoke at school, partly because I just couldn't speak to other lads and also as Martin and Lucy weren't an item back then. We encountered one another several times as our best friends were hitting it off and now, surprisingly, we've become friends. He has a wicked, dry sense of humour. We agree about a lot of things school-related. He also has some funny, endearing little habits – pulling his lips right into his teeth with his cigarette and making an exaggerated popping sound when he pulls it out; rocking back and forth on his seat whenever he's shouting at the TV and a repressed snickering-giggle when he laughs that sounds like air escaping from a punctured tyre. The first male friend I've had in years. He passes me the spliff at last. I think I'm falling in love. He's straight. The last thing I need, with everything else on my mind. I take a long, deep drag. And another. And another. And another.

Easy Does It

The distant sound of a car travelling along the adjacent main road, somewhere out of sight, whispers through the afternoon hue. A faint, insignificant murmur. The noise of its steadily-rumbling engine builds a pleasing crescendo as it gets closer, louder, peaks in a brief, whooshing-roar, before shrinking away into the distance, back to nothingness. We're all familiar with the sound of a passing car, nothing novel there. But now…this everyday sound is somehow…different…more intimate…noticeable, like rediscovering a long forgotten favourite song. Was it noisy? What is 'noise'? A cyclist rolls by. Rhythmic exertion and the whispered-hum of singing spokes. On his way to somewhere terribly important. Birds settle on nearby branches, dart their twitching heads here and there, shooting cute little glances all over the place. They burst into song and take flight again with effortless grace; soft feathers caressing and coaxing elevation from the still summer air. People talk. Disembodied words drift through the warm summer air; ephemeral, idiosyncratic sound-waves with a life all their own. Suddenly such mundane, everyday phenomena casually float into consciousness and glimmer in the senses before the mind can assemble the heavy, greasy machinery of thought, judgement or labels. Perception is drawn-out and gently-focused. Tension leaves the muscles like a slowly-deflating bouncy castle. A cascading burst of calm spreads within, reaching each and every corner of being, pacifying all mental traffic, slowing thoughts to a leisurely, meandering, snail's pace. Those feelings of shock, regret, the bottomless pit of shame…they're still there…somewhere, but somehow…a little less loud; more distant, less troubling, just like the sound of the car as it trailed off into insignificance… as we…just…chill…for a…a…what was I thinking about? Ummmm. Oh wow, another bird. A slight breeze. Hair a gently rustling dance. A thousand little exquisite things you'd not normally notice. What a lovely day. Blissful, childlike grins paint across faces. Eyes settle into a bloodshot-glaze. Repose envelopes us. Everything's okay. We're here and we're now and not a lot else. Please call back later. Our Ability-to-Give-A-Shit-Department is currently offline. And we're suddenly quite hungry…

Sitting on the concrete, melting into the garage wall against which I'm leaning, I'm more comfortable than I ever thought possible on such hard surfaces. Interactions are suddenly so much easier. Eye contact is made before the mind can freak out in a flurry of danger-signals. Some of these lads are not to be trifled with. We're on good terms because I know Dan and Martin but the need to be careful of how I'm coming across is, usually, a constant concern. Usually. Right now, unease itself has sunk gently down into a manageable little lull, like a fart that's not quite ready to come out. Something to be dealt with…later. If I remember. Looking at the bloodshot eyes of Mike, my brain can't quite conjure up all that scary context that usually surrounds him, that must always be so carefully navigated. Instead, I just see the eyes of a young lad who's just as stoned as I am; whose 'normal' thoughts are probably as delayed and indistinct as my own. No longer a dangerous, potential threat to be cautiously tiptoed around: no, just another human being. A person. So it is with everyone present. Words, looks and giggles float gently through the air and into consciousness like everything else, unhindered by evaluation. I somehow lack the energy, even presence of mind, to be painfully aware of each and every mannerism, of the potentially 'gay' inflections of my voice. It all just shrinks into indistinct…distance. It's like seeing everything and everyone for the first time, with fresh, open, pacified eyes. Our group chats at a serene, meandering pace; we giggle helplessly at inconsequential nonsense, laughing for what seems like hours before anyone can articulate what the joke actually is. A stroll to the shop in search of the miracle of food becomes a hilarious slow-motion, epic pilgrimage of comrades in arms; united in the simplicity of the here and now. To let go and be part of a group without being continually on edge and having to compensate by acting like an obnoxious clown. To belong. It's heavenly.

Late summer soon flowed into early autumn; a premature cold-snap brought a chastening wind that stripped the trees of their browning leaves. The nights drew in. During the ever-diminishing daylight hours, while everyone else was busy at school or work, I was painfully bored, constantly pinning for Dan and always looking for something to fill the empty hours. The evenings couldn't come quickly enough.

My parents and I had a meeting with the local education authority to determine the best course of action. Sitting in the office of Mrs Jameson, a local Educational Psychologist, it was decided that I had Attention Deficit Hyperactivity Disorder, or ADHD, and decreed that, instead of returning to another mainstream high school, the best place to conclude my GCSEs was at Oakwood, a local Pupil Referral Unit. I'd heard all sorts of rumours about that place but luckily Martin, Lucy's one true love, was a former attendee.

It's fair to say that Martin was professional juvenile delinquent. Aged just sixteen, he'd been arrested tens of times since the age of ten, for everything from Drunken Disorderly Behaviour to shoplifting to fraud and was banned from driving before being of age and yet was out driving a new car each week. Like myself, he was never one for getting into fights, although his track record in every other area made mine look almost unblemished. He knew every trick in the book and just about every unsavoury character our side of the river. And he knew all about Oakwood, so Lucy asked him pick me up in his latest illegal ride one day while she was at school. Suffice to say, I wasn't busy. He recounted all sorts of entertaining stories about the place, all designed to put my mind at ease but, somehow, I wasn't reassured. I wasn't a seasoned delinquent like him and, perhaps more importantly, I wasn't straight. Obviously we didn't discuss *that*. Instead I pretended to be reassured. Then we found a car park in which he could teach me the basics of driving. Illegally, of course.

Things around the dilapidated cul-de-sac weren't as fun or lively as they'd been late in the summer; marijuana was relatively rare at the best of times and fewer of Dan's friends were keen to come out in the cold, dark evenings. But, thankfully, Dan was quite the socialite, so was always happy to have company, which I was more than happy to provide. Sometimes we'd meet with others to knock back a few litres of cider on a street corner; other times we'd all squeeze into Martin's latest car and tour the streets, stereo ablaze. But most of the time, it was just Dan and myself, hanging around the cul-de sac, sharing cigarettes and putting the world to rights. I *had* to see him daily, hear his voice, see those piercing blue eyes peering over the rims of his thick glasses, however futile and alienating my affections were. We argued a lot. I was very intense and probably got on his nerves. But we stayed close. We even got stoned together in my room a few times. They were great fun, despite continually hating myself for wanting something I knew I couldn't have. But, in the midst of the swirling cauldron of self-loathing and bottomless regret, he was the one thing that kept me going.

The weather grew even colder, the days still shorter. Martin got through an MG, a Metro, a white van (into the back of which about nine of us squeezed on Halloween with booze, spliffs and a few other substances), a couple of Escorts and a Montego. Things became more dramatic; Dan and I were arguing ever more; I was arrested, for the first and only time in my life, with Martin in one of his cars, and we saw less and less of the extended group. A few of Martin and Mike's scarier associates began frequenting the area, being recently released from prison. They soon fell out with them and, before long, we found ourselves in a full-on car chase – six of us squashed into an old hatchback with a near-empty tank – that screeched to a halt on a petrol station forecourt and Martin's window was kicked in with the rest of us still sat inside.

By Christmas, it had become too much. I was still on bail, had a court date set for the New Year and was now walking the streets terrified of running into any one of those scary ex-prisoners, especially since one of their minions had recently punched me, quite unprovoked, in front of them. It felt very much like I was circling the edge of a dangerous whirlpool; that an already-bad situation could easily get so much worse. When Dan and I fell out again, and I knew it was time to move on. I was starting full time at Oakwood in January. Time for a clean break. But I missed him like crazy. And I missed those carefree times getting stoned, too.

Oakwood Pupil Referral Unit

"I really wanna try Skunk. And Squidgy Black. Can you get any?"

"Yeah, I can get 'em. Easy."

"How much?"

"You should probably only get a little. It's *really* strong. I'm not bringing it here, though. No way."

Louis, our IT teacher, has momentarily left the room and, as usual, Kayleigh and I are discussing cannabis. I don't have many contacts in Worcester; Those I did have, I've lost touch with, and I've been ripped off more than once. Chatting, on a daily basis, with the bright, enigmatic, law-unto-herself Kayleigh, she's often mentioned smoking of the kind of legendary, exotic weed the kids in Worcester only ever talk about. She does it all the time. Daily, even. Sometimes we even discuss it in the presence of teachers – Oakwood Pupil Referral Unit is a *very* informal place.

The word on the street was that Oakwood was a school "for all the really, *really* bad kids". Martin's reassurances had done little to assuage the daily inferno in my gut, especially when taken with *other* comments I'd heard over the years: "There're some scary fuckers there!" "Even the hard kids get bullied at Oakwood". As my first day on campus rapidly approached, a freefalling apprehension joined the usual cauldron of shame, regret and anxiety.

One evening, about a year earlier, shortly after first going off the tracks at school, I was spending the evening with my then newfound female friends at a local youth club, when a lad named Ed Norwood suddenly showed up. He was a former rogue pupil at our school, expelled eons ago, way back in the distant past of Year Seven, for behaviour *far* worse than mine ever was. He clearly hadn't liked my newfound popularity among the girls as, once most of them had left and we were sat by the window, he spent a good ten minutes intermittently hitting me across the legs with a length of thick, plastic drainpipe, threatening far worse violence if I dared to move. A few others nearby, including the staff member in charge, shot concerned glances in our direction and uttered a few uncomfortable interventions from across the room, but they knew as well as I did it was pointless. Ed Norwood was another one of those lads you didn't stand up to, from another 'hard' family. Back when he was still at school, even Adrian Watson wouldn't have crossed him. The only thing that could be done was let him get on with it and hope he got bored. Eventually, he did, but not before leaving a good spread of purple, redraw bruises across the top of my thighs. It was rumoured he was now a pupil at Oakwood, as was another guy by the name of Glyn Powell, who'd punched me in the face down at the racecourse one night when Lucy and I were attending the Bonfire Night Fayre, presumably because I was there with her (since we'd not met before). I was a sensitive, scared fifteen year old in the closet, in trouble for erratic and disruptive antics at school, but the one thing I definitely was not was a hard nut like those lads. So, yeah, there was a plummeting-to-certain-death level of anxiety about going to Oakwood, garnished with a cold, mortal dread that I was walking into a lions' den that'd make my High School days seem like a jolly holiday. A school *full* of Adrian Watson types, and I a piece of fresh meat to be ravenously torn apart. I couldn't have been more wrong.

Down a quiet, inner city back street, tucked away in the far corner of a tiny plot of land, Oakwood Pupil Referral Unit was a ten-roomed porta-cabin. If you walked quickly enough across the entrance hall, the art projects in the display cabinets would shake. Kids unable to attend mainstream school were taxied in from all over the county. There were about fifty on the register but only half that number in regular attendance, all fourteen, fifteen and sixteen year olds in Years Ten or Eleven. We were grouped, not according to our Year Group or academic ability, but rather, according to our behavioural problems and overall profile. The rumour-mill-roll-call of kids with infamous reputations was entirely accurate: both Ed and Glyn were there and in *very* good company. Continually swallowing back the urge to vomit, the rocketing-nerves experienced on the first day were enough to make me feel close to passing out, but, I was soon to discover that Oakwood was very different to the average school environment.

No uniforms were worn and most teachers were addressed by their first name; classes contained around six kids each, and good behaviour meant we were allowed off site at lunch for a smoke. The school day began at half nine and finished at half two and each lesson was fifty minutes long. The whole place had a friendly air about it that was, at first, a huge surprise. Even Glyn and Ed were congenial in this relaxed environment. Coming from the same area of Worcester, Ed and I shared a taxi, along with Gemma, an old girlfriend from infant school who'd been battling Chronic Fatigue Syndrome for the last four years. Everyone was incredibly amiable on the ride in. It was bizarre. It soon became clear that, at Oakwood, there was a common, unspoken understanding that everyone was there due to their own unique problems that made fitting in with the mainstream school system nigh impossible. Some kids attended because they had a tendency to get into fights and throw furniture at teachers; some, like Gemma, had Chronic Fatigue Syndrome while others had various mental health problems or learning difficulties. I was a back-chatter, class clown and chronic truant, but not given to violence, so I was grouped with kids with similar issues. Although there were occasional outbursts, the staff had a firm but fair, informal relationship with all the kids, that kept everyone under control and made for a pleasant learning environment. In my group was an enigmatic, outspoken, individualistic girl, from out of town, by the name of Kayleigh. We'd both started attending at around the same time. And today, yet again, we're talking weed:

"So, how will you get it to me then? Shall I come to Droitwich?"

"Yeah, why not? I can show you how to roll a spliff properly!"

"Yeah, that'd be good!"

Even through our affected adolescent aloofness, Kayleigh and I are both visibly pleased to have finally agreed to get together outside of school hours. Neither of us has made any real new friends in this place and we've been having these cannabis-centric chats for several weeks, so it's clear we're both pleased with the arrangement. I've admired Kayleigh from day one for her individualistic, often outrageous dress sense, fierce intelligence, dry sense of humour and beautiful singing voice so, for me at least, the act of getting stoned is really just a cover for making a new friend.

A Welcome Break

Trips to the sleepy suburbs of Droitwich, the small, nearby town where Kayleigh lived, soon became a regular occurrence. Our initial point of convergence had been weed, but it turned out we shared much common ground. We'd both been academic highflyers before going off the rails, which had perplexed almost everyone around us; peers, parents and teachers were all utterly bewildered by our sudden waywardness. While I'd been expelled from a comprehensive, Kayleigh was "asked to leave" a prestigious private school, sent to a local comp, where she struggled to cope, stopped attending and was subsequently sent to Oakwood. Neither of us was particularly proud or boastful of our behavioural track record, unlike many of the other Oakwooders. We'd just had enough of school and it transpired that it, too, had had enough of us. Our taste in music was similar and our issues quite complimentary: while I often struggled to talk with people my own age – especially other young men – Kayleigh had profound difficulties interacting with adults. So she'd deal with any teenagers we encountered, while conversing with folk over the age of thirty was my job. For all the common ground, however, our time together was overwhelmingly spent under the influence of THC. Kayleigh sometimes expressed concern that our friendship was only the result of our mutual green friend but nothing could've been further from the truth. I really enjoyed her company; her devil-may-care individualism was a breath of fresh air. That was the one thing we didn't share: I always dressed, spoke and acted to blend in, to avoid drawing attention to myself, while secretly wishing I had her courage. I really admired her for that. She wore her own bespoke melange of styles: a fitted, dark-mauve velvet jacket; flares with trainers, elaborate and imaginative make up. She always said whatever she thought, in the presence of absolutely anyone, and seemed to care very little what others thought of her. She was easily the coolest person I'd ever met. Nonetheless, we did get really, *really* stoned. All. The. Time.

Going about my business in and around the local area, I was forever looking over my shoulder. Sometimes I'd hear my name shouted with a kind of gleeful contempt – *"Rich Willoooooows!!!"* as though my name itself was some kind of obscene insult. It was usually kids from high school, some of whom I'd never so much as spoken to, whose names I didn't even know. Other times it was high pitched, homophobic cat-calls: *"Queer!"*, *"Bender!"*, *"Gay Boy!"* and so on. Having spent so many years trying to avoid the other lads; and striving to remain unseen on those long, boring days of truancy, I knew every last nook and cranny of the neighbourhood for at least a square mile. If I wanted to elude anyone, I usually could. A master of clandestine transit. It started with that smug sense of satisfaction at the age of thirteen as I'd pop in and out of town first thing in the morning during school holidays, while the other teens remained in bed, or walk onto the playground *just* as the bell rang. As the situation deteriorated and I veered off the rails, however, it felt less like a sneaky advantage and more like a refuge from all the drama. Now I'd been expelled, gotten into trouble with the police, and was avoiding so many more specific individuals, like Martin's ex-prisoner associates, it was closer to a kind of grim segregation. I felt like a rodent, forever on the run, darting in and out of the cracks, avoiding ubiquitous predators. Worcester seemed like a warzone. Too many Adrian Watson-types I just didn't know how to deal with. Too much drama and gossip. I was sick of it.

In Droitwich, I was an unknown quantity - free of rumours, stigma and reputation – just Kayleigh's quiet stoner-friend. Splitting time between there and the new, much better school environment of Oakwood was a tremendous relief; Kayleigh's quiet little suburban corner of Droitwich was the perfect place to finally relax - with the *perfect* medicine. Occasional stoner-sessions in Worcester with Dan, Lucy, Martin and his mates had led to some wonderfully laid-back chillouts now and then, but with Kayleigh - whose older boyfriend had some *serious* contacts in Birmingham – I discovered the joys of skunk weed.

Chilling her room, listening to music, walking to the shop, or just enjoying the long bus ride to Droitwich – skunk rendered the whole world like the inside of a brightly-coloured Van Gogh painting, alive with soft, luminous, blurry-texture and sublime, beautiful, idiosyncratic meaning. Time would slow to a gentle pace, a delicate glow emanating from everything around; imagination and intuition making sweet love with one another, morphing endlessly in exquisite half-formed notions. Consciousness itself would transmute into a gently-rippling sea, twinkling in brilliant sunlight. All the unpleasantness inside - the constant vigilance of dangerously gay mannerisms; that still-reverberating shock that, yes, I really had been expelled and possibly screwed up my life permanently; the rising alienation and isolation as I watched friends going through the normal teenage motions of sex and relationships, while I remained frozen in the closet, and an increasing feeling that I was an effeminate freak of nature - all of it just slipped away like a barely-noticed landmark quickly receding in a rear view mirror. We were transported to another planet, filled sensory depth: bright colours, echoing, idiosyncratic textures and hypnotic scents. It was a world where music had unheard of levels and revelatory dimensions; a place where our troubles were little more than an obscure, out of reach constellation. There were still problems, big problems I hadn't the faintest idea how to even begin dealing with but, for now, I was free: free of that awful school, those awful kids and the screeching cacophony of white noise inside. Problems could be dealt with another time; a time when I had the energy to move a single muscle or articulate a single thought. Right now I was just fine, thank you very much. And soooo hungry…

Those Were The Days…

That spring, the final few months of mandatory education, was easily the best of all my schooldays. Gemma's CFS had gone into remission, enough for her to start walking again, so she was soon hanging around with Kayleigh and I, along with the occasional cameo by other kids from the PRU. Mostly, though, it was just Kayleigh and me….and, of course, our Little Green Friend. We divided our time between Droitwich and Worcester; I knew all the idyllic little hideaways down by the brook where we could roll our spliffs in tranquil seclusion, (*not* the godforsaken bush I used to hide in) and frequenting them *with* someone, with a purpose other than hiding from the world, was sublime. Lush, green leaves catching the vibrant sunlight as they softly rustled in the breeze; the quietly chattering ripples of the brook – all a resounding orchestra of exquisite brilliance amidst the pacified-haze of cannabis. There were times when we could only get hold of the weaker stuff – hashish or ordinary weed – and, although their impact wasn't as potent now that I was a skunk connoisseur, it still made a wonderful difference.

Kayleigh knew all the nooks and crannies of her suburban estate, including a couple of small, disused barns atop a hill – one frequented by skaters, resplendent with inventive ramps and colourful graffiti; the other, empty and rustic, with a dusting of dry mud that covered the floor, relatively untouched. The latter was our favourite haunt. We were always getting stoned, yes, but also continually swapping mix tapes and chatting about music, even taking a small stereo on our travels (this was in the days before mp3s, Bluetooth and smartphones). Smoking so much weed so often, it was getting a little harder to get quite so blasted as had previously been the case, but that simply made it more rewarding whenever we did manage to acquire a really good batch that could hit the spot. I was aware that I was smoking it a lot, practically every day in fact, but the world without weed was always that same old alarming, confusing place. Planet Weed was *much* nicer and, after everything that'd happened in recent years, I decided I'd earned a nice, long break.

For the first time in what seemed like an age, I had a simple, pleasant and uncomplicated social life *and* I wasn't getting into trouble at Oakwood or at home; at least not as much as had been the case in 'normal' school. There'd been the occasional argument with teachers along with a small amount of truanting, but on the whole, I was settled, happy and actually *wanted* to be there. The so-called "ADHD" behaviour – for which I received absolutely no treatment whatsoever – was tapering off, dissolving somewhere in the cloud of thick, green smoke in which I now lived and, frankly, the disruptive behaviour I *had* engaged in, back at high school, paled in comparison to that of many of other Oakwood kids. At last I felt able to learn comfortably and was, subsequently, much less disruptive. I quickly developed deep affection for the Oakwood, lamenting only the fact that my time there was to be so short. I also quite enjoyed my newfound identity as a 'Stoner'. It was a *much* easier, more tranquil category to inhabit than that of the introverted geek or the obnoxious tearaway. There was just one problem…

My Little Green Friend

Midway through an overcast June afternoon and I'm lying on the bed in the spare room of Kayleigh's house, half asleep, in a stupefied trance, once again stoned out of my brain. The thin, pale yellow curtains are closed. Kayleigh wasn't going into Oakwood today either and, when we spoke on the phone, although she didn't mind my coming over to get some hash, was keen to stress that she'd be busy with other things. Hash is nowhere near as nice as skunk. Firstly, it comes in a heavy, browinish-green block that has to be burnt and crumbled. Doing so scalds and stains the fingertips, and it burns that much hotter while smoking. The hit itself isn't the soft, psychedelic glaze of skunk, but more of a dull, sluggish-numbness; it slows the world down but doesn't illuminate it all that much. Lying here, lacking the energy to move, it suddenly dawns that today will be our last official day of lessons at Oakwood. I'll have to go back on site to sit the exams, but classes, as of today, are officially over. Kayleigh, being six months younger than I, will be returning in September. I won't. This was supposed to be that all important, momentous last *ever* day of school. I'm missing it because the only thing I could think of when I awoke this morning was getting stoned. I *needed* to; Nothing else even registered, let alone mattered.

Spring has raced on into summer, just as my cannabis use rolled on into full-blown addiction. I've built up a serious resistance, and it's taking more and more of the green stuff to slip away from the self-alienation and loathing, social awkwardness and an increasingly strange detachment from…from…just about everything. Whenever the effects wear off, the return of those jarring feelings is rendered ever more painful…and *potent*. Before the weed, I could just about steer the mental ship amidst all the stormy crap inside, if only barely…just enough to muddle through the day. It was hard, even demoralising, but not impossible. Now, it is. Without the glaze of ganja, everything returns to consciousness that much stronger, brighter, louder and harder to ignore. Deafening. Jitteriness and unease around others is getting worse than ever before; harder to even *try* and get a handle on, however shakily. Before cannabis, social unease elicited a horrible internal storm, but I remained at least physically in control. Now, however, it's that much worse and increasingly accompanied by palpitations and throbbing, draining headaches. So I get stoned every day to navigate this weird wide world that's always been so problematic; especially as it increasingly feels that important part of my mind is beginning to disintegrate in the daunting and disquieting face of adulthood, looming *just* around the corner.

Everyday noises – the slamming of a door or rumble of distant traffic – are becoming inexplicably unsettling, even disturbing. Simple visual stimuli like streaks of paint on a wall or a scratch on a desk can be weirdly annoying and distracting, for no obvious reason. I'm getting irritable again, arguing with Mum and Dad once more. On the odd occasion I argue with a teacher or skive off, it's always hot on the heels of a few days of weed withdrawal. And…there are the thoughts. The ideas. Jarring, unnerving notions about myself, my immediate environment and those around me keep emerging from nowhere, parking themselves in my mind; during lessons, while talking to Kayleigh or even alone watching TV or listening to music. Those intrusive maybe-monster-thoughts of childhood could at least, to a certain extent, be placated with strange rituals and the avoidance of shadows, some of the time. These new thoughts, however, such as *"I'm not fully connected to the words coming out of my mouth"*, *"The world isn't real…or I'm not"*, or *"I'm a weird, genderless freak"* just appear, only to settle in consciousness for hours, sometimes days. I seem to have less ability to resist or dismiss them, as though certain defences have been permanently lowered. It's a perpetual dissonance; a delayed train with nowhere to go; idling, unable to leave the station, spewing out poisonous, black diesel smoke, hour after hour. Really weird and more than a little annoying. Experience has taught that obsessing about weird thoughts is useless, counterproductive, so I resolve to not pay them any attention until they fade away, which it's proving more and more difficult as their intensity never seems to recede – like floaters stuck on eyeballs, gate-crashing every image. Getting stoned yet again helps a little, although it's getting ever harder to find that same, pacifying hit that was so liberating just a few months ago. Muscles are still zapped of energy; motor functions still stupefied, but my brain doesn't settle quite so easily; instead it keeps wandering into places it doesn't like…or belong…or know how to get back from. Nonetheless, it's still easier to distract myself under the influence than when sober.

Kayleigh, having smoked the stuff for much, much longer than myself, has warned several times about its downside, even complaining that it's ruined her life. I can't imagine what she's talking about. Weed takes everything away, transforms and expands consciousness, makes the here and now not just bearable, but *enjoyable*. Life's full of shit, but you can't blame that on the ganja. It's the one thing you *can* count on. Most of the time.

I can't blame my Little Green Friend for these strange new thoughts and life's wider problems, no, it has to be the fact that I'm suddenly sixteen, completely in the closet and still a virgin; the pressure of approaching exams; the chaos and drama of the last few years and the looming spectre of adult life – anything but the weed. It's my ally. The one thing I could count on to calm me down. My Little Green *Best* Friend. So I'm still smoking it like it's going out of fashion. The intensity of those weird, unwelcome thoughts at least abates then for a little while, allowing me to return my attention, to an extent, to the here and now. But it's not the same as it was. The world now is less of a Van Gogh and more of a series of strange, unexplained, poorly-shot photographs. And problems, while still kept at bay by My Little Green Friend, just about, are much, much closer now: less a distant, unreachable constellation; more an inconvenient overcast of grey clouds sluggishly seeping overhead, ever lower, the air becoming thicker, more laden. Still, that at least is better than when I'm sober, with the headaches, disinterest, confusion, regret, alienation, short temper and the blinding brightness of everything.

So here I am, prostrate on the bed in the spare room of Kayleigh's Dad's suburban semi, too stoned to move or think straight. Kayleigh's downstairs, arguing on the phone with her boyfriend, Gaz. The potent June sunlight has broken through the clouds outside and now works on the closed, yellow curtains that glow with each onslaught as I lie, zombie-like, in a balmy afternoon sweat. I'm disgusting.

I had hoped to get some sleep here but the sun's glowing intrusion seems to be heightening the unpleasant realisation that I've missed the last day, as if somehow shining on it. Illuminating the truth with a mocking cruelty. That all-too-familiar feeling of falling, fast. The "Oh shit, I've messed up again" is happening in painful slow motion as the glaring burns down. It's a far, far cry from that carefree, warm summer afternoon on the kerb outside Dan's house.

All those years; all that work I put in before things went awry; the aspirations, the bullying, the friends and enemies, the endless wishing for it all to be over…today would've finally salvaged the situation, drawn a line under all of it, at a school I enjoy and belong in. At last the elusive End that felt like it would never come. I'm ready to move on, but nonetheless, I love Oakwood. It's provided a salvageable ending to this whole bizarre story. I should be there. I *want* to be there. With all the other kids before we go our separate ways, out into the world. Instead I'm lying on a bed in the suburb of another town, sweating, tired, confused, with a dull headache, with more of those nasty, trains-of-thought rumbling into my head, parking up, impassive to all attempts to dismiss their thick, black smoke.

"I'm not a real person."

"My sexuality is an unnatural abomination."

"Nature is mocking me. Agreeing with these thoughts."

The journey was never meant to end like this.

Reality Check

Clocking Off

A Saturday afternoon, in July of that same year, and the gruelling eight hour shift on the packing department is at last nearing an end. The department occupies the entire top floor of a huge, windowless warehouse of corrugated metal, something along the lines of garden shed meets small aircraft hangar. My station is one among hundreds of identical others: a corner-desk-like structure with no seat, adjacent to a raised conveyor belt that runs the length and breadth of the entire room, bearing plastic gondolas filled with catalogue orders for packing to each and every station. A vast, automated Santa's Workshop, sans festivity. Gondolas rumble down from the conveyor into each station via a small slope of squeaking, rattling wheels, banging to a halt in front of each worker, ready for packing. Next to the slope is a computer screen, attached to a scanner and small printer. Beneath the desk, in regimented slots is an assortment of different sized plastic packing bags. Take items from gondola, scan, place appropriate number in designated bag, seal, print label and place onto the other, unseen conveyor, running beneath the haughty one that brings the goods. The parcels disappear into the darkness for dispatch to wherever. Repeat, ad-nauseam for eight hours.

I worked throughout my school life – four paper rounds followed by a weekend market job – but I never imagined any job could be *this* awful. Boredom on a near-spiritual level. My expectations hadn't been high, but like Lucy and many others I know, I took the first job I could find the minute I was legally able to work. It's *so* crap. I need money. For weed

Across the vast expanse of workstations, rumbling gondolas and swirling dust, mounted on the far wall, is a small clock. It scrapes slowly through each and every excruciating minute and now, finally hits five o'clock. I exit the cell-like pen of my workstation and join the horde of humanity slowly filing out of the department, down a long, narrow corridor, through the security gate and out onto the sunlit concrete of the car park. Fresh air. Freedom. *Relief.* Not only at escaping the purgatory of the Saturday shift, but also because tonight I'm off to Droitwich. The paper rounds and market job used to pay between fifteen and twenty pounds a week but yesterday I received my first ever wage-debit of eighty pounds and know *exactly* what to buy first; A whole half-ounce of hash. No weed available at the moment but I'll settle for a nice big measure of anything-I-can-get. Kayleigh said she'll be busy with Gaz, her weed-dealer boyfriend, so I can stay for one spliff and then they're off out. That's been happening a lot lately. Kayleigh's been spending more and more time with Gaz; Lucy with Martin and Gemma with her boyfriend Alan. Dating. The all-important Coupling Prerogative of normal, natural human beings. Of people not inhabiting The Closet. I've lost touch with most other people from High School and Oakwood. Wouldn't know what to say to them now. Increasingly, I'm finding people who don't smoke weed difficult to relate to, as though they inhabit an entirely different, more stressful world where everything moves too fast and is entirely devoid of meaning. Entirely. The fact that more and more of those odd, broken down trains-of-thought have been stuck in my mind of late doesn't help either…their idling-grumble and chocking black smoke a constant source of annoyance…even worry…

Flies in the Ointment

Sitting on the back seat of a huge, old Mercedes bus as it roars and rattles its way along the main road from Worcester to Droitwich, I stare out at the passing fields with a distracted frown, and try to ignore my reflection in the window. It's become more than a little foreign of late. Alien. Unsettling.

I prefer this view: the grazing fields between Worcester and Drotiwich – simple and unchallenging…relatively speaking. The ride out through the city centre, followed by the suburbs was unnerving: people getting on and off the bus, talking, looking around; the view of folk walking along pavements, going in and out of buildings, driving their cars – the hustle and bustle of life – lately it's all seemed strangely remote, otherworldly. I understand it a little less each day. It's all so overwhelming, as is much external stimuli these days; my already-cluttered mind ever occupied with strange thoughts and *horrible* unshakable intuitions.

"I'm not connected to the words coming out of my mouth. Or those in my head".

"I'm a weird, genderless freak".

"My body, so suddenly adult, is completely alien to me".

Those were the annoying little ideas that kept invading consciousness at Oakwood. Greater amounts of weed were needed to pacify them; to drift off into pleasant, stoned contemplation of other, more agreeable nonsense. But since Oakwood ended, since sitting exams and having no sense of whether or not I've so much as passed them, getting a crappy warehouse job and doing little else with my time but smoke weed, those kinds of thoughts have been creeping and nesting in more and more. And more.

The taunts and jibes of high school had always been largely ignored. I felt uncomfortable, often vulnerable when hearing them, yes, but their actual content? It hadn't bothered me all that much. Those obnoxious dicks were only saying such things to impress their mates and besides, they weren't gay, so how could they possibly know what they were talking about? Sexuality wasn't something I gave much thought, beyond privately enjoying all the inevitable adolescent attractions and desires. What it all meant…well, that was something to be dealt with later, once clear of the slings and arrows of outrageous high school. I just had to get through it in one piece. So yes, the ever-present homophobic jibes were difficult in a social context, but their actual themes? Water off a duck's back. The edifying elixir of spirituality also had a similar dynamic: it was always so private and idiosyncratic. There were countless unanswered questions, for sure, but while in the throes of school and all its drama, they could be deferred for another, easier time. Now, however, those years of comments, insults, jeers and unanswered questions about God are somehow creeping up on me, moving in on my stoned brain inch by inch, winning new territory each day. The neutralising effects of weed aren't nearly as reliable as they once were: the ability to respond to thoughts while stoned remains inhibited, as do all useful filters and coping mechanisms. That's very much the other end of this double-edged, green sword: Unnerving ideas arise and take root before they can be intercepted, responded to or even ignored. Their instantaneous emotional effect cascades through mind and body before I can scramble a half- baked, barely effectual response. So now the homophobic taunts so casually ignored have returned, internally, and with a vengeance, demanding at last to be dealt with. What if really *am* just a repulsive, effeminate, freak of nature? Was their hostility justified after all? And those deep, edifying feelings of transcendence that got me through the hard times…was it all just the deluded story of a desperate teen? Throughout the bullying, and the bad behaviour of those wayward days, I always knew I harboured no real, genuine animosity for anyone. The subtleties of private spirituality had tutored me thus. Unconditional Love was deep, profound and empowering. What if, all that time, I'd just been talking to myself? It'd been such a profound and important part of life and now, the thought it could all just be a tragic lie bores into my head, day by day, just like the homophobic thoughts; burrowing beyond rational discourse, slowly eating away some deep, essential parts of my psyche before my very eyes. A slow-motion disintegration of the self, as I watch, and feel, these thoughts take hold, with a deep horror and despair at the loss of control of my own…identity. I'm not who I think I am; the world isn't at all what it seems. And, for good measure, there's a recently-acquired, fungal scalp infection nestled in my hair, its raised, bumpy rings throbbing away. Very much the crowning glory of all there is to dislike about my body. It blushes too much; overreacts to the presence of males; it's the reason I'm gay and, therefore, the reason I could never fit in or avoid unwanted attention at school. And now these itchy, mucusy, fungal-mounds that pulsate, leaking their sticky, watery discharge from my scalp, seem a fitting external symbol of the slow rot setting in below the surface. I'm a rotting corpse, somehow still sentient, watching and smelling its own putrefaction first hand.

These aren't the intense, quick, vivid intrusive thoughts of childhood – of the snowman, the gremlins and a thousand other phantoms – that vanished by day, and by night, could at least be clumsily fought with a mixture of strange rituals and elaborate avoidance. No, these thoughts are non-visual, slow burners, penetrating that much deeper, sinking a little further into flesh each day; sulphuric acid raindrops slowly burning drafty holes into my bones. Not all of the thoughts have an obvious, rational origin, either:

"Everything in the world is an illusion that only I can see"

"…thoughts, feelings, sensations are a fragile veil, thinly covering the horrible truth that none of this is really happening."
"Everything we see is nature's cruel joke."

"I'm not supposed to be this person. No good. A waste of oxygen; a lump of mindless flesh."

"I am mould."

"I don't look like myself."

"My voice is coming from somewhere else."

"The only thing I'm good at is screwing up my life."

They all sink in, further and further, reflecting back as they manifest in consciousness during even the slightest, most mundane, perceptions, from brushing teeth and tying laces to riding this bus. All wrong. All haunting this waning equilibrium. I feel increasingly detached, yet horrified and highly anxious about this disquieting deterioration. Lucid drowning. I'm peering nervously into a vast, infinite blackness that just gets bigger, deeper and harder to ignore. There's a strange urgency to this burgeoning despair, as I feel myself losing my grip on reality, whatever that is, on a daily basis. I can't wait to get stoned and just turn it all down.

The bus exits the main roundabout, on into the outskirts Droitwich. The seat bounces at little as the wheels scramble over a pothole. My body moves a little with the motion. The thoughts don't. I'm dizzy with confusion and a little sick. Maybe it really is the weed that's the problem, but what else do I have to keep me calm? Everything else has gone wrong.

Pass (Bad) Time With Good Company

I decant at Droitwich and walk the winding, leafy, suburban streets to Gaz's flat. Everything's weird. The shapes of houses, texture of pavement slabs, the sounds of car engines, the sight of people talking, even the summer air itself. None of it makes sense. The rumbling of those idling trains-of-thought now gridlocked in the station is with me all the way. Bothersome. Soon it won't matter, as today I'm buying half an ounce – the largest amount I've ever purchased. Forty quid's worth. A proper grown up amount. The two-storey, red-brick building where Gaz lives soon comes into view. I push the door to the communal stairway as the unmistakable, pungent, cat's piss-and-orange-juice stench of burning skunk cascades down from his first floor flat, filling the entrance hall. It was once a reassuring scent, the intense aroma of a potent incense heralding the journey to some faraway, exotic land. These days? Not so much. I'm sick of the smell of weed, and increasingly concerned by the way it commands me. An odd-yet-familiar sense of inertia gropes menacingly at my consciousness as I haul my weird, gay-ape, lethargic legs up the stairway and shuffle down the walkway to the appropriate door. I give the coded-knock and disappear into the low-lit, smoke-filled flat. Why am I doing this? *"My thoughts are not my own"* Oh yeah, that. I'm bolted by the iron bars of my own inadequacy into a fairground ride I'm no longer enjoying. Keep your hands inside the ride.

Inside Gaz's first floor bedsit-flat, with its permanently-closed curtains, low-lighting and smoky ambience, the conversation is superficially genial: who we've seen, what music we're listening to – the everyday, inconsequential small talk of people who get stoned together. I can't stay long, as Kayleigh and Gaz are off out soon, doing 'couple-things'. As we puff away and chat, the intense, jarring sense of profound disjointedness and alienation grow stronger and louder within. It's getting worse in the presence of others, particularly other blokes:

"I'm a freak of nature. I don't belong in this world."

I'm repulsed by myself; this suddenly-adult body, androgynous voice and shameful mannerisms, especially in contrast to Gaz, with his low voice, beard, masculine carriage and natural, appropriate sexuality. We dress similarly but, while the cap, jogging bottoms and sports-brand t-shirt suit his laddish air…on me? They're a joke; a bad disguise, barely concealing shameful femininity and psychological weirdness. A shoddy spacesuit for a lost, dying alien. The notion burns itself deep into my mind, flesh and soul; infecting all other thought, word, sensation and interaction. I take another drag and try to act normally.

The hash is beginning to hit, but doesn't seem strong enough. Or is it too strong? Can't tell. I'm slowing down, relaxing…a little…but my mind is so fragile. Small palpitations judder in various places, the kind one wouldn't ordinarily pay much attention to, but now, it's as though someone or something else is causing those little random ripples – playing bursts of irregular rhythm in veins and nerves to taunt the disembodied spirit inhabiting them. Breathing is similarly alien and disjointed; a heaving-and-hissing mass of unconscious flesh that sixteen years ago congealed somewhere in a dank, misty swamp and I, a strange parasitic anomaly growing atop it. Another dark intuition booms:

"The blood in my veins isn't my own. It's a disease. Life is an infection and I'm no more than a talking piece of mould. I'm disgusting, inside and out."

This is so horrible. I try my best to ignore it. Focus on the conversation. But those strange, inexplicable irritations with the surrounding environment are back again: the streaky paint that covers the walls *feels* like something…unpleasant, just by looking at it…as though it's *itchy* somehow. The texture of the carpet, the knitted zigzag pattern of the throw on Gaz's sofa, they're viscerally bright and loud, despite the closed curtains and quiet music. The carpet doesn't look any different to the last time I was here, but somehow feels like a semiconscious lagoon of microorganisms. Burgeoning? Or dying? Either way, it feels horrible. And the jagged-yet-regular patterns on the throw are angry, as though their dimensions and contours are shouting into my brain. This problem is definitely getting worse. Something's very wrong. I wish I was back at Oakwood, enjoying the best of all my school days. Now, I'm teetering on some eerie cliff edge in a thickening fog.

I don't let on. Years of meticulous micromanagement of every last gesture and expression at school, have made me a master of the tranquil façade. I keep chatting amiably with Kayleigh and Gaz while these strange, disconcerting notions take possession of my consciousness; moving in, deeper and deeper, claiming more and more of reality as their own.

"I don't recognise the words coming out of my mouth. They're not my own. Software transmitted from somewhere else, by a being that doesn't even know I exist."

Everything – inside and out – appears as a lie. Kayleigh and Gaz are part of the lie, which is why they're happy…or I'm the lie, which is why I feel this way. But I'm still highly lucid. I know enough to recognise that my grip on reality is slipping…loosening…crumbling…disintegrating. I'm stood at the edge of a reality-bending black hole, have no idea how I got here or what on earth can be done about it. It's terrifying. Physical manifestations fight to the surface: vertigo, watery saliva and tangible nausea. As I quietly, internally, freak out, the weird alien-blood in my veins races with the intrusive rhythm of someone else's heartbeat. The sweaty fungal infection throbs with the pulse. It itches and leaks beneath alien hair. My scalp is crying. I shudder. Better have another quick spliff before heading back. Do Kayleigh and Gaz have time? Not really, so I'll be quick. God, I wish he had some skunk. This hash really isn't hitting the spot.

Reality Check

The next day I awake in a sticky sweat with a pounding headache. On returning home late yesterday afternoon, I disappeared into the dusty humidity of the attic, where I smoked copious amounts of hash out of the skylight well into the small hours, trying in vain to numb the dark theatre unfolding in my head.

Sweating and drowsy in the July heat, I pull my dressing gown over my weird body and shuffle downstairs. The motions of my limbs as I descend the ladder to the first floor and then the staircase to the ground floor are a strange, clumsy, dissonant dance; someone else's movements, happening inexplicably to this body, whomever it belongs to. The fungal scabs have hardened overnight, and now fresh, sticky discharge leaks out beneath their crust, soaking scalp as my head throbs. Disgusting. The weird thoughts are waking up, too. Trains still noisily idling. I stagger into the kitchen and gaze up at the old floral plate-clock that's been hanging on the wall since time immemorial: two thirty in the afternoon. Great. I'm such a fucking loser. Why can't I pull myself together and do…do…*what?* School is finally over, all my friends are busy living their normal, heterosexual lives, as nature intended; I'm unsure if I've even passed my exams and now all I've got going for me is a god-awful factory job that's so desperately boring I feel like head-butting the wall to numb the relentless tedium. Somehow I have to sort myself out; figure out where it all went wrong and what on earth is to be done about this vomit-stain of a life. But right now, this afternoon, I'm a swirling mess of disintegrating mind.

The now terrifying thoughts, awkward questions and disquieting physical and emotional reactions they elicit are all there, every single one, in full flow. Without anything to pacify them, they all scream in my face. I can barely think. Utterly zapped of energy and motivation, I need to take the edge off this freak show before I can cope with anything else. I eat breakfast, take a cup of tea out into the garden and smoke a fag. The glaring sunlight is at it again; brightly and cruelly illuminating the discordance and despair in my mind, amplifying it a thousand-fold, just as it did as I lay on the spare bed at Kayleigh's Dad's house, just a month ago. I finish the fag and then drag a sweaty, disgusting, confusing body and mind back upstairs. Better keep the blinds closed today.

The bright afternoon sun glowers onto the attic skylight, burning a golden, laser-like frame around the edges of the drawn blind. Still taunting. I sit at the old plastic camping table next to the skylight, open it just a touch and grimace as blinding sunbeams pour in. The wobbly old table is strewn with the messy detritus of last night's solitary session: smelly, oily flakes of old tobacco and ash scattered around emptied out fag-butts; crumbs of crumbled, burnt hash etched onto the plastic surface; a large packet of cigarette papers; stray matches – some burnt out, others yet unused – and a couple of broken lighters. The sight and smell are repulsive. In the close, ubiquitous, greenhouse-like heat of the attic, I sweat some more, and fungal discharge creeps over my scalp, soaking up hair-roots. Despite the heat and sweat, I remain in my dressing gown so I don't have to see this disgusting body. Fragile and hopelessly on edge, I start building a spliff. The humid summer air has gotten into the gum of the papers and the bastard things won't stick. Helpless exasperation further fuels the horrible notions, jarring intuitions and worrying sensations. They burrow like alien spider-worms, tentacles frantically grasping at something crucial, central to identity. Further attempts at rolling are fruitless. Not a single one of the papers will stick. The last thing I want to do right now is dress this horrible, balmy body and drag it through the glaring afternoon sunlight to the shop, much less brave the mind-bending confusion of human interaction. Why is this happening? My head is awash with deep confusion, repulsion, fear, regret and despair. I just want *one* little spliff to take the edge off. I start to cry. The internal cacophony threatens to build into a crescendo. I reach behind a chest of drawers for my home-made bong, pack the gauze with the tobacco-and-hash mixture from the half-built spliff, top it off with some extra, pure hash for good measure and pull myself a strong one. And another. And another. What a way to start the day. But I have to get free of these awful feelings. The third bag of thick, snot-coloured smoke hits the back of my throat with bonfire intensity and I cough it back up with aching lungs, watering eyes and a horrible, nauseous-spinning sensation. That'll do for now. I plonk myself down on a foam mattress-chair and wait for my head, and the room, to stop spinning.

After a few more nauseous, giddy moments, slumped in a squashy-foam chair-mattress, throat still reeling, I decide a little music will help. Wobbling lethargically on all fours, across the floor, through dusty-dizziness and over to the stereo, I know just the song to lift my spirits. 'Floribunda' by the trance group, Mother's Pride; the 'Tall Paul' remix – a particular favourite during those heady days of spring, hanging out with Kayleigh, without a care in the world. A million years ago, now. Nine minutes long, it starts with a steady, driving beat, interspersed with ethereal, echoing calls from a provincial-sounding children's choir. A pounding, melodic, electronic bass kicks in and meanders along beneath a bass-y arpeggio as the track builds. Almost four minutes in, this all cuts out as the evocative, electrified-panpipe chords come in, over a background of ambient crowd-cheers. The motif loops over and over again, building as the beats and children's choir come steadily back in, before all exploding together in a beautiful, uplifting, splendorous crescendo that catapults the heart and imagination effortlessly into the stratosphere and beyond. The piece then eases steadily down: chords briefly alone once more before bowing out, arpeggio-beat comes back in and the choir chant just a little longer as the track fades at last to a close. It's a stirring masterpiece, suggestive of vast, sun-soaked planes, resplendent with vivacious life. Just what the doctor ordered. Motor skills already stupefying, I clumsily remove the shining CD from its scratched case, put it into the stereo, select the track and slither back to my chair, awaiting musical solace.

The beat gets going just as the effect of the bongs are seeping into consciousness. Muscles melt into a drugged-atrophy as I sink deeper into the foam chair, a discarded ragdoll. Light and colour grow garish and lurid. The musty-haze of the attic takes on a thick, tactile quality, as though the stale air is somehow a part of consciousness itself. The coarse, synthetic texture of the purple-grey carpet is becoming self aware. The hard-lifelessness of the walls take on a strange echo that obtrudes into ordinary sensation. That third bong was probably one too many. Idiot. Feel a little sick. Just give it a minute…

The stereo speakers pound out the driving beat with laser-sharpness as the echoing choir begin their haunting refrain:

"Oooh laaaayah…"

Something's wrong. The rousing musical patterns are there, yes, but are oddly…dwarfed. As if the sounds are being absorbed into a matrix of distortion amid the close haze of the attic. The air itself shimmers with unseen chaos.

My brain throbs with heat…pulsates and spins in a nauseous-swirl; the dull-plateau of hash stupefaction nowhere to be found. Instead, the weird thoughts and sensations rapidly grow louder, clearer, more immediate, as though the thoughts themselves are taking on a life all their own; staring, blinking…stirring with predatory-poise. A cold chill goes through me. Just ignore it.

The thick, humid, afternoon heat is closing in. The fungal-scalp-rings pulsate and itch, AGAIN. I scratch them, annoyed. They're horribly sore. Going to leak now. Disgusting. I'm so fucking *irritated*. But too weak to be angry in any cohesive way; just a hot swarm of disparate, negative emotions colliding in the stuffy air. I'm sweaty and useless and disgusting and inhuman. Jolts of soul-scorching self-hatred and despair flash through me, ten times brighter this morning…I mean…afternoon.

"Oooh laaaayah…"

The disquieting sensations neither peak nor settle; instead they grow volatile …inflammable …deadly. The bad thoughts stir themselves further as the poisonous emotions heat up in menacing-agreement. This just isn't the time for my useless brain to be sabotaging something as simple as enjoying a good trance track. I. Need. This. Boost.

"Shut up!!", *"I'm disgusting,"* "Just give it a minute to settle. The music will soothe soon enough." *"Not really here",* "Shut up! JUST SHUT THE FUCK UP!!!"

The beat races on. The pounding bass kicks in. Weirdly, worryingly, it powers through the air and pounds away at my scalp and the outside of my skull; a remorseless, predatory-rhythm, determined to break in. Tangible. Alarmingly real. The arpeggio gets going. It has a piercing eeriness I've not noticed before, an ethereal thundering that could tear down buildings. Darting up and down the scales, swirling around the room, it relentlessly punches thousands of tiny holes, all over my body. Head, limbs, torso, face. What the hell is going on? This is awful. The living-thoughts and incendiary emotions become fully sentient, freeing themselves from my control, scurrying around beneath my skull, frantically searching for an exit. Body temperature rising, sweat erupting from innumerable pores, I resolve not to take these hellish apparitions seriously. Among the menacing sounds and salivating thoughts, the intermittent call of the evocative choir cuts through. That at least sounds and feels the way it should…sort of…*please…*

"Oooh laaaayah…"

"I'm not real…I don't exist…I have no consciousness."

The beat and arpeggio break though. Thoughts and emotions burst from the confines of my head, dart around the room and explode into terrifying superposition. They dance independently, menacingly, in the walls, the carpet, taking invisible possession of the air, of the thick, ubiquitous ambience of the attic. Fully sentient. Independent. Predatory. *Alive* . They move in on the reverberating music.

"*Ooo leeeeyah…*" BoomBaDa BoomBaDaBoomBaDaBoomBoom "*Ooo leeeeyah-madelhah…*"

"*This body is a disease. Heaving mass of inanimate matter. Blood is alive. I'm not. I don't exist. It pumps through an infinite void.*"

I feel them seep through the stereo casing, into the machinery beneath; the circuit boards, the rapidly rotating CD, the shaking speakers. There, they multiply and magnify, gathering pace, strength, clarity, identity; the music a runaway catalyst for their life-force. They seize possession of the song and its floating voices. The choir come to life somewhere inside the stereo. Sentient. Thinking, feeling, singing. At *me*. They *know* these horrible thoughts are real. The only truth. They feel them with deep, sure, spiritual-conviction. The spirited voices sing them with piercing-vividness directly, tangibly, into the deepest depths of my brain and bones, mixing and mingling with the swirling headache as it pounds at the inside of my skull. Something is very seriously wrong here. A wave of terror flashes, touching head, neck, torso, limbs, toes and fingers as adrenaline starts to spike. A nauseating, rhythmic-fusion of beat and blood pulsates the fungal lumps.

"*Ooo leeeeyah…ooo leeeeyah-madelhah…*"

In seconds, annoyance becomes flaming fury. Moments later, speechless fear. This isn't right. Something important in my mind is under siege. This track is the one thing that's *always* guaranteed to lift my spirits, high as they'll go, but now, it's a dreadful incantation, bringing the horrors out of my mind and into the air itself, possessing reality, drowning out everything else, as the watery-weeping of fresh discharge oozes from my scalp, in time with the music.

It's time to *fight*. Not dismiss or ignore, as I've been trying to do the last few months, but actually *fight* these ridiculous, irritating ideas. They're *not* going to ruin my favourite song, today of all days. *I'm* the one in charge here, not some stupid shitstorm of obscure nonsense. I concentrate, with all the obstinate defiance I can muster, on recalling the edifying feelings this track *used* to illicit; the soaring, joyful uplift of sweet sensations. I find the memory of them: the joy, elation, the intangible inspiration, and *force* their memory onto the sound, to drown out *everything* else. But I'm so stoned, the desired notions slip and slide helplessly around in consciousness, vague, messy, indistinct, out of focus. Taking a deep breath, I try again, hard as I can. Superimpose the good thoughts over the bad. They instantly dissipate, puffs of smoke on the wind. Empowered by victory, the evil, living-thoughts swell further in their tempest of chaos:

"I'm not alive. I've died. A fading echo of extinct consciousness. Feedback loop. I'm trapped in this breathing-corpse. The fungal lumps are thinking, disgusted with their zombie-host."

The air, the speakers, the choir, the beat, the arpeggio – all are one with the horrifying thoughts as, with glaring clarity, they tear clean through all attempts at positive focus, like bullets shattering glass. Toxic, flesh-burning waves of horror and shock shoot though me; muscles involuntarily taut, electrocuted by an outside force. My heart palpitates. A cold sweat oozes from every crying pore. The beat, arpeggio and choir race on:

"Ooo leeeeyah…ooo leeeeyah…" BoomBaDaBoom BoomBaDaBoom BoomBaDaBoomBOOM**BOOM** *"…ooo leeeeyah-madelhah…"*

This is bad. *Really* bad. I should turn the track off. Anaesthetised by hash, gripped by shock at the unfolding hellscape, I can muster neither thought nor motion to reach the nearby remote. I stare at it, paralysed, horrified, stuck in the foam chair like a fly in the fleshy jaws of a Venus fly trap. A short, electric drum roll signals the end of this section of the track as the beat, bass and arpeggio cut out, leaving, for a faction of a second, no sound but the chilling echo of the now taunting choir, just in time for the onset of those beautiful chor-

Oh God.

The living choir go silent as the resounding chords kick in. They're possessed of an invisible, burning light, a ubiquitous, resonating laser, eviscerating the entire room. They burn deep into mind, body and heart, to the very bones, incinerating every last shred of resistance, of self. My stomach now a bottomless pit; muscles frozen in terror.

The living-thoughts explode out from the speakers and multiply a thousand times; a jungle like cacophony of horrors swirling, racing at light-speed, riding ethereal chords into every single atom of the universe. The orgy of deadly impressions at last reaches my heart, and kills me, dead, beyond all doubt. Space and time vanish beneath the murderous, resonant music.

"I don't exist. This body is unconscious mould. Alien. A virus that dreamt it was human. Fungus is alive; I'm not. Blood in these veins is conscious; I'm not. It doesn't know I exist. I don't. Thoughts not my own. Words are living-lies. Body breathes but I don't. Air is poison. Homosexuality a vile curse. There is no consciousness. Reality isn't there. Existence doesn't happen. People aren't real. I'm watching myself die."

The bottom drops out of reality itself. All remnants of ability to respond to or intercept this psychic Armageddon disintegrate. Emotion becomes sizzling sulphuric acid. Every last inch of mind unravels as I watch in enraptured despair.

The beat comes back in, its thundering pulse hijacks the rhythm of my beating heart and racing blood. The deadly, radioactive rhythm, pounds mercilessly through every object in the room, each atom of air, every last inch of flesh and petrified psyche, out through the walls and window, to the sky and beyond. Taking full possession of all perception; touching every last dimension of reality with its remorseless hammering.

None. Bada. Of. Boom. This. Bada. is. BOOM. Real. BADA. I. BOOM. Don't. *BADA*. Exist. *BOOM.* Nothing. *BOOM.* Ever. ***BOOM.*** Happened. ***BOOM BADA BOOM BADA BOOM BOOM BOOM.***

There's not a thought in all existence, but for this eviscerating beat, touching every last atom of the universe, erasing all of existence, of reality itself.

Despair gives way to unadulterated terror, everything impossibly vivid-yet-distant as my body drowns in a tsunami of its own adrenaline. Physical reactions out of all control and beyond anything I've ever experienced or thought possible. A thousand car crashes all at once. Nerves tearing apart. Brain temperature swelling to critical mass; a skull about to erupt from rocketing internal pressure…

"Ooo leeeeyah…ooo leeeeyah-madelhah"

The hypnotic refrain of the choir re-materialises over the beat and chords, reiterating the self-loathing thoughts, magnifying them a thousand fold, filling the empty universe with their diamond-clarity. I'm a disgusting infection. I'm dead but trapped inside this body, watching its decay, *tasting* it, powerless. My sexuality is a deadly disease. I'm not a person. Never was. Thoughts are a malevolent curse. The ground and walls are breathing; I'm not. My racing pulse massages the scalp-fungus from within and it thinks as it oozes fresh, watery discharge, resounding, crowning agreement. With every beat, chord and choral harmony I *feel* every single idea as an absolute, visceral truth, to my very core and beyond, baptizing my entire being with deadly despair. The sun shines a blinding, laser-like frame onto the edges of the drawn blind. Celestial agreement. I am the music and the floor and the dust and air and the sky and this empty body and dead mind and these thoughts are the *only* reality.

Beneath a blinding sun, in a humid attic-bedroom of a suburban house, a human male body, loosely wrapped in a damp dressing gown, shakes and sweats, its head pounding with thundering terror. It barely knows where or what it is. A torturous-ensemble of trance music, thoughts and death consume it, claiming all consciousness. Everything that ever made sense to it is gone; burnt to ash, carried away on a nuclear wind. Just before the peak of the dance track drops away to a lonesome, driving-beat, its heart breaks. A tide of vomit threatens to burst forth. It has to get out of the room. Right. Now. Breathless and drowning in pounding adrenaline, it somehow manages to pull itself onto all-fours, crawl through the thick ether of hellish sounds and cursed consciousness towards the stereo, the trailing beat throbbing with a new, cursed reality.

The trembling, clammy body somehow manages to climb down the attic-hatch and onto the ladder. Shaking, sweating feat fumble down each rung in something resembling coordination. A disparate, perturbed consciousness, trapped inside the body that carries it clumsily down, rung by rung, into a first floor box-room of the house. As feet connect with carpet, the consciousness is suddenly possessed by an overwhelming and all-consuming, visceral urge to hurl the body at the nearest window. The clarity and force of the impulse is epic, almost irresistible – akin to rage or laughter that cannot be contained; a phenomenal, swelling, murderous rage directed at its own flesh. Walls, furniture, sunlight and carpet echo in, resounding symphonic agreement. *Do it.* The consciousness doesn't want to, but the power of the urge is terrifying and potent. It's going to happen.

A mortal fear fulminates through the fleshy mess, rousing just enough strength to resist the urge, leave the room and descend a nearby staircase. The urge trails the body, louring over consciousness with each disconnected step. It shuffles in terrified shock and despair into a living room, climbs onto a sofa. There it lies…foetal…trembling… for an eternity.

Get a Life

At some ill-defined point along a vast, timeless expanse of nothingness, the effects of hastily-imbibed cannabis begin to trail off. The shaking of the body starts to slow. Colour and texture lose some of their terrifying edge. Consciousness gradually coalesces back into identity. With limbs. Bones. Skin…insides…sensations…thoughts…words. But the unadulterated shock remains. At some point, I manage to pull myself up from the sofa. Mixed fibres and cushions. Floral patterns. A machine for sitting. *My* feet then make contact with *the* carpet. Coarse texture…a little springy. For standing on. I tread with cautious coordination from living room, through hall and into kitchen, looking around for…reality. Walls are just walls again. Sky is outside. Something like orientation has returned. I'm me again, inhabiting my horrible body. Something called a cup of tea. A cigarette. Everything is back where it should be, however jarring and wrong it feels.

I spend the rest of the day in stunned silence. That night, brain and nerves redraw, sleep eludes me. I walk along the brook at six in the morning, the grassy valley of my old paper-round, smoking the last of my hash with a new pack of rolling papers. I'll be throwing the rest of my half-ounce away. I hate myself for smoking it and I'm glad this will be my last ever spliff. This stuff is poison. I come to the conclusion that what I experienced yesterday was a 'Whitey', at least in part (for the uninitiated, a 'Whitey' is the toker's equivalent of drinking too much, spinning out, falling over and vomiting). I've had a couple before, but the effects were nowhere near as intense and were weathered with relative ease. What happened yesterday was…different. A coach and horses ran roughshod through my entire being, shaking me to the core, and beyond; reducing important parts of my mind to dust. Something very, very important has been compromised. Destroyed. Lost. Feels like it's a combination of my identity and spirituality; disconnected, severed…defiled once and for all. A seismic shock that's changed everything. Forever. Still reeling, the whole world upside down and inside-out, I walk home and finally get off to sleep about eight in the morning.

Over the next week, trundling mule-like through the endless, infinitesimal minutes of each warehouse shift, I set what's left of my mind to work on figuring out how on earth I can ever move forward. Those awful sensations and ideas, now branded deep into the fabric of my brain, remain in consciousness all the time, superimposed onto everything else; every thought, feeling, sensation, object and encounter are stalked, haunted by them. Still, without the magnifying effects of THC, I can at least function. To a degree. I'm irrevocably sad, and painfully detached, every minute of every day. It feels unmistakably as though, on that awful afternoon, something crucial inside snapped: all optimism, energy, resilience and zest for life were torn out; something integral to life itself reduced to a pile of cold ash. Something inside erupted; the horrible thoughts became reality, exploding mercilessly into the world, burning everything. The incident bore deep holes into my heart and mind that I can't seem to close, out of which a steady stream of life gushes out, a cold wind rushing inside in its place. I have to pull myself together, get a life and somehow overcome this strange, psychotic depression. I'm miserable, feel guilty that I've let myself and others down so completely, ashamed of my behaviour, drug addiction, my strange mind and most of all, I feel like a freak of nature for my homosexuality and totally lost without that indefinable spiritual feeling that was once so crucial, so uplifting. Now, everything is heavy, burdensome and utterly pointless. Repeating the endless parcel-packing ritual in my designated alcove of the vast, stuffy, windowless warehouse, I contemplate what it might take to feel human again. To feel alive. At all. It seems a long way off – the bewildering uncertainties and confusion left in the wake of that weed-induced breakdown appear as a mountain so high I can barely see the summit. I decide that what's really needed is to regain a sense of connection; to be part of something I can feel good about. In all those stressful school days of unsuccessfully micromanaging life, in the vain hope of avoiding confrontation; the intense frustration of rebellion; getting expelled and diving headlong into the ultimately dubious world of cannabis, it seems I've steadily, progressively disconnected from my own life. Time to do something about it. The only thing I can envision really losing myself in – in a positive, productive manner, for a change – is singing. I can't sing very well at the moment but Kayleigh, who has an exquisite, soulful voice, is always telling me I can, it's just a question of working on technique. Seems like a long shot but the idea of being lost in song, to be both making and experiencing the music simultaneously, being *part* of it, perhaps even in a band, might just provide enough of a stimulating, transcendent feeling to remedy all the panic and despair that now stalks every waking moment. The trouble is, even if I were to develop my voice to an acceptable standard, I'm far, far, *far* too self conscious to even consider singing around others, let alone perform. I hate my strange, apologetic, genderless voice; my big, protruding ears, rounded shoulders and skinny body. There are deep self-loathing and confidence issues to resolve – many of which were either ignored or repressed during the school years, when the priority was just getting through the next day. I sense the level of confidence required to really pursue this dream will take a long time to develop, in my own bizarre case. In the meantime, I *badly* need to get a life. ASAP. Each day begins with that same residual shock and despair from the psychotic-Whitey, a crippling alienation from absolutely everything and everyone, including myself, along with a deepening despair and shock at the way my mind had disintegrated so rapidly, so *entirely*, that I doubt I'll ever be the same again. Now it seems everything good in the world needs a clearly defined reason: laughter, excitement and even straightforward concentration feel slippery, fleeting, draining…even dangerous. In the past, whenever I was lucky enough to experience these first two, fully, I always lost the plot, became overexcited and ended up in serious trouble. I'd dearly love to talk to someone about all this insanity but feel utterly baffled as to how I'd find the language, let alone the courage. Considering just how elaborate, strange and intense all the chaos in my head is, I fear I'll find myself parked on a psychiatric ward indefinitely, written off and never again taken seriously. No, I have to find a way out of this waking nightmare by myself. The only way to do that is to venture back into the real world and get a life. Go to college, make new friends, have things to do, stimulate my brain, and, at some point, start coming out to existing friends. And keep well away from that awful weed. It's time to start growing up, and get back to the real world.

Project Hope

I apply to the local tech college and, given my near-phobic reticence at the prospect of actually studying performing arts, opt instead for academic A-levels. Exam results pending, I hope to have something resembling a life in a few months…I tell Kayleigh about the awful psychotic-whitey and express my intent to never touch cannabis again, but she has other ideas – "What are we going to do if we don't get stoned?" – suggesting that I'm simply more measured with future doses. The prospect of hanging out with my best friend without the usual THC hit fills me with the powerful fear of being socially awkward, mute, unlikeable and ultimately alone; the semi-conscious notion that there must always be some kind of precarious payoff to gain so much as a modicum of cachet with just about anyone. I relent and agree to get stoned with her again, but be very, very careful.

Summer drags on forever. Four-hour shifts at the warehouse every evening except Wednesday, and the snail-paced eight hour shift each Saturday. I get up at ten each morning, walk a neighbour's dog and try to keep busy. A huge, emotionally draining life laundry takes place over several weeks – most remnants of the recent past of high school and Oakwood are either thrown out or stored away. I make regular visits to a local music memorabilia store and acquire a few gems with which to adorn my newly revamped room; their glamorous sheen providing a reminder of those distant, future goals; of being immersed in music and purpose, of the idea that the future might yet be salvageable and the past not repeated. I buy all the equipment I might need for college and smoke just a moderate amount of cannabis at the weekends with Kayleigh. Smaller, controlled doses and weekday abstinence mean some of the old medicinal effects are back, if only a little. For a couple of hours a week I'm able to take at least some of the edge off that sinking sadness that's infected everything since the breakdown. I remain scared of getting too stoned and wonder why I still need it at all, until Monday morning comes and a little more light disappears from the world. No, cannabis isn't the answer – getting a life is – but it can still provide the odd break, if used sensibly. After all, getting a life is going to take everything I've got, so, why not have a little smoke? Still, I wish I didn't need it to relax. There's just so much confusion and despair. I'll stop completely at a later date, when college is well under way. It'll be easier then. Surely.

Most nights I sit in the attic-room and fantasise about what college might be like, and about my long term goals – the immersive escape of imagination provides a small balm for those sad feelings that just won't fade. A very small balm. Something vital has gone. I feel wrong. The world feels wrong. Life's simple joys like laughter, spontaneity, enjoying music, a film or a conversation with a friend all seem cruel lies. I miss them terribly but they can no longer be trusted – all part of the lie, along with sentiment and emotion. Occasionally laughing or a spontaneous chat with a friend feels somehow sore, as though any connection with my insides could jeopardise my entire thought process once again. I'm so heavy and out of place all the time. Each day begins with this feeling, from the moment my eyes open, and it stays with me right until I fall asleep each night. The colour hasn't exactly gone from the world, it's just that I no longer recognise or have anything to do with it, like some faraway, exotic and dangerous place, where nothing is what it seems. I've been expelled from this thing called 'Reality'; I'll never again be a part of it, and unsure whether I even believe in its existence any more. The emotional consequences of such convictions leave me feeling as though I'm hauling a giant stone boulder everywhere I go. And those strange, nauseating intuitions from that awful July afternoon – extreme distortion of and alienation from self, environment; from everything and everyone around – remain painfully close at all times, threatening to overwhelm my brain once more at the opportune moment. Thoughts that I'm a mindless lump of mould stalk consciousness day and night; either it's the truth and I'm the only one who knows or else there's something very, very wrong with me. Project Hope is the fight back; the deployment of all remaining resources against this strange malady. It doesn't make much of a dent over the summer, but that's the whole point of getting a life – to climb out of this godforsaken hole. God, I can't wait until college starts. I miss not having this level of crap in my head. I miss the real world.

A Study in Red

A Study in Red

The long, gruelling summer finally crawls into September as, at long last, college begins. Out of purgatory and back to the world. That's the plan. I have a deep, nagging feeling that college might never fully heal the black hole within – it seems able to swallow whole absolutely everything in life – but at the very least it'll help take my mind off it; something else to focus on and a direction, hopefully, towards one day, somehow, maybe, feeling okay again. Kayleigh's managed to persuade the local educational authorities to let her split her time between Oakwood and college, so she'll be around a couple of days a week, and there are a few other familiar female faces from school, so it doesn't seem *too* daunting. Immeasurably important, yes, but not quite the deep end.

Worcester College of Technology occupies a handful of mid-twentieth century modernist buildings, mostly along the east riverbank, just shy of the bridge. I spent my high school work experience week in the library here, so the huge concrete, cubist structures aren't entirely unfamiliar. The town centre is just over the road, and the twinkling tranquillity of the river a stone's throw in the opposite direction, the across the main college car park. Intellectual and social stimulation in congenial surroundings. Structure, routine and a direction in which to go: the perfect place for Project Hope.

The first few weeks are a tentative success. Pushing the jittering-nervousness and weird thoughts to the back of my mind, I find I can chat with others outside, amidst the hustle and bustle of the main entrance concourse that serves as the unofficial smoking area. Providing I'm with someone I already know, that is. This is a different ball game to Oakwood or School. Most students are here by choice and, being largely of the academic ilk, finally freed from the confines of high school; the atmosphere is rowdy, a tad over the top, but largely congenial. I struggle to talk directly with other lads, as whenever any other male speaks but a word to me, I find myself speechless and frozen to the spot, a rabbit in headlights. But, as Kayleigh or one or two other girls are usually around, I can at least skulk on the periphery of conversation without too much awkwardness. Nervous and over-excited but otherwise okay. At the end of the third week, Kayleigh and I sit on a riverside bench on the Friday afternoon, chatting about our experiences thus far. We both agree that each week has been progressively better than the last. A good start all round. Movement in the right direction. Things might even be looking up.

A few short weeks into the academic year, however, the days still bright and warm, atmosphere buzzing with September-optimism, something happens in an English lecture that brings all forward momentum to a *shuddering* halt.

Red Alert

Being back in a classroom environment after everything that happened at school, Oakwood and the mental shit-storm of the summer, was quite an intense experience. I put most of it down to start-of-term-nerves but, a few weeks into the course, as most other students appeared to be settling in well, I remained *very* uncomfortable. There was something about being in an enclosed environment with groups of other teens that stirred in me an inexplicable unease; a feeling I was woefully out of place and jarringly separate from everyone else. The liveliness of lectures, group discussions and casual classroom chit chat always rendered me insanely self-conscious and on edge, as if an unseen, unspeakable danger lurked somewhere close by. I put it down to my weird brain, the residual effects of weed and this strange depression. Give it time.

At high school, English had always been my strongest subject; in fact, just a week or so before being expelled I'd achieved my first ever A* for a coursework assignment on Macbeth. Although there was no one especially familiar in A-level English, the lecturer and head of department happened to be Gill, the mother of an old friend from school. A mid-height, middle aged lady, somewhere in her forties, Gill always seemed to wear the same white blouse, long, pleated skirt and high heels. A smallish pair of thin, round glasses framed her intense-yet-wise eyes and a curly-bob of thick, dark hair sat atop her head. Her somewhat familiar presence was reassuring.

Passing through the heavy cloud of cigarette smoke on the outside concourse and in through the main entrance doors, one found the humanities building was laid out a lot like an archetypal school. Long, bright, sanitary corridors lined with classroom doors; stairwells at each end and a smallish performing arts studio on the lower ground floor.

Through a small door at the bottom of the main stairwell, at the start of the lower ground floor corridor, tucked away in a corner next to her office, Gill's well-lit classroom was a sanctuary of tranquillity amongst the noisy rabble of college. The far wall was lined end-to-end with large windows overlooking the car park as it sloped down to the tree lined riverbank beyond, backlit by sky. This magnolia-walled room with its light brown corduroy carpet was arranged differently to the other classes, where the setup was often the traditional rows-of-tables facing the board. In English we sat behind a large U-shape formation of desks along the edge of the room, with Gill often perched casually on the edge of a single desk in front of the whiteboard. All faces could be seen across the open plan seating. Despite being a stickler for getting work in on time, having everyone's attention and pushing each student for their best work, Gill nonetheless maintained a calm, informal environment; the no-drinks-in-class rule was openly flouted and her contemplative, meandering discourses away from the syllabus were often engaging and profound.

During one afternoon lecture, however, one little detour down digression-lane tripped a wire…

Ten minutes into the lecture, Gill takes us down another pleasant side road, this time on the subject of stereotypes and their limitations – a matter close to my own heart. A handful of other students wear looks of glazed disinterest, but I'm listening intently. She suddenly alights on the topic of gay stereotypes:

"…And typically, while many people might expect most gay men to be quite fay, camp and effeminate as, for example, Julian Clary is in his stage act, in reality that's often not the case at all."

The moment Gill's soft, meditative voice sends the phrase "gay men" floating through the air, into the ears of everyone present, my face immediately burns a red-hot crimson. No sudden build up of anxiety before the fact, no chance to divert my attention away from the awkward subject just in time; my face is instantly afire with glowing shame before I can so much as think. A cycle of panic kicks in: I'm alarmed and feel weirdly exposed at what's happening, gripped by a sense that not only does my blushing betray the truth of my sexuality, but every self-loathing thought of repulsion and shame I've ever had, *including* all those messed up ideas from the breakdown in July. <u>Everyone</u> can see that I'm gay; that I feel like a slimy little faggot-abomination, a freak of nature *and* that it's all true; the redness of my face a flaming beacon, brilliantly illuminating every last insecurity for the world to see. It's as though my skin has peeled away, and a harsh, silent judgement fills the air, stabbing deep into exposed organs. Nerves afire with danger signals and I'm so rigid I can barely move, let alone think. And, of course, such sensations inevitably perpetuate the excruciating redness of face. Petrol to a flame. My scalp tightens and I feel myself sweat. Every muscle tense. Almost breathless, I grit my teeth and curse internally. ShitShitShitShitShitShitShit. Fuck. Bollocks. Should I ask to be excused? Make up some dubious malady?

No. That'll only draw further attention. Too scared to glance around the room to see if anyone's actually noticed; my gaze is fixed on the desk in front of me in trancelike terror. I'm rooted to the spot. The burning facial temperature continues; an unending moment of flaming shame. Body a boiling pan of scalding adrenaline. Soon it's as though there's nothing else within the room or indeed myself; no air, no thought, not even gravity; everything temporarily obliterated with a terrifying cocktail of danger and shame. For god's sake, when will this pass? I finally understand the old cliché of wanting the ground to open up and swallow you whole. I feel dizzy and, oddly, violated in some strange way by my own body…or brain…by this red hot, burning face. I wish I could pass out. At least then it would be over.

The redness eventually subsides as breathing and pulse start to slow. I glance at Chloe, the girl to my right. She's staring straight at me and slowly blinking in a way that's impossible to read: is this empathy? Surprise? Distaste? I can't tell. OhFuckOhFuckOhFuck. Shit. Why did this have to happen? No one else appears to be looking in my direction right now but how can I be sure they didn't see? A gushing waterfall of humiliation and anger rushes through me. Panic and a sudden, intense-exhaustion set in. I spend the rest of the lecture on a knife edge, barely able to speak; mouth sandpaper- dry; throat shrinking and concentration levels close to zero. Every thought, word, sound and movement pummel the senses at with industrial force. There's a sharp pain in my head. My body feels spent with the adrenaline, like I've just been hauled out of a near-fatal car crash. Did anyone else see? It felt in that moment as if any sense of privacy or personal boundaries fell clean away, and some terrible chain reaction was dangerously close to ignition. Will rumours start to circulate? Will people shun me? Thoughts race out of control. I just want to get away from this humiliating ordeal to somewhere safe. When the lecture finally ends and I step outside, the sunlight and fresh air flood the senses; reassuring and overbearing in equal measure. I feel sick. Violated.

Exhaustion grows worse, as if all life has drained away. I'll smoke my fag somewhere quiet, away from the main building. I just want to hide.

Contagion

Despite all attempts to dismiss or ignore the blushing incident, shockwaves reverberate for several days. The fragile, superficial confidence of those first few weeks is shattered, leaving only an acute weariness in the presence of other students. Before the incident, casual conversation was something of a nervous dance: *really* intense but ultimately bearable. Now, however, I find myself impossibly on edge. Standing on the periphery of idle, break-time conversations, I can think of all the things I'd like to say to join in, but find that everything that comes out of my mouth somehow passes through a, distortive filter that renders the sounds ugly, jarring and hideously out of place; those self-loathing thoughts from the summer made flesh, externalised for all to see. Before the blushing incident, I was highly anxious in social situations. Now, I'm downright terrified.

I'm furious with myself. Why and how have I overreacted to a simple incident of blushing so *completely*? Everyone feels a little embarrassed from time to time – it's a normal part of life – so why had there been such terror and why on earth couldn't I just forget about it? Try as I might, I just can't seem to haul my brain and nerves out of this funk; something inside is acting like a petrified animal that cannot and will not cooperate, under any circumstances. It's pathetic, debilitating and utterly infuriating. I tell myself to give it time. What else can be done?

The first term marches on through autumn, towards Christmas. English lectures become a bizarre mix of much needed intellectual stimulation and knife-edge nerves. Gill's discourses, along with the books we study remain wholly engaging, and there are good and bad days, but the fear of another unexpected blushing-trigger and the inner trauma that goes with it continually hijack my attention. I begin reading ahead in the texts in search of any potential trigger-words that might arise. No direct references to homosexuality turn up but a few risqué phrases elicit a powerful plummeting feeling and slight headache, even when sat reading them alone in the safety of home. In eighteenth and nineteenth century literature, the use of the words "gay" and "queer" occur now and then, in their former context, as do the more old fashioned, romanticised ways of describing close male friendships. Each example I come across evokes a sense of precarious relief, found in the knowledge that it's currently several chapters away and so we won't be looking at it for weeks. I can relax, for now. In tandem with this is a slow-burning, burgeoning dread that sooner or later, the risqué word will inevitably be read aloud in class. A strange contagion-effect takes hold: During one lecture, Gill discusses the "joyful" tone of a particular piece of dialogue. "Joyful" is dangerously close to "gay" (as in "gaiety"). Being so desperately on edge in class, just the word "joy" soon starts to evoke an unsettling, distant thunder. A louring tempest troubling the horizon. The same is true of words that simply *sound* like trigger-terms: "Hay" and "Day" join the ranks along with "Seer" and "Queen" as they all sound or look vaguely similar to contemporary terms for homosexuality. Of course, it's all on a spectrum, as nothing elicits that quicksand-panic with the same harrowing-immediacy as the word "gay" itself, but, sometimes just a glance at vaguely connected words or synonyms elicits a quiet tremor within. Other times, tangible-quivers and tremors ripple through my chest, stomach or scalp in the middle of a lecture for no obvious reason. Often, as Gill reads this week's chapter aloud, I'll be several lines ahead, scanning for danger, just in case there's anything I've missed. When we do eventually begin our final approach toward those much anticipated danger-words, an accelerating, silent panic sets in as we traverse the prior page, followed by free-falling desperation as we turn over and work through the penultimate paragraph. Each second is a little less safe the last. I brace myself. Sometimes Gill stops reading, just short of the trigger, to reflect on the text or indulge another tangent. It's excruciating. When the dreaded word is finally read aloud, I frantically fight to distract myself from the rising body temperature, stomach somersaults and throbbing headache by gritting my teeth tight and rapidly repeating words and numbers in my head. Twentyninetoiletattendants. Moonbootsale. ShitShitShit. ShutUpShutUpShutUpShutUpSocks. Or I force myself to answer random, internal questions: How many people live in Birmingham?

TwoMillionTwoMillionShutUpTwoMillion. Bollocks. It's weird, horrible and does nothing to calm the panic but it does, somehow, manage to keep me from actually blushing, most of the time. Other times I do blush, but at words like "Scene" – one part of the phrase "Gay Scene" – that couldn't possibly have any meaningful context to anyone watching. Nonetheless, the feeling that every manic thought and shameful emotion is on display, for all to see, remains crystal clear. All the time. And all this from one simple, ostensibly innocuous blushing incident back in September.

What is *Wrong* With Me?

Close to Christmas, Kayleigh starts truanting. I remain as depressed as ever, Project Hope yielding almost no result so far and, in many ways, making everything that much more gloomy and confusing. But as hard a slog as college is, I *have* to make it work, so joining Kayleigh on the Truant Express isn't an option. I just can't face going back to that old life of the stoned-loser with nothing to do but sit in the attic, smoking weed and going steadily insane. But we keep in touch, hang out and even come out to each other – She confides her bisexuality, a fact about which I had no inkling whatsoever and I my homosexuality – so we have plenty of new topics to discuss. But not having her around at college much of the time does make things harder. Most other familiar female associates have by now either left or transferred to another course in a different building. The few that remain are usually busy chatting and laughing with new college friends amidst the smoky-din of the outside concourse. But for my nicotine addiction, it becomes a no go area. Standing amongst the adolescent chatter, leaning against a wall or railing, not knowing where to look or even how to stand, I desperately want to join in overheard conversations, but those crippling feelings of social danger from that first blushing incident howl inside, frightened wolves on a stormy night. All the bad thoughts I have about myself, the weird ideas from the breakdown over the summer, all of it, swarm around inside, pushing at the surface, threatening to project themselves outwards via body language or my weird, gay voice. It's *all* true and it'll *all* come out. Then people will know what a fraud I am; a weird, messed up, shrivelled little freak. I fight to push it all down or just plain ignore it, but everything springs instantly back up; a demoralising game of mental whack-a-mole. Occasional conversations with kind-hearted, well-meaning people bring on the usual headaches, charged-tension and cold sweat. The concourse includes a small bridge over the staff car park below, just before the entrance doors. Sometimes, with the stress of it all, weariness morphs into thoughts of throwing myself down onto the concrete. Not deliberate 'I-want-to-die' thoughts; more like a part of my brain suggesting an efficient way to make the gruelling discomfort stop. Utterly ridiculous, but also worrying, insofar as it adds to the sense that I'm generally no more than an insane basket-case. Once the cigarette's finished, I go inside, downstairs, into the toilets just outside Gill's class, shut myself in a stall and wait for the next lesson to begin. It feels just like high school; like everyone else is part of a 'normal', cool alumni I can neither access nor fathom. I've become the strange, self-isolating mute once again. Unable to cope in social situations. And yet this *isn't* high school. I'm not being bullied. People here may be rowdy and cocksure, but they're also mostly friendly and individualistic. So what on earth is wrong with me? I decide it must be something to do with my sexuality. Much of the self-consciousness, self-loathing and even the terrifying, macabre thoughts of the breakdown last summer all seem to centre on this notion that I just don't fit it; don't belong. So it must all have something to do with being in the closet. If only I wasn't gay, none of this would be a problem. But I am. I'm gay and in the closet and sitting here, literally locking myself inside a stall, waiting for the sound of the teenage hoard to signal the beginning of the next lecture. Just like hiding in that bush on the field or timing my arrival to co-inside with the ringing of the school bell. Hiding away, yet again. In the closet. Figuratively and literally. This is getting ridiculous.

Shortly after the Christmas break, Kayleigh drops out. I call her from a tattered old red phone box in town one cold and wet February morning during the fag break. She won't be coming back to college. She's pregnant. She's excited, scared and confused but she's going to keep it and so won't be on campus for the foreseeable future. I'm baffled and worried. Baffled that she's gotten pregnant in the first place and worried that she won't be able to rely on Gaz, her weed-dealer boyfriend. And, selfishly, worried for myself. Another eighteen months of college without my best friend coming in a couple of days a week to take the edge off? I'm feeling more alienated by the day. Weed use started creeping in again over Christmas and the weird-intensity of English lectures and general social paranoia has made it seem once again an appealing balm. I know it ultimately isn't, but after all the insane fretting, the headaches and all the studying, short term relief is as short term relief does. Now isn't a good time to stop. Things are too hard at the moment. I can't believe Kayleigh isn't coming back.

Project Hopeless?

Things don't improve. College without allies becomes overbearing as the paranoia and word-watching descend into farce. The list of dangerous words and subjects grows almost weekly until concentrating at all during lectures is nigh impossible. More than ever I feel like an irredeemable outsider; a freak unable to socialise, fit in or just enjoy being young. Or anything about life. Project Hope was supposed to mobilise against the terrifying meaninglessness, confusion and crushing depression, and now, six months in, it's close to crashing and burning completely. College was to be the way forward and instead it just seems to be confirming all the worst thoughts I have about myself. I feel like a failure as a human being; unable to enjoy even the simple things in life. The one thing that could penetrate all the colour-draining sadness was hope for the future, but as college is becoming increasingly unbearable, it seems there's not a lot else to feel good about or look forward to. Thoughts are becoming dangerous again. My emotional state is plummeting still further into a kind of manic desperation and, frankly, it's scary.

Gill's daughter is also a student at the college and old friend from high school. Although we don't really see each other off campus, and on campus she's quite the social butterfly, we still chat now and then. She knows something's been up for a while and, although I'm deliberately vague on detail, can see it's getting worse so mentions it to Gill who, in turn, relays a message back to me that I can hang back at the end of English on Friday for a chat, if I'd like. That particular lecture is a little different; the painful social unease like a thousand itching boils all over the skin is there, as usual, but it's joined by a quiet foreboding: a feeling that something significant is going to happen at the end of the hour. Something concrete and final. Admitting to the problem. I can no longer deal with it alone and just knowing I can finally open up and talk to someone is a huge relief, but that knowledge does nothing to abate the sinking feeling of having to face up to things I *really* don't want to. I don't want to be gay, depressed or have all of these strange social handicaps. I just want to be a casual and nonchalant student like almost everyone else. But I can't. So it must be done. The lesson finally ends and the rest of the class file out. Gill sits on the edge of her usual tangent-table in front of the whiteboard; I stay in my usual seat nearest the door. And we talk.

That First Step

Gill and I spoke for about an hour, mostly about depression and the services available in and around college. We didn't go into too much detail but just to discuss it with someone was nice, not to mention reassuring. Gill referred me to a counselling service at a nearby youth centre, where I met a lady who made us both a cup of tea and brought in a plate of chips. Telling a complete stranger about my sexuality was a gruelling leap of faith: It takes a good few minutes of long, excruciating silence, racing heart rate and frantic wringing of hands to get the words out. A lump the size of a fist in my throat and liquid-dread boiling out of every pore. I stare at the floor, rub my temples, flesh like jelly and in a low, quivering voice mutter the words: "I'm gay." Just saying it aloud feels like a thousand things at once: breaking through a stone-wall; jumping out of an airplane; confessing to a terrible crime; pleading for acceptance; walking through the high street naked; wandering into no-man's-land; risking everything. I stare at the floor a few moments more before forcing my gaze up to gage the counsellor's reaction. She smiles, nods reassuringly and seems empathetic. Halfway through the session she suggests referring me to her friend Colin at the sexual health centre, as he's more experienced with this kind of thing. I agree, she makes a quick phone call and we continue talking for around an hour.

Colin. A man. Another male. Discuss my homosexuality with a man. Maybe after that I could jump from a plane without a parachute? He sounded professional and unassuming over the phone, so I agreed to the appointment, but the prospect of having to go through 'The

Announcement' again with another complete stranger, a *male* stranger no less, is daunting to say the least. But these problems loom large as ever and certainly aren't going anywhere, so I must do what I must.

About a fortnight later I'm sitting in the reception of the Worcester Sexual Health clinic. In a quiet back street, just outside the city centre, is a small, modern office building, built to look like a row of old townhouse terraces. The clinic occupies the third floor. There are a handful of cluttered desks in three of the four corners of the reception area, some with staff behind them taking calls, tapping away at computers. Several small windows are hung with half-open venetian blinds, grey February sky peering gloomily through the slats. Every visible surface is covered with stacks of leaflets and out of date magazines. I'm sitting on a small sofa, not daring to move or look up beyond the occasional, nervous glance, when a ridiculously tall man enters the room (I'm 6ft 1, so anyone taller than me is "ridiculously tall" in my eyes), wearing dark jeans, office shoes and a pastel pink shirt. He chats quietly to the young female receptionist before approaching me with the words "Are you Richard?"

"Yes" I nod nervously and bite my lip.

"Nice to meet you Richard, I'm Colin. Shall we go through to my office?"

I follow towards a door at other end of the reception room. We go through. I can't quite believe this is happening. Inside, a partition wall with windows and more venetian blinds – these ones are, thankfully, closed – separate us from reception. A large desk sits against the far wall, again strewn with innumerable leaflets, an office chair next to it. I sit on a padded chair opposite, half-dazed with the weight of what's about to happen. Colin asks if I'd like a cup of tea. I accept and nervously scan the many informative-posters that line the walls while awaiting the brew. Some are about contraception, some about drugs, others about HIV, homelessness and so on. Many display helpline numbers. The matter-of-fact-ness of their subject matter is at once alarming and reassuring. But not distracting enough. Have I really got to go through The Announcement again? I think so, yes.

Colin soon returns with a scalding-hot cup of tea and the session begins. The ritual announcement is hard in much the same way as with the last counsellor, it takes much longer, as though there's even more gravity to it this time; more at stake. I'm in the Sexual Health Clinic, about to tell another male that I'm gay. It's terrifying. But, being so central to everything right now, it has to be done. His response is calm and empathetic. Nonetheless, my stomach and brain turn cartwheels. He soon segues onto other areas: questions about my life, relationships, hobbies, habits, and much more besides, taking notes all the while. It takes some time to cover the whole picture but we manage to go over a lot of ground in the first session, which lasts for three and a half hours. He also asks about how I'd like things to change, what said changes might look like and how do we get from where I am to where I'd like to be? Offloading in this way, in so much detail and with Colin's searching questions, empathetic looks and unassuming tone, proves a huge relief. By the end of the session, much has come out, and my nerves are almost settled.

I sit on the bus home, in a messy-cloud of cynicism and guarded hope. It's going to take a lot to convince me this awful situation could ever change: that since the cataclysmic break down last summer I could ever again be myself around others, let alone confident and self assured; that my sexuality hasn't completely ruined my life; that this penetrating sadness could somehow be overcome. But, for the first time in a long time, it feels like a genuine, if remote, possibility.

The Final Rush Hour, Part V

Blushing. Fucking blushing. The undisputed bane of my life. No other problem has ever been so persistent, resilient or destructive in my life. I often think that if only it wasn't for the blushing problem, I might have found a way through all of this, in the end. But it cuts through everything; boils all emotion and reason to an all-consuming, unbearable heat.

The traffic creeps steadily away from the river, along the east side of the racecourse, slowly winding around the corner and up the hill by the old, empty hospital and coming to a brief standstill by the new police station. The ineffable joy fades a little to the background. Will I be brought back to this neck of the woods later on, handcuffed in the back of a police van? There'll be no acting calm then. Not that I care…or at least I don't want to. Getting closer now. Once I'm out of the city centre traffic it won't be far to the industrial estate, and an end to all of this. I reckon I've got about twenty to thirty minutes left in the frugal protection of this car and the anonymity of the morning commute, although I wouldn't be surprised if something suddenly kicked off right here and now. White-hot fear courses fiercely through my body like a scalding steam. I don't fight it. Drunk with disorientation, pins-and-needles tickling beneath the surface of every inch of skin, but, no longer trying to control any of it, there's still that deep sense of relief. Of release. How strange it is that so many hyper-intense, contradictory feelings can inhabit me, all at once. I fought so hard, for so long; to control fear and despair in the hope of rediscovering and cultivating those old, edifying feelings of spiritual joy and calm. They were supposed make everything okay again, but were nowhere to be found. Today, however, they've abruptly returned and swirl among the more familiar terror and trauma. No one emotion wins out; it's a bizarre sunshine storm of flaming hailstones and exquisite snowflakes. I'm so messed up. It wasn't supposed to happen like this. Joy isn't doing its job properly. I pass the twenty four hour petrol station at the top of the hill, turn left at the lights and into the corridor of old houses and shop fronts that lead out of the city centre. Glances at the same old familiar shop windows and pavements stir memories of a time when just walking around here was akin to walking on the air itself. So much deep spiritual joy and strength; gone when most desperately needed and, at last, returning today, on this day-of-days, when it's far, *far* too late. Sometimes I wonder if that was the core problem: the search for long-lost Joy ultimately caused more difficulties than it ever really solved…in the end…but it was *so*…incredible…

Zenith

Zenith

On a beautifully clear June night in the summer of 2000, I'm driving home from Kayleigh's house in my first ever car – Nan's old 1979, Mark II Escort – doing little more than thirty as the tank is once again close to empty. Gently meandering along the narrow, winding, rustic A-roads that make up the quieter, scenic route from Droitwich to Worcester, I notice everything inside and outside the car is bathed in the ubiquitous, sublime, slivery glow of the moon. Each little leaf on every tree; the rolling fields that flank the winding old road; the roofs of occasional houses, the road surface: *everything* basks in twinkling moonlit radiance. There's not another vehicle in sight. It's one in the morning…or possibly two…or two thirty…I can't be sure. First, because this beloved old banger has no clock; second, and much more significantly, my conscious mind has finally ceased to turn. Still as the small, roadside puddles that shimmer silvery reflections of the vast, infinite light show of the night sky; the occasional thought just *barley* skims the surface of this tranquil mind. Almost unnoticed, such thoughts simply float on by and recede quietly into the distance – inconsequential landmarks on a delightful journey to nowhere in particular. Driving is a simple, effortless joy; gears changed and corners turned with such gentle ease it's like watching myself do it all in some pleasant dream. Nerves are completely and utterly settled as each breath sings in, then out of my being. I'm *deeply* calm, filled with a serene, exquisite, unspeakable joy.

This delightful drive began in much the same way as every nocturnal commute from Kayliegh's suburban sanctuary: with a residual stoned-feeling after another of our regular spilff-and-singing sessions. Kayleigh gave up the weed while pregnant and we don't smoke anywhere near as much as we used to but nevertheless, I still prefer to wait for the effects to more or less wear off before driving home. I've developed the habit, of late, of continuing singing by myself throughout the seven mile homeward journey; sometimes to whatever CDs are in the car; other times just ad-libbing random tunes and lyrics, always in the vein of a simple, positive, spiritual sentiment. This newfound hobby has the wonderful effect of cultivating and augmenting an already buoyant mood into a gentle crescendo of sublime, blissful ecstasy. I've been making the night time commute in this manner for some months now, and tonight, I've reached my zenith. The signing has stopped. Now I'm just gliding along, barely a thought in mind, enjoying the view with the most tranquil smile on my face. I couldn't *be* more relaxed: mind utterly empty; heart overflowing with radiant love and light. Even the gentle motions of the steadily-rumbling car are a sublime dance of kinetic poetry. I'm the happiest I've ever been. Ever. Depression is now a distant, obscure memory from some long-forgotten tale. I honestly feel that everything will be okay from now on. More than okay. Positively blissful.

Slowly but Surely

The final months of the first year of college had been a little less than awful. Certainly nowhere near as difficult as was the case when I started seeing Colin at the Sexual Health Clinic. I might even have gone so far as to say they were almost pleasant. There was still so much about myself I wasn't comfortable with; so much confusion and sadness, but, in our regular sessions, Colin and I were beginning to unravel some of the tangled mess. It was all about coming to terms with my sexuality as a young adult and finding ways to be myself around others. We also discussed the blushing fears, but not the really, really weird thoughts or weed use. I assumed they were all tied up with being in the closet so rarely brought them up. Suffice to say, as the bleakness of winter gave way to spring's flowering beauty and then on into the verdant brightness of summer, the edge was beginning to ease off of the depression and anxiety. I felt able to stay at college a while longer and, in those final few months of the academic year, I was really, unexpectedly, enjoying the GCSE History class…

Wise Old Bob

A-level English and Media studies had been continually torturous, but GCSE History was another matter. Having dropped History when given the choice at Oakwood, I'd taken it up again at college for a few reasons. It was a favourite subject at school until we alighted on the GCSE syllabus in Year Ten, focusing mainly on topics like crop rotation and other farming methods, none of which were even remotely engaging. The college syllabus, by contrast, was twentieth century history; far more interesting. My erratic, unreliable and often unpleasant brain demanded so much energy that I doubted I could cope with three, full time A-Level classes, as was the norm at the time, so the one-year GCSE course at college seemed a more workable, realistic option. Also, Kayleigh had been allowed to split her time between Oakwood and college so, once again, that feeling of being a social abomination in need of a chaperone meant I leapt at the opportunity the moment she expressed an interest in the history class.

The History classroom, situated at the far end of the first floor corridor, was something of a backwater. The only human traffic passing the always-open door consisted of staff visiting the adjacent History office. The room itself was small, and much more like the archetypical, old fashioned classroom than most other college classes. Faded, pastel-pink walls with scattered scuff marks interspersed with patches of peeling paint; wood-effect, laminate flooring, dusty and probably older than any student or staff member. A single row of small, high-up windows connected the back wall and the ceiling; in front of them were three rows of tables facing the big, old bureau-style desk that sat in front of an old-fashioned, dusty blackboard. With the little windows behind us and nothing going on in the corridor outside, there really was nowhere else to direct one's attention. This hadn't been a problem with Simon, our twenty-something Thursday afternoon lecturer - he of the bohemian dress sense and dry humour — he easily held the attention of the class. On Fridays, however, we had two hours with old Bob Jameson. Bob was a short, slightly plump, pastry-faced older man with short, thin brown hair, a stereotypical tweed jacket and round glasses thick enough to withstand all but an atomic blast. Venerated by colleagues and either giggled at or ignored by students, he was very much the clichéd, old-fashioned, academic professor. A wise old owl among rowdy teens. While Simon conducted most of his lessons standing up, chatting *with* the class in a lively, engaging manner; Bob, by contrast, would routinely sit at his desk, remove his blast-proof glasses and simply talk *at* the class in a hypnotically-boring monotone, rubbing the bridge of his nose throughout. The latter teaching style, coupled with the penned-in setup of the classroom meant that when Bob was in charge, you either had to busy yourself taking notes or the suffer slow mental torture of timeless boredom.

The course began in September with about eight students, but by mid spring there were just two of us left as all others, including Kayleigh, had gradually peeled away. Simon was eventually reassigned to teach another class on Thursdays, so Sadiq and I had four hours a week with Bob. On paper, it sounded boring. It wasn't. With just the three of us in the room, lectures assumed a more conversational tone, the syllabus quickly covered and soon Sadiq and I were able to pick Bob's inexhaustible, encyclopaedic brain on almost any subject we liked. We discussed science, history, religion, theology, metaphysics and much more besides. Bob was an atheist, Sadiq a Muslim and I, at the time, an agnostic, so the conversations were both fascinating and illuminating. Many of the burning questions that arose around the time of my hash-induced breakdown were now casually explored though our conversational forums. What I took from them was ultimately that "no one really knows the answer to such questions", which seems obvious, but after Bob's tour de force of all subjects philosophical and spiritual, that truth really hit home. After all, if Wise and Well-Read Old Bob couldn't be certain, then who could? Spirituality was starting to seem like an exciting, blank canvass, limited only by the extent of one's imagination.

Epiphany

Counselling sessions with Colin continued into the summer, and I gradually began feeling just a little more comfortable in my own skin. I remained wary of others my own age, especially other lads, but was at least beginning to get a few things off my chest, accept myself a little more and not feel quite so fatally-phobic about blushing or discussing sexuality. Coupled with Bob's weekly forums, some of the gloomier clouds were at last on the move. Thoughts felt a little lighter, less threatening; emotions less draining. There was even a vague hint of a glow of optimism in the mix, mingling among the less pleasant mental traffic. A good deal of insecurity and confusion remained, but I was at least beginning to feel halfway human again. Then one overcast afternoon in early July – roughly a year to the day of that mind-shattering breakdown in the attic – something amazing happened that was to change things forever…

Carrying a steaming mug of tea, I wander down the garden to the little alcove between Dad's wooden tool shed and the large, vibrant forsythia bush. I park myself on the plastic chair, and light up a nice strong spliff. College finished for the summer just over a week ago and the job I have lined up at a local cake factory doesn't start for another week or so, so I'm enjoying just chilling out. That's all this spliff is for. There's a distinct lack of inner tempest today; nothing particularly harsh that needs to be dulled, per se, which is unusual. In fact, between Colin's searching questions in counselling and Bob's fascinating answers to my philosophical enquiries, my mind has, of late, been gently opening like the petals of so many daisies in this garden.

A few things Bob has said, have been lingering pleasantly in my thoughts. Statements like: "The bible isn't literally the direct word of god, but rather the accounts of the witnesses present at the time of Jesus", "Science tells us how but not why" and "A lot of the more mystical traditions seem to converge on the notion of heaven being a sense of oneness with god, an act of merging, rather than a specific place or dimension". So too has an idea I've recently come across while watching a documentary on Sikhism: the notion that "god is inside you. Inside everyone." Thoughts of god not approving of homosexuality, or of the concept of god being irredeemably flawed, have taken a back seat to these glittering, exciting new notions. The latter have been engendering a burgeoning, warm-glow within, which is pleasant, to say the least. The perfect subject matter to mull over in the garden, with a mug of tea and a nice skunk spliff, on a July afternoon.

Sitting comfortably on the plastic garden chair, in the relative seclusion of the alcove, I puff away as skunk's pacifying-crescendo gently enters consciousness. The world slows down and takes on that more immediate, softer, brighter, richly-sensual texture that only good weed can deliver. I mull over the inspiring ideas a little more. Still so many unanswered questions, but conversations with Bob have opened my eyes to the notion that much of spiritual and philosophical matters remain unsettled and uncertain; essentially a matter of opinion. As the skunk begins to lull the jittery-whirrings of the brain, and the many shades of garden-greenery begin to shine with psychedelic brilliance, the warm-glow within answers in kind, swelling to newer, sweeter depths. Buoyed by this development, I open my mind a little more to the new, abstract ideas and possibilities gleaned from Bob's class. A few shimmering pennies drop. ...We simply don't know...Ching! ...god is *inside* you...Chiing!...Some mystical traditions converge on notions of conscious immersion, Oneness, Nirvana. Oneness itself is god. God is *inside*. Chiiing! Oneness is inside. A delicate, tingling sensation dances around inside my brain, up and down my spine, beneath the surface of my skin; flickering and fluttering in random places with gentle excitement. Chiiing!! Now quite stoned and in a somewhat playful, experimental mood, I open my heart and mind, just a little, to the possibility that the old, transcendent feeling I used to cherish so much is maybe, possibly, somehow, still around…buried beneath the pain. Where the Oneness is. Ching! Ching! Ching! The tantalising, transcendent glow of old comes just a *little* into focus, as though a long-lingering fog is beginning to lift. So many nagging doubts and questions remain, but this new perspective is awakening something…something so fundamental to life, to *feeling alive*, that such misgivings can, frankly, damn well wait for the time being. Radiant daylight becomes more apparent; its ubiquitous, tangible warmth envelops me. The fresh summer air so caressing and sweet; the sensation of the plastic chair supporting my body; the beautiful, diverse textures and colours of the garden; the life that lives inside this body…I open up to it just a *tiny* bit more…

As I gaze out from the tranquil seclusion of the alcove, at the innumerable bright green blades of grass and gently-waving leaves of the small conifers opposite, they suddenly take on a wholesome, tantalizing hue. It quite literally touches my heart, imbuing the senses with a delicate, subtle feeling of *all* the textures of the garden. I lift my sight to the softly-undulating branches of the old oak tree in a neighbour's garden, feeling their gentle whispers as I discover the same brilliant hue glowing there, too. I continue glancing around and feel it radiating from the coarse rooftops of nearby houses like a gentle heat. It reaches all the way up to the milky-white clouds that fill the overcast, afternoon sky; their fluffy textures caress consciousness itself. In a single instant, a shimmering oneness is suddenly apparent in everything…*everything*…including…*me*…

The gentle-tingling gives way, exploding into the ubiquitous hue. It imbues all, from grass to sky, cascading its glowing-oneness though my body; a nourishing light touching every cell, organ, thought, sensation and emotion. The pain, self-loathing, anxiety and despair – all, and much, much more besides, are alighted upon, without exception, by this incredible, indiscriminate glow that now to connects everything with…with…*everything else.* Tantalized with excitement, I pause for a moment. This seems unmistakably like the spirit, the presence or 'god' of old, that used to console my heart in troubled times and lift it skyward in others. So dearly beloved and desperately missed. And yet, I can't recall it ever being quite so bright, brilliant or immediate as it appears right now, in this very moment. There's a new…edge to it. Could it be possible? Have I really found it again? What if I just…

Throwing caution to the wind, I fully embrace the glow. In an instant, its brightness explodes in my heart in a supernova of joy, bursting thorough flesh, bone, blood, brain and skin and out from my body; blazing an ecstatic, buoyant brilliance through the chair, the forsythia bush, the grass, the conifers opposite, nearby buildings and trees, to the low-hanging clouds and far, far beyond. My heart overflowing with rejoicing love as all of creation, at once ablaze, echoes the sentiment in triumphant symphony. I'm breathless and speechless with ecstatic joy. The world, no, the *universe* has been comprehensively illuminated, switched on once and everything in existence shimmers with unspeakable radiance.

No tears fall from my eyes; no rapturous proclamation of religious devotion, no, I simply sit, enraptured, enveloped in a bright, lucid trance of warm light; revelling in the indescribable brilliance that sparkles absolutely everywhere. I'm *alive!* Edifying joy swells, and filling every inch of my being, shining even on the doubts and insecurities, vastly reducing their potency to a vague, almost negligible shadow. They *can* and they *will* be allayed in time. I now have that power.

An overwhelming, unavoidable conclusion shines within: that tangible something I used to call 'God' has clearly and unmistakably returned, yet somehow more immediate, potent and uplifting than ever before. Throughout the last year, feeling itself has been slowly suffocating beneath a dark, immovable oppression but now, all at once, it's fully liberated; a delightful flourishing with a brightness beyond words. The edifying sensuality of feeling, the exquisite subtleties of the world, stretch to every cell of my being. It's *back*. God, I've missed it so much. It's like waking up, as though seeing this incredible world for the very first time.

I remain in the little alcove between the wooden shed and the hue-rich forsythia bush, ensconced in the plastic chair and enraptured in bliss, for what seems like a delightful eternity. Quietly, joyfully, I slowly reacquaint myself with the thousands of sweet, idiosyncratic delights of the world as they gleefully dance through the air and into consciousness. They flirt with perception while playfully defying definition as I marvel at how much brighter they shine, this time around. Weariness and insecurity lurk on the periphery, almost sulking in envy. This just isn't their moment. What exactly this newly rediscovered 'thing' is, what's causing it and what it all means, I'm not entirely sure. Such questions can wait, for now. The summer air is exquisite; the softly-rustling summer leaves whisper sweet nothings to my heart; the birdsong a sublime symphony of bliss…

After a long, rejuvenating rest in the alcove, an amazed smile stretched across my face, I eventually rise from the chair and wander carelessly inside, peaceful and intrigued by this bright new incarnation of that nice old feeling. I did it. I found my spirit again. The world is alive with light.

Back to Life

The epiphany, peak experience, or whatever it was, trailed gently off shortly after I returned inside. The resilient insecurities returned: being in the closet, addicted to weed, the feelings of discomfort with myself and in being around others, but what happened in the garden on that otherwise unremarkable July afternoon left a robust buoyancy in its wake that insecurities just couldn't eclipse. An elixir. A sense that, although so many obstacles lay ahead, life need not be quite so dark and hopeless after all. I no longer had to deal with it all alone. Now my mind had rediscovered its sweet companion and playmate. The residual glow remained, and it seemed entirely up to me what, if anything, I wanted to do with it.

The summer job in the nearby cake factory stated shortly afterwards. It was a hard slog – endless hours of repetitive production-line work in which time had little meaning, *but*, the glow remained – it didn't exactly render the work enjoyable per se, but keeping its light close at heart made a marked difference. There in my mind, body and heart, was a simple, natural glow that reflected back in every object and individual in the factory and, indeed, the world outside. It was inevitably mixed with the more difficult thoughts and emotions, but I increasingly found I could 'mine' it for strength and catharsis during those long factory shifts, reaching within to find an exquisite, fertile glow that provided a gentle and uplifting strength.

College resumed late in September and the social unease was ever present, but, as with the factory, that buoyant, inner glow provided a gentle, quiet confidence on which to build. The same was true of the unfathomably boring part time call centre job I started that October. Slowly, gently, bit by bit, through all the ups and downs, that 'alive' feeling, providing I remained open to it, proved an edifying elixir with which to move forward; not an instantaneous, all encompassing rapture of religious proclamations, sweeping all before it in blind faith, but, rather, a gradual, accumulative integration of a more joyful, hopeful way of life, providing one choose to remain mindful of its radiance. Mine the gold within. Much of life remained daunting – that 'Freak of Nature' feeling still lingered, rendering social encounters perpetually challenging, not to mention the fear of blushing at the slightest thing, and fear of my mind disintegrating again the way it had in the attic just over a year earlier – but, as the glow provided enough strength to put one foot in front of the other, I slowly began believing that gradually, in my own time, maybe, life's problems could all be faced after all.

I passed my driving test in the autumn and spent ridiculous amounts of time driving around in Nan's noisy old car, singing along to the CD player to work on my vocals. Being one of the first among my school friends to pass, there was plenty of company for the first week or so, during which time I hardly set foot in college. Since the car served as a portable practice-studio in which one could make as much vocal noise as one wished, it was just too wonderful not to do so. After the first week, many faces disappeared, but Kayleigh remained. And we sang. We sang and sang and sang some more. Whenever driving alone, vocal practice took on another, more personal dimension. Improvised vocal-hooks, fashioned initially as simple exercises, quickly morphed into freestyle mantras: a phrase, word or simple vowel sound playfully repeated and re-shaped through differing rhythms and keys, cultivating and augmenting not just my voice, but the ever-burgeoning subtleties of the inner glow. I did this as often and for as long as humanly possible, and although those dark, troubling feelings of despair, confusion and insecurity lingered in the background, this new hobby meant the nicer, calmer, more buoyant feelings were steadily gaining ground. Eventually, counselling sessions with Colin ceased as it was clear I was feeling much better than had been the case back in February. It felt a little scary, going on without his support, but nowhere near as daunting as would've been the case before my recent, game-changing epiphany. Now, I had hope itself on my side.

Can't Fight the Feeling

The autumn term of college came and went, as did the spring. With the glowing elixir within, always there to draw upon, each challenge of daily life was weathered with more quiet confidence than the last. I was happier more and more often and found myself increasingly carried away by the whole absorbing process. Soon, college appeared an inconvenient distraction; time that could be better spent cultivating the edifying spirituality that was, by now, paying dividends. That was, after all, the point of all this: what Project Hope had always been about. Studying A-levels had been the path of least resistance – the easiest and most sensible option in a very dark and difficult time – but the spiritual awakening had changed all that. The ability to feel alive had returned with gusto, and lingered so much brighter and sooner than I'd ever hoped. Studying increasingly seemed an irritating diversion from something so much more profound and crucial. From the one thing that mattered most. The spectre of another psychotic breakdown like that of less than two years prior, along with the suffocating depression and anxiety that had followed, continually loomed in the back of my mind; a terrifying and disastrous outcome to be assiduously avoided at all costs. Project Hope *had* to succeed and, if that meant college took a back seat to this transcendent 'thing' that actually *worked*, so be it.

I felt sure that singing and spirituality would eventually conquer all demons and insecurities, but I had to be sure; to put the hours in. Cultivating the glow wasn't just for the sake of hedonism. No, the bewildering, chilling, mental and emotional chaos of recent few years was painful and all-too-familiar. The prospect of everything going south again, as it had done at high school and again shortly after Oakwood, was *very* motivating. Up to this point, I'd struggled to function in numerous 'normal' situations for so many years – from going to sleep at night as a child to coping around peers at school and the cataclysmic mental fallout that followed the weed addiction – there was just no way to envision myself moving forward into adult life without this newfound spiritual strength. I simply couldn't cope without it. The last few years of struggle had proved that. Emphatically.

Singing and driving, working in the call centre and occasionally going into college, inner-confidence and self-love blossomed with the spring and on into the brightness of summer. Something truly amazing was happening. I felt deeply grateful that things were going so well, psychologically at least. But the further I climbed from my hole, the greater was the fear of falling back in again; the emotional destitution that went with it and the epic amounts of strength required to climb out time after time after time. Thus, what began as something delightful, uplifting and curative became an absolute necessity of the utmost importance. I couldn't afford to make all this progress only to see it slip away yet again. No, adult life beckoned and spirituality simply *had* to be a fundamental part of it. It became non-negotiable.

And so, whenever the house was empty, regardless of whether or not I had lectures to attend, I'd get stoned and sing. Despite all the healing that was going on, cannabis remained very much a necessity for focus. A couple of bongs eased concentration and relaxed the muscles necessary for singing. I knew it was stupid to be skiving off again, bombarding my brain with THC, but reassured myself that I was doing something inherently good for my mental health *and* working on my voice in the process. Once my mind and voice were in good shape, I could quit the weed for good. Continuing on this path was all that mattered. So it was all I did. And the deep, edifying glow grew and grew and *grew*, filling mind and body to overflowing, daily.

Despite several attempts to get back on track at college, by the time the second academic year concluded, I'd missed too much of the syllabus and thus thrown it all away. But it didn't matter: I'd finally found, and freed myself from that dungeon of misery that once seemed so inescapable. And now, the elixir of life was filling me to overflowing, all the time. I'd wake up each morning, buzzing with life and drift off to sleep each night in a state of gentle bliss. Project Hope had succeeded in ways I could never have expected. Whatever happened from, now on, everything would be okay.

Mission Accomplished

And so the faithful old Escort chugged its way through countless springtime nights, on into summer, with me at the wheel, singing, night after night, week after week, month after month, quite literally to my heart's content.

Driving joyfully and aimlessly around the idyllic Worcestershire countryside, though each starry night into the small hours, singing my way to blissful serenity, my entire body was continually absorbed with incredibly subtle –yet–potent sensations of sweet transcendence, love and numinous joy. Flutters of delight would gently flutter inside, as half-imagined thoughts of infinite positivity playfully rippled through consciousness. My insides were an ever-glowing light show of blinding colours; edification evolving into ineffable ecstasy. Every atom of existence joyfully hummed with blissful incandescence. The last lingering remnants of fear and sadness slipped quietly away, into the sealed vaults of distant memory. I was *truly* happy; sublimely calm and increasingly confident. Really confident. Too confident? Perhaps. Whenever problems or distress came my way, I found I could resolve or heal them simply by holding the glowing elixir of life close to my heart and singing until I felt better. *Much* better. I was now beyond healed. Nigh invincible.

I kept the part time call centre job after leaving college to fund my driving-and-singing hobby. I had now come out to most of my close friends and although I remained dependent on cannabis, I was at least reducing the overall amount consumed. The strong hits of bongs and pipes were increasingly a thing of the past, replaced instead by spliffs. Soon I'd be able to come out of the closet completely – then everything would just fall into place and I could finally start to live life. I wouldn't even need the weed then…I just *knew* it. The past year had changed things forever. For the better. It was high time I found myself a boyfriend and got on with life. In mid August of that year, a good looking young man named Tom joined our team at work…

Fabulous, Darling!

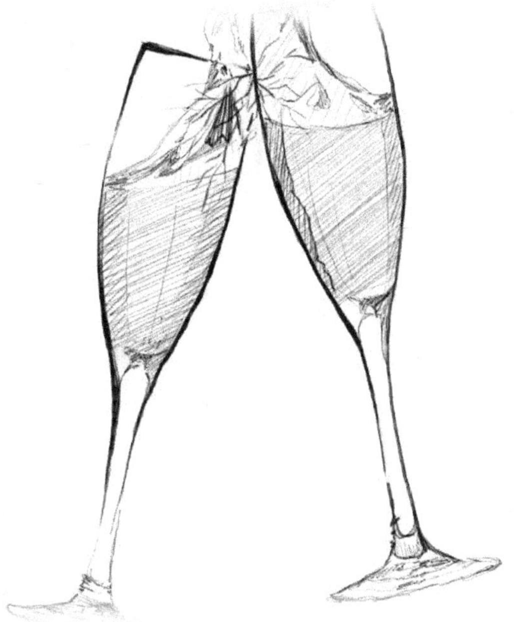

Fabulous, Darling!

"Lie on your front?"

"What for?"

"I wanna try something."

"What?"

"I just want to poke around."

"But I told you I don't wanna do that yet."

"Don't be stupid, Rich, I'm not even wearing a condom and without lube…"

"Then…why?"

"Oh, for God's sake! You have to try these things if we're ever going to get anywhere as a couple. You really have no idea, do you?"

I stare at the wall and let out a bewildered sigh.

"What do you mean 'poke around'?"

"Y'know, just explore it a little bit, that's all. I promise that's all I want to do. You'll like it"

That, I very much doubt.

"Alright, but that's all. Nothing else.

"Honestly, Rich, you have no idea. This isn't how it works even if I was about to put it in."

Halfway down a quiet, narrow back-street of small Victorian terraces, residents' cars parked in so tight they're almost bumper to bumper, is a small, cold student house. The front door opens straight into the tiny, musty-smelling living room. Cold-white woodchip walls embellished with the occasional scratch; a blotchy, blue-grey, shag-pile carpet and an old, striped green-and-navy, slightly damp, three piece suite. At the other end of the room is a typically long, narrow, Victorian terrace corridor, passing an old, cramped dining room, now repurposed as a bedroom, before leading, eventually, to a small kitchen and bathroom beyond. To the left of the corridor is an unfeasibly steep staircase, covered down the middle in tattered purple carpet and at the top of the stairs, directly above the living room, is the bedroom belonging to my boyfriend, Tom. Inside, it's the quintessential student room: beneath posters of indy-bands, 'ironic' humorous postcards, photos of memorable pissups and other assorted memorabilia, the same woodchip lines the walls, painted lilac. Atop a desk, leaning against the wall, rests a huge, wooden-framed mirror (Tom is *obsessed* with his appearance) facing the single sash window on the opposite wall. Next to the desk is a cheap, canvas wardrobe filled with the latest fashions. The ceiling light is enclosed in a dark orange, paper-star lampshade, so the room is never brighter than a dim glow. Along the wall adjacent to the door is a set of bunk beds. Tom and I are on the top bunk. Through the thin, bamboo blind, a cloudy, early evening sky hangs over the opposite terraces. The October nights are drawing in, stealing away the last warm remnants of summer and, increasingly, Tom's bedroom patience.

Reluctantly, cold from the autumn air that creeps in through the half-open window, limbs and heart heavy with frustration and dread, I lie on my front as requested. I honestly don't want to but Tom's been unusually affectionate this evening so I feel obliged. His moods can't be taken for granted. So yeah, *really* I don't want to be doing this but have learnt from experience that too much resistance soon elicits a bitter, annoyed, vitriolic outburst from my beloved. I do love being close. I love it when we kiss and engage in a bit of light foreplay. But Tom always wants, no, *needs*, to go further and faster within a matter of minutes, and becomes <u>incredibly</u> irritated and impatient if I either don't want to or can't relax. That part I hate. I hate that he's always in such a rush. The trouble is, I've got so much invested in this relationship that I let him push me around more than I know to be wise. I worry about the relationship abruptly ending and it all having been for nothing. Tom's the first guy I've been close to – *really* close to – in years. When things go wrong or wires get crossed there's a voice in the back of my head whispering that it's probably all my fault – just that old hypersensitivity and inability to 'get' the way other guys communicate. There's another voice, outside of my head, that resoundingly agrees with such sentiments. That voice belongs to Tom.

So here I am, once again, going through the motions as best I can, painfully uncomfortable as Tom 'pokes around', and getting increasingly annoyed with myself for not enjoying it the way I'm supposed to. The way Tom says it should be. The way I thought it *would* be…

Come Out, Come Out, Wherever You Are

When Tom first strolled onto the telemarketing department, I was hunkered down in the throes of some serious overtime. My utterly useless gaydar had this new guy down as yet another young, attractive, straight guy; Unattainable eye-candy. No doubt he was riding the Stop-Gap Express like most of the rest of us. Over a few short weeks, following lots of nudging from a handful of female colleagues on the department to whom I'd come out, I got to know Tom, who in fact turned out to be gay.

Tom was two years older, and his story quite different; he came out aged fourteen, almost as soon as he'd realised his sexuality, and had notched up nine serious relationships by the tender age of twenty. A fully-fledged, out-and-proud gay man, living the student life at Worcester University, Tom appeared a shining paragon; strutting where I merely tiptoed. Myself, prone to deep, elaborate flights of fancy, I turned my imagination to the idea of the two of us in a relationship and, as one might expect, each fantasy was alive with bright colours, near-tangible 3D images, surround sound and sublime orchestral music. A typical, clichéd teenage infatuation. We didn't have a tremendous amount in common at first but, if nothing else, it seemed high time to make some gay friends. I wanted to come out myself pretty soon. Up to that point, I'd been doing so gradually, gently and successfully: one friend at a time. Even Mum and one of the neighbours knew. Then I did something really, *really* stupid.

Having spent some time getting to know Tom, meeting his outrageously camp and in-your-face older friends, things seemed to be going well – but nothing remotely intimate had passed between us. I got the impression that he either wasn't interested or was put off by my open admittance of a total lack of experience with guys in any capacity whatsoever. On the night of his twentieth birthday house-party, Tom drank himself into an early bed. Downstairs, his best friend cornered me and repeatedly insisted that he was, in fact, very much interested. Still, nothing happened. Nevertheless, by now I was so intoxicated with rose-tinted dreams of hoped-for romance that I was barely able to think straight (dah-dum!). The following Saturday Tom and I sat together during the morning shift and, through a heady mix of desperate excitement and blinding frustration at the ambiguity of the whole situation, I came home and decided it was time to come out of the closet. Right now. It might just bring the two of us closer. It didn't feel at all like the right time, but all I could think of was how much I wanted to have a boyfriend. So I did it.

It didn't go terribly well. Although, in the end, everyone was ultimately accepting and supportive, that wasn't the case on that momentous Saturday afternoon. There was shouting, tears and harsh words and, by the time it was over, I was deeply upset; mostly over some of the reactions I'd received, but also, at least a little, at the way I'd rushed one of the important days of my life for potentially dubious reasons. Coming out had been going so well until that point. Nonetheless, I got what I wanted: that night I slept on the spare bunk in Tom's room, stayed there for two weeks straight (such an unfortunate turn of phrase!), by the end of which we were officially an item.

Out and About

Following the coming out debacle, I told close friends: "You can tell who you like now, I don't care anymore." At work, and related social events, it was soon common knowledge that Tom and I were an item. Everyone was supportive. Nonetheless, it was more than a little daunting going from the prior, easy-does-it approach to suddenly being out to absolutely everyone, overnight. Watching how casually Tom would openly discuss his sexuality, seeing him interact easily with straight guys – he was very much my role model and mentor. This latter role he seemed to enjoy…

In those heady, early days of the relationship, Tom was continually complimentary, always heaping on the praise: "You are *so* beautiful", "You're so nice, intelligent and funny", "…so much more down to earth than all my other boyfriends" and I basked, gleefully, in the twinkling spotlight of his adoration.

Very much a follower of fashion, he even began dressing me in his clothes, as, at that time, I wasn't exactly keen on going home to retrieve my own. My dress sense prior to coming out had always been very much about blending in and, beyond the occasional bright shirt, not making too much of a spectacle of myself (although I did dye my hair bright green just before Tom came along, probably a clear sign I was already pushing at the closet door). Now I became his fashion doll, resplendent in the very latest sartorial trends. Friends and colleagues commented on the sudden, stylistic transformation. Before Tom, I'd always politely greet people on the department, but chatting, confidently, causally, to anyone and everyone was another matter entirely. Now, under Tom's tutelage, I'd quickly become a confident, snappy dresser who could easily pass the time of day with anyone on the department and beyond. Tom remade me in his own hyper-styled image and the positive reactions from others, not to mention all the new work-friends, came thick and fast. I lapped it all up, the cat that got the cream.

Our first kiss had been quite abrupt. Being so inexperienced in every way, I couldn't even imagine how to initiate so intimate an exchange. Upstairs in Tom's room, a few days after coming out, I heard my name, turned around and suddenly found myself being kissed. It was a little odd. And rushed. I'd expected this moment to be filled with a romantic, erotic-rapture, set to sweeping symphonies as almost every film, TV show and pop song had suggested would be the case. Manic thoughts like "Oh my God, this is finally happening", "He *does* like me" and "Am I doing this right?" filled my head and aside from the nerves, I felt a little detached. He tasted strongly of wine and cigarettes, but then, I imagine, so did I. Soon we graduated to the bed. The nerves remained pretty high but Tom was patient and kind – we didn't do a great deal, then snuggled and slept.

Drip, Drip, Drip

The less-than-complimentary comments started a few weeks into the relationship. Initially presented as innocuous, well meaning observations like: "I do think you're quite naïve about a lot of things…like sex," or "I think you've got a lot to learn, but, y'know, in your own time…long as you don't take forever" and so on. Always said with a smile and presented as a kind word, entirely for my own benefit, they came with increasing frequency and were soon touching on anything from my taste in music, ambitions, the last remnants of my own dress sense and even much of the company I kept. At first it seemed that Tom was the concerned boyfriend, my best interests at heart, trying to enlighten me for my own sake, but the tone steadily changed. Gently spoken interventions from a worldly-wise boyfriend soon became impatient digs.

"Take that fucking sports top off, you look like a fucking Worcester townie!"

"Why are you so uptight? You're so anally retentive, it's a wonder you're even in a relationship."

These were the rarer comments, at first. They tended to conjure that old feeling from school that I'd unintentionally made another social faux pas. They were hurtful and felt unfair but, thankfully, the majority were still just silly little comments and digs that I knew didn't matter. But there was nonetheless a flippancy and insensitivity about it all, along with a reach that seemed unnecessary; soon the tiniest detail about inconsequential things such as my shoelaces (yes, my *shoelaces*) or my parents' taste in home décor were being constantly derided for no apparent reason other than the fact that Tom disapproved and had *every* right to point these things out. Silly little things. Far too innocuous to matter. They *didn't* matter. It was all for my own good. Over time, however, I found myself adding more and more items to the list of 'silly little things' that I shouldn't, or rather wasn't allowed to mind about, at least not if I wanted to stay in Tom's good books. Ever disguised as inconsequential trivia and yet always with that same, derisory undertone. Every single day: drip, drip, drip. But it didn't matter. I was being too sensitive, as Tom would often point out. I was in a grown-up relationship now and had to learn to take things on the chin. At least, if I wanted to stay with Tom, that was. After all, I was always the one that was too much of this or not enough of that. Privately, I reasoned that, as my spirituality had brought about such immeasurable and exquisite bliss, a little dig here was nothing; not an issue in the grand scheme of things.

Comments soon became outright insults, justified as 'banter'. At this time, I was still very literal; prone to give or take sarcasm in entirely the wrong context and not keen on others taking the piss "just for a laugh". I couldn't always tell the difference. Tom seemed to enjoy this. Comments like, "Make me a cup of tea, shit lips", along with the endless public impersonations, mocking 'songs' about me and flippant digs were quite hurtful. Tom could see I wasn't enjoying them, but continued all the same. This being my first ever relationship, and having recklessly rushed out of the closet in the process, it naturally felt there was so much riding on it; on making it work. Increasingly, I found I was pushing parts of myself aside – parts I knew were important, but could wait for the time being – just to cope with being with Tom. My sensitivity, opinions, even simple preferences like which film we were going to watch or whether or not to stay in that night; all had to be carefully managed so as not to displease the boyfriend and evoke his increasingly public ambivalence about our relationship. If I got things right, and he was in a good mood, he might even be nice. I soon found I was even distancing myself from my spirituality – its gentle, soothing inspirations now so out of step with this paragon boyfriend of mine and his obnoxious mood swings. Weed helped. He drank so much I figured it didn't matter for now if I got stoned every night. Getting, and staying, in Tom's good books was what mattered. But it was never enough. Soon he became openly hostile in his put downs, public and private, which probably had something to do with our sex life.

Just Relax

Tom's patient, gentle manner in the bedroom began to sour less than a fortnight after our first kiss. Having not so much as held hands with another guy before, it seemed natural to me to explore intimacy at a comfortable pace and, ideally, via affection. Tom wasn't overly keen on this approach: He wanted all clothes removed, more or less immediately, and I was expected to be totally at ease because, after all, what was there to be afraid of?

Very much the extrovert, Tom was in many ways everything the stereotype dictated: the most fashionable clothes and makeup; an ardent fan of every Bette Davis film ever made; a dry, risqué sense of humour and, perhaps most importantly of all (to him at least) a penchant for discussing his sexual conquests as loudly and candidly as possible with anyone who'd listen. His Uni friends were a frequent, keen audience:

"Have you two done it yet? Well, why not? What *have* you done?"

"When did you do that? How many times?"

"Have you sucked his dick yet? Has he sucked yours?"

The level of detail about which they enquired left absolutely nothing to the imagination. And they certainly didn't wait until I was out of the room. Tom's initial response had been that, while in the past he'd always gone straight for third base, this time he was happy to wait a little while, spend some time getting to know each other. Initially. But, after a few weeks, as the relentless barrage of candid questions continued, Tom's response changed to him simply shooting me a contemptuous, sidelong glance and saying nothing, or just shaking his head in bitter disappointment. He was also quite happy to discuss intimate details of my anatomy with his friends, in my presence, whether I liked it or not. As far as he was concerned, I *should* like it, or at least be okay with it. His increasing impatience, and the crude forums with his friends meant the pressure was continually on, and rising. But, despite my sincerest efforts, I couldn't force myself to be comfortable. Kissing for more than two minutes; getting used to being touched without having to take everything off straightaway – such caveats seemed reasonable enough to me, but Tom *hated* them. His bedroom manner may have been patient and kind during the first week or so, but it soon changed to casual, passive-aggressive digs…

"Well, maybe you're just not meant to be with a man."

"You're obviously not a sexual person."

…shortly before graduating to irritated, impatient barbs, rolling of the eyes and outright venom…

"For fuck's sake, Rich, just get *over* it. You're *so* uptight and anally retentive. How're ever gonna have a fucking relationship with anyone if you're like this?"

"This is fucking pathetic. I've never met anyone like you. You need a good cock up your arse."

…And much, much, *much* more besides. More than once, I was told that if I wanted to be in this relationship, "we <u>have</u> to do certain things" and that was that. If I wasn't quite ready or wasn't enjoying said activity, I was "neurotic", "frigid" and "probably not gay". Such comments inevitably raised the stakes and made relaxation that much harder, indeed, nigh impossible. One particularly unhelpful comment Tom was fond of making was "the more you resist, the more it turns me on". So it was *my* fault for not being comfortable. It was making him want it all the more. Intimacy with my boyfriend was now a dreaded chore. Although I was frequently annoyed, often downright insulted, with and by his behaviour, Tom had an uncanny, almost artful way of turning it all around to imply that it really was all my own fault. After all, there was nothing wrong with him; he was the one who'd had several "grown up relationships", he was trying to be patient, but I was making it *so* difficult. And there was so much riding on this relationship: if it abruptly ended then I really did come out of the closet and distance myself from so much that mattered to me, for absolutely nothing. No, I had to make this work somehow. Take it all on the chin and try my best to get on with it. Tom reiterated the conditionality of his interest and commitment on many occasions. Maybe it really was my fault for not being "fun" enough, or "sexual" enough, or whatever else I wasn't enough of? How lucky I was to have a boyfriend that would tolerate so many of my ridiculous, infuriating faults.

So here I am, lying naked on my front, on the top bunk, not really wanting to but cooperating once again for fear of pissing off my "highly sexed" boyfriend. He's "gently poking around" as he puts it. I try to enjoy it but ultimately all I'm doing is lying there, eyes shut, feeling really uncomfortable and hoping he'll soon be satisfied enough to stop. The pokes and prods around the outside edge of my anus are getting sharper, more forceful and invasive. As he pushes himself hard against my skin, there's very little about it that's gentle. It feels…insistent. He keeps saying "Just relax" in a low, slow, almost whispering tone…there's something creepy about it. I'm tense. Consumed with dread. I don't want to be doing this. Please god, he'll soon be satisfied enough to stop. A couple of times he pushes at my anus with a little more force than I'm prepared to tolerate. I reprimand him. He's done that with his finger more than once before, and became irritated and bitter when told to stop. But right now, he's not wearing a condom and hasn't got permission to do anything more than "poke around", so I tell him to back off. He does as he's told and says again, with an amused tone, that he "wouldn't to do it without a condom in any case." Then, suddenly, he *does*. For a split second I'm dumbfounded, in shock, almost unable to believe what's happening. The world suddenly falls away. But the pain brings it home. His penis is inside, a good few inches. What the *fuck* is going on?!

"Ow! Ow! Tom, what are you doing?! Ow! TOM!?"

After a few seconds he abruptly withdraws.

"What the fuck are you doing?!"

"Oh sorry, Rich, dunno what happened there. You must've just relaxed for a second or something. It can happen."

The pain in my rectum is pretty intense, but the shock, bewilderment, anger and incredulity far outstrip it. I'm almost speechless, beside myself with disbelief. What the fuck just happened?

"What do you mean 'it can happen'?"

"Sometimes it can. Like I said, you must've just relaxed for a second. It was just an accident. Nothing to worry about."

There's something strangely casual and unapologetic in his tone. He seems almost amused yet disinterested in what just happened, as if it really was nothing. I stare at him. So often I worry about how I'm coming across in the bedroom; if I'm saying or doing anything that might upset him and bring on the hurtful comments but right now, in this instant, I'm at one with the suspicious, reproachful stare that's burst across my face and burns itself into Tom. His tone immediately transforms from indifference to sweetness:

"Oh, Rich, it's okay. These things happen from time to time. You really have no idea, do you? Aw, you're such a sweet baby, bless you. So naïve. It's okay"

His face is suddenly alight with empathy; his voice doting. This is the first time he's expressed any real kindness or affection in weeks. He hugs me and tells me it's all okay. It's comforting to see his kind side again after so many weeks of tension. We get dressed and go downstairs to watch a film. I tell myself these things happen. There's still so much about having a sex life I don't understand. If I'd just go all the way with him, as he suggests, this probably wouldn't have happened. It feels like it was at least partly my fault. Tom's had nine boyfriends before this relationship but I'm the first who's needed to take it slow. I suppose I should think myself lucky he's so patient and accommodating. I'm annoyed with myself. These things happen. My arse aches for the next four days.

Fabulous, Darling!

The next couple of months are an emotional rollercoaster. Tom has a few strange episodes that begin with his drinking in the daytime and suddenly insisting he has to "sort his life out", right here, right now. A frantic attempt to drastically rearrange his bedroom ensues (I'm not allowed to help) and soon he's trapped in a chaotic mess of furniture and paraphernalia with a manic, unhinged look in his eyes. In such moments, all attempts at talking or reasoning with him make him that much worse and he abruptly starts shouting, screaming and smashing his furniture until the room resembles a bomb-site. After the first episode, he apologises and explains nothing like that has ever happened before.

Following the second outburst, I talk with one of his Uni-friends, who confirms that's not actually the case. Our relationship becomes ever more turbulent. Although we manage to find bedroom-activities that please us both sexually, Tom remains adamant that it's still not enough as we haven't gone all the way. His increasing unpleasantness towards me makes the prospect of relaxing and trusting him enough to do so all the more remote. I start to stand up for myself – returning his public and private jibes with a few of my own, but this just encourages and emboldens his venom. In public, mutual friends find our bickering side-splittingly funny but in truth, each hurtful comment or 'hilarious' character assassination cuts a little deeper, adding to the feeling that I really am just an unlikeable, neurotic mess, not good enough to be in a 'normal' adult relationship; a burden on poor Tom. Somehow, he's gotten deep inside my head. I reassume my old casual dress sense and get roundly shouted at. Tom's drinking increases, as does my cannabis use. Profoundly. Now, of all times, isn't a good time to stop. His Uni-friends' prying-curiosity about our bedroom activities continues, and on the one occasion I attempt to casually mention his recent, clumsy "accident" he cuts me off, saying something along the lines of: "Oh for fuck's sake Rich, will you just shut up?! We've never done it and if you think that was anythin', you really are just fuckin' clueless, so shut up, alright?"

Tom dumps me. We get back together. He dumps me again but we continue our bedroom encounters. We go round and round like this until Christmas. Sometimes he confesses, "I can't help loving you" and other times "You just don't float my boat". The first breakup has me crying hysterically, almost inconsolable. Old school friends come to the rescue with soothing words. They help me through it, but throughout the break ups, make ups and everything in between, there's something very wrong going on inside. Having been dressed and socialised by Tom, and been physically intimate with someone who expresses such contempt for me, and having jettisoned just about everyone and everything he dislikes, a worrying feeling that I've lost my identity starts to grow. The calm, quietly-confident, optimistic and joyful Richard from the summer is long gone and in his place is an anxious, bitter and confused cliché. After a few months with Tom and his friends, it I'm now defined entirely by a shallow notion of my sexuality and this exacerbating relationship. I even started working full time at the call centre so we could spend more time together. I've become trendy, bitchy, judgemental, obsessed with my appearance and utterly miserable. I smoke copious amounts of weed and cigarettes and drink almost as much as Tom. There's an odd and unsettling inertia about the whole thing, as though I no longer have any control over my place in it all. This is my fate. Life outside of the closet. This is how a gay man is in the real world. Who I'm supposed to be. Apparently. It's Fabulous, Darling.

Tom travels back to his family home for Christmas and I resolve to use the time to get back to my old self. It's tricky. Oddly, I can no longer remember much of who I was; why I used to like certain kinds of music; why and how I thought the way I did - all those little things that made me who I was just a few short months ago. It's now no more than a distant dream. I go through the motions, dressing my own way, listening to music *I* like and catching up with old friends, but none of it registers or means anything. I remember I have certain ideas; believe, feel and enjoy certain things, see certain people and just how happy I was but now, whenever I try to reconnect with any of it, it feels as though everything needs to be signed off by Tom. Everything. Every song, each item of clothing, place I visit or opinion I form, Tom's scowling disapproval haunts my thoughts, mocking and debasing from within. Each and every thought is stalked by an invisible sentinel, whispering in Tom's voice: "That's just bollocks. You're full of shit." I've internalised the more unpleasant parts of our relationship and now he sits like a constantly-scathing demon on my shoulder. My whole life and identity have revolved around this messed up guy for just a few months and now it's all over…it seems there's nothing left of 'me' to return to.

Tom returns to Worcester in the New Year as the humdrum of the call centre shifts resume. We remain 'friends' The public bickering also returns. The bedroom activities do not. My identity still so tethered to his own, I now feel strangely compelled to compete with him; to keep up somehow. He cuts down his alcohol consumption; I do the same with weed. He goes on a diet; so do I. Buys new clothes; so do I. And so on. If I don't keep up with him, I don't know who I am. I'm a lesser version. A botched carbon copy. Pale imitation. That's all I know anymore. Most of what went before is long gone and all that remains is this unpleasant, weird, crushing reality. His constant digs, however, get too much: sometimes we get stoned at his place with a few friends from work; under the influence of THC, Tom becomes an outrageous pantomime dame and keeps the room gleefully entertained by tearing into me like never before with an elaborate, scathing routine. Impressions, anecdotes, jokes and the gleeful sharing of confidences come thick and fast and have everyone rolling with laughter. He *really* gets into it. The degree to which he's able to divine my deepest insecurities and broadcast them around the room in hilarious parody is almost diabolical. It cuts deep. I try to give it back or at least shrug it off, but he's unstoppable when in these 'fabulous' moods. It increasingly seems he can utterly destroy me; reduce me to less than nothing with his words, reach inside, pull out my innards and use them as props with which to entertain his adoring public. There's a near-tangible feeling of each and every scathing witticism sinking through my skin, into my head and bones, taking root. They nestle deep within, becoming my truth. The guy who initially brought me out of myself and became a post-coming-out-mentor can seemingly snatch back every last morsel of outward confidence and grind it to powder beneath his uncompromising heel. It's really, really hurtful, yet still at least partly my fault for being either "too sensitive" or not "fun" enough. After all, it's really just banter. Eventually it gets too much, so I stop associating with him altogether. I quit the call centre job and disappear up to my bedroom in a thick cloud of cannabis smoke. Back where it all started. My head a confusing, depressing mess once more. Confidence plummeting. Again. How have I ended up back here? I don't even know where to start.

My Spirit Used to Wander Here

Having finally staggered from the rollercoaster, head still spinning, it seemed high time to finally reconnect with that old, life-affirming spirituality. Get back to my old self and leave this whole sorry drama in the dust. But I couldn't. Search as I might for those old, sweet thoughts and intuitions, nothing penetrated the confused, depressed-stupor in which I now found myself. I threw out most of the Tom-approved clothing, returned permanently to listening to the music *I* liked; resumed contact with all old friends and drove around singing. None of it registered or moved me. At all. Bewildered, I could no longer recall what it was *about* the music I'd once enjoyed, or the reason for the thoughts I used to have. My memory contained a vague, sketchy-outline of who I'd once been, but it seemed a badly-drawn blueprint of some other person. Not myself. I no longer existed. Music went through me like a cold wind rushing through a rusted fence. Watching TV or listening to others talk, I was utterly detached, all sights and sounds seemed either a million miles away, or else glaring, loud, disorienting. Nothing anyone said, about anything at all, made any sense. So much of the language around and within me was a meaningless jumble of unrelated sounds. The cold, dark, barren winter soon gave way to a warm, blossoming spring and I felt nothing but regret, confusion and crushing numbness. A zombie-corpse with random fragments of memory, pretending to be a person.

This was utterly terrifying. Escaping the bottomless doldrums of depression had been beyond hard last time, and now, here I was *yet again*, only this time with almost no bearing whatsoever. No real context or starting point, just an impossible sense of confusion and numbness. Once again it was time to mobilise against my own mind and emotions; find a way to pull them, kicking and screaming from the abyss. Wonderful.

I spend the next eighteen months wandering aimlessly from one temp job to another and another and another, mired in deep ruminations day and night, trying to figure out how, where and why it all went so horribly wrong. Not only the relationship with Tom, but also how it was that I lost so much of myself in the process, and why I can't seem to find it again. Where did it all *go*? Some remnants of human emotion begin to return. A sentimental pang here, a spark of life there. But they now seem so…dangerous. And I've no idea why. Thus they're quickly swallowed by the vast vortex of confusion and despair. It's as if the whole experience of that first relationship has lobotomised me; I struggle to trust my own mind and have to have much about the world explained by friends. Why is this funny? Why is that sad? What's nice about that? Like a child with no experience of the world. It's a slow, gruelling, almost static process, until, finally, in June 2002, I land a temp job in a rivet factory where I'm left to my own devices most of the time, sorting and packing rivets in a dusty corner of the old factory…

The Final Rush Hour, Part VI

Tom. God, what a mess that was. The following eighteen months were really hard, and more than a little infuriating since, on paper, there was so much to be happy about. I was a young and healthy man in the peak of life with so much ahead of me, only with a mind that refused to work, to function, that seemed to scorn at and sabotage everything. And yet this was as *nothing* compared to the years that followed – once those mortifying intrusive thoughts showed up, with the deadly danger they invariably evoked, they changed everything for the worse. And now, of course, that danger is perilously close. Less than a mile away, in fact.

The bustling city centre is now about a mile behind me, so it's just a case of navigating the inner city and suburbs…then it's a straight shot to…to…to god knows what. To the industrial estate where I currently work. And the reckoning I've been running from these last four and a half years.

Won't be long now. A sinking, whirlpool-sensation mingles in among the inner-tempest of dread, bewilderment and elation. Fear is *really* starting to heat up, frantically transmitting red-alert signals and concentrated stress hormones to every last cell. I taste danger in the air as clear as the crisp, spring breeze as it flows in through the open window. I could throw up all my insides and pass out at any second. Impending, unavoidable doom reverberates through the world. But, thankfully, all the newly-liberated beauty remains. The trees bask blissfully in the exquisite morning air; birds sing and dance merrily from branch to branch; even the smooth, tarmac surface of the road glows with a soft, subtle beauty. I feel *all* of it, every last inch, just like I used to. It's overwhelming and divine. The only impenetrable concrete to be found now is outside my body, lining the pavement, where it belongs. But the raw emotion it had encased within my gut nonetheless seems very much the reason I could well be en route to imminent execution. Too much sensitivity. Too much thought. A brain that can't cope with the world. With people. With life. Why can't I just stay in this car forever? Or, even better, switch off all this crazy shit in my head? It's not fair. But the wringing of hands won't help now. It never really did. Fast-flashing memories of school days, the malevolent snowman, juvenile delinquency, medicinal-skunk, singing, feeling alive, not feeling at all and the onset of blushing phobia have provided no great insight I can glean. I have no idea why I am the way I am. I turn off the main road at the mini roundabout. The edge of town coming ever closer. Through suburbs, past the out-of-town retail parks as HVGs rattle noisily ahead to the looming industrial estate. So close. There's a deadly heat up ahead, and I a scurrying insect actually *approaching* the eviscerating flame. Throat closes a little more. Mouth dry as sandpaper. Poisonous adrenaline running so high it's a bad drugs-trip. The final precipice is closer; almost in sight. Flashbacks of the past haven't made much sense of anything. All I can really say about why this day-of-days has finally come is that things have been deteriorating for months now. Seriously. That's all. I returned from Edinburgh hoping for a fresh start. Something went horribly wrong…

Fiends Reunited

Home, Sweet Home

For all its breathtaking beauty, Edinburgh had not been the place to find myself and finally get clear of so many personal horrors. Quite the opposite, in fact. Mum and Dad had come to visit, late in November, I'd broken down in floods of tears and finally ended the deafening silence of four years.

Now the private hell was, apparently, over, there seemed little reason to stay so far from home. In three months, I hadn't made a single friend (deliberately), had no family for hundreds of miles and had almost maxed-out two credit cards, just to get by. Mum and Dad were very understanding and supportive when, sobbing, I'd told them about the heartbreaking intrusive thoughts I had day and night; the constant fear of being brutally killed for blushing that robbed me of sleep; the deep depression and subsequent difficulty in feeling much beyond panic, anxiety or sadness. They didn't condemn me as a monster. They finally understood what had been going on all these years. I was a catastrophic mess, and living and working three hundred miles from home in a tiny little hovel had made things even worse. It was time to go home.

The Honeymoon Period

Moving back into the family home after three months of misery – not to mention barely eating, sleeping or washing properly – was like checking into The Ritz. Hot baths, cupboards full of food, a decent TV signal and multiple-room-living, the very height of luxury. Greatest of all was the miracle of having finally broken the battered sea-wall of isolation by telling someone what I was going through, *and* living to tell the tale. Mum and Dad hadn't condemned me or recoiled in righteous horror, called the police or summoned an angry mob; in fact they'd been very sympathetic and totally supportive. Those four long years of knowing I had a very serious problem – one I needed to confide – but was so viscerally afraid of talking about…I was certain that awful holding pattern would remain for the rest of my days; that I'd never again be close to anyone, be honest or open up in any way. I was wrong. I ran out of options, strength and ideas; broke down and told them everything. And they were okay with it. It was a huge, immeasurable weight from my shoulders. Annoyingly, and somewhat surprisingly, however, it didn't stop the constant vile intrusions or inconsolable paranoia in the presence of others. Not. One. Bit. Nor had the atrophied range-of-human-emotions, encased in visceral concrete, budged or even shrunk a little. And, of course, those strange, disconcerting tension headaches in the left side of my brain were still there – neurons trying desperately to communicate something that just couldn't be allowed. It always seemed, throughout the last four years, that the terrified-isolation was the main problem – the suffocating, toxic catalyst that had turned an intense and horrible problem into an impossible one. Surely, once I opened up and confessed, the pressure valves would burst open, hiss industrial steam for a few hours and then, finally, I'd be able to relax and, at last let go. Stop worrying about the intrusions and watch gladly as they'd ebb away into insignificance. That was the redemptive promise that made actually telling someone so unavoidable, wasn't it? Up to a point, yes. I was no longer alone, suffering in petrified-silence, but all the horrible mental traffic was still *very much* in play. It was bewildering to say the least, but still I was glad to have overcome that impossible obstacle and found compassion, rather than hideous death, on the other side. And that was wonderful, whatever the current situation. Give it time. The threshold now crossed, it still seemed hopeful the problem would ease away soon enough. Patience and optimism. Just what the doctor ordered.

Perhaps the most important lesson of my short time up north was the importance of keeping busy. The runaway-ghost-train of mental problems, always so tiring and demoralising that, all too often, I just wanted the world to piss off and let me rest in relative safety. Living alone in a capital city, going into work each day no matter how tired, suicidal or terrified, taught me that, while the demands of responsibility didn't even begin to touch the problem itself, having things to do least stopped it from festering *quite* so much, especially since these thoughts and feelings remained, no matter what I did. Also, I was by now increasingly suspicious of the practice of rumination. It was arduous, impossible, robbed me of what little sleep could be gleaned and, crucially, had almost no long term impact on the problem. In fact it made it worse. I might find myself pathologically drawn into it more often than I'd like, but I was no longer convinced it was doing the situation any good. So on my first day back in Worcester I went straight to the temp agency and landed an admin job at the local council. Mum and Dad were quite surprised, but I was sure that keeping busy would see me on my way to mental health.

The new job at County Hall was another basic admin gig; this time in a huge, 1970s, modernist complex: red bricks, flat, grey, metal roofing and endless rows of huge windows, all set in a wooded nature reserve on the outskirts of town. Being the County Council hub, it was a crowded workplace. Every office, small or large, was crammed with people at desks, elbow to elbow, and our huge, first-floor department was no exception. My charge was to assist Helen – a finance officer for the Older Persons Team branch of Social Services. Helen was a late-middle-age Newcastle woman with short, thin, mousey hair, glasses and a head that tended to wobble whenever she was agitated. Which was often. On the first day, I was assigned to shadow another temp whose job was similar to my own. Short and slim with thin, dark, shoulder-length straight hair and a proud, almost regal carriage, Hannah's bright blue eyes shone out of her freckled face, brimming with enthusiasm and intelligence. She struck me straight away as the kind of down-to-earth, straight-dealing, polite, confident person that effortlessly commands respect without any air of pretention. I liked her instantly. We had a lot in common: both exactly the same age; grew up in Worcester (but attended different schools); both recently returned to our hometown after a brief hiatus elsewhere (Hannah and her boyfriend had just returned from Australia to apply for permanent visas) and, along with similar tastes in music, we also seemed to share an open-mindedness, sense of humour and intellectual curiosity about anything and everything. Until now, Hannah had been doing the job I was about to take on, was about to assume a few more responsibilities in the office, all the while undergoing the lengthy process of applying to the Australian authorities in hope of returning. I really admired her enthusiasm and drive. We went on fag breaks together and chatted endlessly. It all seemed so apt: a busy job and a new friend – a great way to move on from the drama of the last few years. All the old demons continued to poke at consciousness, but I remained upbeat. The routine and distraction, minus the stresses of living in splendid isolation, were a breath of fresh air. I really liked working at County Hall. Sod my mental health problems. *They'd* have to put up with *me* for a change.

Fiends Reunited

Throughout the darkening days of December, I managed to struggle on, trying my level best to focus on work, ignoring the same old troublesome shocks that raged in the weird brain sat atop my shoulders, savouring the fact that the worst was well and truly behind. It *had* to be. Or so I thought. *None* of the horrible violent, sexual or offensive intrusions, intense paranoia, ominous fears of blushing or that same old weary, tired-sadness, none of it, had even started to trail off by Christmas. Not one bit. I'd been home over a month now, and nothing had changed. In the New Year, as the decorations came down and the daily routines resumed in the cold mornings of January, that much-hoped-for healing was beginning to look like it might not be on the cards after all. In fact, the exact opposite was proving to be the case.

Keeping busy with work in a huge, packed office filled with stressed-out public sector workers was now causing a brain overload which, in turn, was making all the distressing mental traffic race that much faster. Things had been unbearably intense in the office back in Scotland, but, at least in that environment we'd all sat behind a low partition, separating each pair of desks, creating at least a small sense of personal space. These offices had no such luxury. Sitting elbow-to-elbow in the Council's bustling headquarters was like being squashed with a thousand other nervous wrecks into a slow cooker and left to marinate. Just sitting at my cramped desk, looking at the computer screen, typing, answering the phone or having banal conversations with others about invoices and purchase orders; torrents of disgusting, distracting, mortifying intrusions would tear into my mind, faster and with evermore force. Sexual, violent, racist, sexist, homophobic, xenophobic, destructive and subversive images, words and phantom urges all rushed in, with barely a warning, as they'd done consistently over the past four and a bit years. They were getting worse somehow; not in terms of their content, which was as heartbreaking and repulsive as ever, and couldn't really get any more profane, no, they just now seemed more vivid, intense and frequent than they'd ever been. As their frequency and intensity grew, that buoyant sense of relief and optimism was fading fast, a bewildering mix of anger and desperation taking its place. It made no sense. I'd *told someone* and left weed well and truly behind over the last few years, so why on earth was it not only still happening, but actually getting worse? Here I was, quietly trying to mind my own business, look on the bright side and get on with life but, opening up to Mum and Dad, it turned out, ultimately had no impact whatsoever.

A colleague might walk over to our desk, just as the intrusions were in their full distressing flow and, although I'd fight with all available strength, I'd nonetheless be gripped by an accelerating fear that a 'dangerous' word would soon be uttered in casual conversation. Such terms kept surfacing in my mind, triggering silent terror, regardless of the sincerest efforts to ignore. Words like 'rapist', 'terrorist' or 'murderer' appeared to be somehow 'escaping', transmitting themselves from beneath my skull, darting, laser-like, across the room and straight into the minds of others, *always* threatening to come up in conversation. Specifically because I'd somehow 'put' them there. There were intrusive intuitions and feelings, too: *"It's what I really want. I want to blush, I'm secretly looking forward to it. I want to die because I'm too lazy to work."* And, of course, the usual, unbidden images flashing horribly through my mind: stabbings, inappropriate sexual images, breaking of bones, pushing people down the stairs, derogatory, offensive words and ideas intruding into absolutely everything. *"Bitch."*, *"Whore"*, and *"Fat cunt"*, to name but a few. I was back to frantically arguing with myself while talking with others, flailing to correct or distract myself from the horrors while nervously nodding and struggling to take in any aspect of the conversation at hand. I continuously made schoolboy errors with my work and received harsh words from Helen, her wobbling head turning red, with anger, ironically enough. Once again my own head was a cacophony of deafening white noise: on Red Alert in the midst of every intrusion; terrorised by the *slightest* change in facial temperature, fighting tooth and nail to conceal the ever-present, high-octane panic. I was back to being on a continuous knife-edge in the presence of others, as had been the case like in Edinburgh. Even the impossible feeling that I must confess to the intrusions returned, only now, rather than an insistence that I tell *someone*, it seemed to be insisting I tell *everyone*, just in case the dreaded blushing really did occur. Such demands were obviously impossible, but nonetheless, my apoplectic brain pushed the matter harder than ever. It all seemed so unfair. But I didn't let it stop me from chatting with Hanna; I enjoyed our little chin wags in the smoking room so much that I'd put in an extra special effort to wrestle some kind of fleeting, temporary control for a few short minutes. I paid for it afterwards. Like stuffing all the rubbish in the house into a small cupboard, forcing the door shut and leaning against it to conceal the mess from a guest – the moment you step away it <u>all</u> comes crashing out.

The mental shitstorm raged on at work, day after day, week after week, and the daily onslaught of fight-or-flight adrenaline was more tiring than ever – slowly marinating my brain and further stretching threadbare nerves. I started to wonder if there was something fundamentally lemming-like about this mind of mine; forever working to sabotage my very existence; content only on total self annihilation. The boundaries between where my own thoughts ended and the world began was beginning to crumble – as if there was a gleeful conspiracy between the demons in my head and the people around me. I knew this was utter bollocks, but it was glaringly vivid all the same. HD, 3D, Surround Sound. The lynch-mob that might kill me after an unfortunate, ill-timed blush seemed closer than ever. I could almost *feel* it as a close, unavoidable fate, a louring tempest scowling over the horizon. Groups of angry offices workers gathered outside, including Hanna and Helen; the freefalling-feeling and overwhelming rush of pure, undiluted terror making everything razor sharp…eyes glowering with focused-hatred, burning deadly stares into my flesh. I sometimes wondered if, amid the rabid violence, there'd be an odd sense of relief that it was finally over. I can't control what others think or do, but at least I'd be free of the soul destroying, nerve-rotting, incessant feeling of imminent danger. At times like those, when the deafening, obnoxious mental traffic is at its absolute, uncontrollable worst, the hard surface of a desk has a compelling attraction: one forceful whack on the wood surface – that's all it would take to slip into blissful unconsciousness. I was an old, defunct race car, being driven full-pelt around a poorly maintained race track; engine smoking, wheels rattling, about to come off, and still the accelerator to the floor. At the end of each shift, I climbed into my car with a pounding headache; crazy thoughts and paranoia scurrying through consciousness like busy ants on their expanding hill. I was exhausted, hopeless and had a near-constant taste of reflux in my throat. Day after day. I longed for deep, restful sleep but the old shallow trances and startled awakenings of Edinburgh were back. On one occasion, another member of staff mentioned in passing that I always looked "so calm". Was she taking the piss? Didn't seem so. She appeared to be speaking perfectly honestly. It just brought home the fact that there was something very, very wrong in my head. Something had to be done.

By Any Means Necessary

One typically dreary, wet, cold Saturday afternoon in late January, I dragged myself into town in search of some kind of self-help. A hypnosis CD…a relaxation tape…a meditation audiobook or…or….or…whatever. I needed something, *anything* for this ridiculous, hateful mind. Things were getting beyond desperate. Over the years I'd tried just about everything I could think of, but the problem was only getting worse. What was I supposed to do? A trip to the doctor's still seemed too big a risk. Hypnosis had helped with confidence issues, outwardly at least, back when I was in a state after Tom, at least enough to enable doing some amateur dramatics, so, it seemed worth a try. If nothing else, it might ease the fear of blushing. Going to an actual hypnotist would involve talking to a stranger about the problem – also too risky – so an impersonal recording of some kind was in order.

I wandered gloomily around the bookshops but found nothing of use. On a whim, I tried health shops but again came up empty. As a last resort, I shuffled into one of the many 'alternative' magic shops so popular at the time. Psychic phenomena, if it was real, seemed dangerous for all the obvious reasons, but desperate is as desperate does. Much like the Wiccan shop in Edinburgh, scene of the alarming tarot reading, the establishment I wandered into occupied the ground floor of an old Tudor building: painted-black timber frames warped and bent by the centuries, and lumpy, white, wattle and daub walls. I chatted, through the ever-present mental tempest, with the tall, softly spoken, middle-aged woman inside – dressed like a New Age Sorceress in flowing robes. I typically vague about the problem and, although there were no hypnosis CDs on sale, I left with a subliminal self help CD, titled 'Freedom from Fears' and a guided meditation CD: 'Overcoming Your Weaknesses'. The best I could find. It seemed almost pointless but I resolved to give them a try anyway, lacking any other options.

Meditation had always been pie in the sky. I knew, almost from the onset of intrusions and voices back at the rivet factory, it was something that might help. But whenever sitting down in an attempt to concentrate attention on any given technique, my mind would *always* sabotage proceedings with a flood of worse-than-usual intrusions. In normal circumstances, they could be just barely, clumsily, neutralised with frantically repeated words, hasty visualisations or incessant internal argument – or else I'd distract myself as best I could with external stimuli. Sitting or lying down with closed eyes and focusing on anything in particular, the intrusions would coagulate or 'clog up' in the forefront of consciousness like a backed up sink, the horrors rushing in, colliding with one another, vivid, threatening and terrifying. Terrible fates loomed if I didn't open my eyes and address them in the usual, clumsy, haphazard manner. Meditation probably did hold a lot of promise, but I could never get past the torrent of traumas. How I still longed for the settled tranquillity of weed! But that door remained well and truly closed. Unless I wanted to start hearing voices again. If only I could feel that gentle spiritual uplift from back in the day, or as it was at the factory just before the worst of the intrusions first showed up; then I'd at least have the strength to deal with this thing. But I knew from experience that spiritual feelings couldn't be ruminated back into existence; as all attempts to do only exacerbated *all* the mental problems. No. For want of any other alternatives whatsoever, meditation had to be made to work. Somehow. It was the only option. Doubtless, the same obstacles would present themselves but I didn't want to stop working or socialising so it was time to push on through the proverbial pain barrier. I was furious at the problem for having not buggered off by now and desperate for every reason under the sun, so that at least provided enough bloody-minded motivation to grit my teeth and get through it, the same way I'd seen off The Snowman all those years ago.

Buy Now, Pay Later

The subliminal CD contained a forty five minute track of soft, classical guitar music set to a background of calming waves, with indistinct voices quietly murmuring the subliminal messages. It felt nice, even settling while playing, but the obscure, babbling voices *really* freaked me out and did nothing to abate the white noise they inevitably triggered. So I gingerly tiptoed into the world of meditation once more. I put the Guided Meditation CD on, lay down on the floor of my room and followed the instructions. Being guided felt safer than facing my hideous mind head-on.

Anger and desperation were initially quite useful. Each instructional visualisation – a bright light, a chakra or a golden chord – was threatened by the spectre of manifold intrusions furiously fighting to penetrate, were fought with everything I had. Something in my brain wanted to turn bright lights into radioactive, skin-frying beams, and chakras into poisonous black holes spewing out a thousand ravenous insects. As I sensed the anxiety-spikes that would always herald the onset of intrusions, I drew enough strength from angry-desperation to grit my teeth and force them stubbornly back to the edge of consciousness. *I* was the one in charge, and was saying, emphatically, "no".

The meditation session instructed a visualisation of three 'versions' of myself – mind, body and spirit, joined together by a golden chord – the three of us floated up into the sky, visiting a bright cloud-room for an informal chat about our differences. Naturally, most of our 'conversation' centred on the Mind-Version. As the walls of the cloud-room seemed to heave with latent intrusions and simmering anxiety, I attempted to 'reason' with Mind-Version. It felt a little silly, but, desperate is as desperate does. I repeated the process on Sunday, continually battling back the threatening-onslaught of mental apparitions at every stage of the process, forcing a groundswell of anxiety tenuously under the thin, proverbial rug. I was the boy with his finger in the dyke and, for now, it was holding.

Monday was a revelation. At work, my consciousness was *so* much calmer and felt somehow 'bigger', more open and capacious than usual. There was suddenly room to manoeuvre, space in which to breathe. The phone would ring, a colleague would call my name or utter a dangerous trigger word like 'murder' and, although all incoming stimuli were registering, there was a comfortable time-delay, a safe mental space in which to decide how, if at all, to react. Intrusions still came and went, as did the debilitating feelings of mortal danger, but they didn't penetrate quite so deep into awareness with their usual ferocity. I was able to distance myself from them, if only a little. It was like going from breathing inside a plastic bag to inhaling the fresh air atop The Malvern Hills! Not quite the blissful-suspension of those early days of cannabis use, but, nonetheless, a *big* change. At last, after all these years of hell – something that actually worked!!

So the meditation CD was a no-brainer. If things were to change for good and for the better, it had to be used daily, with steadfast tenacity. There was just one problem, though: the gritted-teeth-resistance approach *always* had consequences. I did it often enough while chatting with Hanna in the smoking room, only to find all mental menaces bursting forth again immediately afterwards. I could wrestle enough control of my mind to defiantly crash through it all and force a fake semblance of sanity for a few minutes in the smoking room, but usually no more than that. The monsters now being fought were far more sophisticated and insidious than The Snowman and his spectral friends; the gritted-teeth approach could only be maintained for so long and the fallout was always horrible. It amounted to nothing more than squeezing one part of a balloon only to have the air pop up somewhere else. I knew this. Nonetheless, meditation was proving so effective, the hope was that I might be able to circumvent the problem simply by powering stubbornly though and meditating as much as humanly possible. This might at least leave me better positioned for the inevitable backlash. Perhaps this was a way forward? It was worth a try. I carried on gritting my teeth and pushing the looming intrusions and rising dread back, so I could practice the guided meditation each night. It worked for less than a week. Soon the intrusions were fully penetrating all resistance and landing with horrifying clarity on every single visualisation. Flies spewing deadly disease nestled into chakras, contaminating them with potent viruses of fear and self-loathing; healing lights turned red hot, sizzling skin to a crisp and, while trying to reason with the Mind-Version of myself, 'he' kept ignoring Spirit-Version attacking Body-Version – drowning, stabbing or pushing him into the visualised fire. Having such horrible images flash through the mind while conscious was bad enough, but now that it was happening while in a deep, trance-like state, in dialogue with my unconscious, it was chilling. It seemed I'd made a huge mistake, inadvertently allowing the pollutions of my conscious mind to penetrate even deeper than was usually the case. After several more teeth-gritted attempts, meditation had to stop entirely. The usual, insidious feeling of something being so very wrong was now threatening to sink down into my bones and infect the deepest parts of my mind and nerves.

Seeing Red

The hard-won benefits of meditation trailed off after a matter of days. Within about a week, the continual barrage of horrifying mind-traffic returned in full force – that useful feeling of 'extra space' in my head entirely gone. Consciousness now shrivelled back to a suffocating immediacy, with the unsettling feeling of it all now penetrating that much deeper. It heightened everything terribly, engendering a sense that I was even beginning to lose the fragile by-the-skin-of-my-teeth control I normally managed to achieve, by the never-ending farce of internalised rituals and unceasing rumination. All, apparently, while "looking so calm". Intrusions, and unwanted psychic 'transmissions' of 'incriminating' thoughts and images grew steadily worse and more dynamic; the litany of blushing-related trigger words again starting to swell and 'infect' one another, just as they'd done at college. "Ripe" sounds and looks similar enough to "rape" and so became dangerous, as did its association with the word "fruit" and so on, forming a deadly chain of potential triggers. Such dangerous words would appear in conversation, each eliciting a blinding flash of mortal danger as I sat at my desk, trying with every last drop of strength to just keep working. My grip on reality seemed to be loosening, daily. The brain in my head wanted me killed and there was almost nothing I could do about it.

Sooner or later my it would create a perfect storm, I just knew it: I'd eventually blush at the worst possible moment, in front of the worst possible person – presumably someone fairly irrational, reactionary, quick to judge and with a penchant for gossip and righteous violence. I'd find myself unable to explain the reason for the blushing without mentioning all the chaotic shit in my head, and essentially stumble into a horrific, fatal attack. The danger was tangible. My hateful lemming-brain *wanted* it to happen. I was running out of strength, ideas, even the ability to care. It felt like my body's natural survival instincts were the only thing propelling me forward at all. Sleep now beyond poor, nerves close to complete burnout; I was losing the battle for my mind. I could *taste* it, the deathly scent of failure in the prevailing wind. The honeymoon period was well and truly over. Then one afternoon, just a few minutes before Five, I walk over to Hannah's desk to make small talk, hoping for a brief distraction from the storm within.

"Hey Hannah. Are you staying late today?"

"No, I'm nearly finished here. Nigel's picking me up at five."

"Any plans for this evening?"

"I'm gonna finish reading my book tonight but, other than that, not much."

"What are you reading?"

"It's an autobiography about a woman who was sexually abused as a child and then again by her husband."

The atom bomb explodes in a fatal flash of light. My facial temperature instantly skyrockets to a thousand degrees. I the overheating surface of my skin glows like a flaming torch. Hannah's eyes widen, her eyebrows raise a little. They quickly contract into a frown. The whole room falls away as a burst of radioactive adrenaline tears through me, every thought of danger I've ever had exploding, a thousand fireworks at once. A physically painful, blinding awareness of this moment, and only this moment, hijacks everything as I feel my limbs turning to jelly and a cold sweat erupting all over my body. I'm in *serious* trouble. It's in her hands now. What she does in the next few seconds will determine whether I live or die. The surprised look on Hannah's face sears itself into every cell of my body. I somehow manage to shakily ad-lib further small talk as she looks back down at her work. For the remainder of conversation she's looking elsewhere, busying herself, looking decidedly guarded and suspicious. Shit. Fuck. It's finally happened. The walls are closing in. Fast.

Lightheaded, trying not to vomit, I return to my desk and gather up my things in an almost catatonic trance; every conceivable alarm screaming in my head, body…in my racing blood. The air in the room has all but gone. Any second now a chain of events will erupt, starting with loud, angry accusations from Hannah echoing across the office, followed rapidly followed by surprised stares – aghast at first but soon angry and vicious – and after that, sheer pandemonium. End of the road. Goodnight World. …But it hasn't happened yet. I walk out of the office with a shaky veneer of outward calm, covering the mental, emotional and bodily cataclysm as best I can but I can tell – can *feel* - that an internal switch has been thrown and by brain and nerves are now *so* far beyond reason. On a rational level I know it's unlikely that anything bad will happen this time, but rationalisations wither and die like flies on a windscreen. Heart thundering like never before. Temperature rising; I feel the change in my blood as stress hormones race out from my brain, pressure-cooking perception in its own white hot terror. I'm often dizzy from anxiety but now my head could quite literally explode. An out-of-control rocket is trapped beneath my skull and will either tear a hole and escape or else explode. Everything blindingly-vivid and dangerous: Every window, each tile in the floor, every object in sight – all around pulsates with ethereal danger. Toxic poison pumps to every nerve and muscle; the runaway chemical reaction making anything more than the most basic motor functions almost impossible. I manage to drive home and explain what's happened to Dad. He's sympathetic but doesn't seem to get quite how catatonic I am. I can't explain it. Don't know how. Panic is shutting me down. Damn this bastard veneer. I've worked so long and hard at hiding how I feel and now it seems as though there's an impenetrable wall stopping me from expressing myself when I most need to, no matter how much I try. I've stunted my own ability to communicate. However I may appear without, I'm spinning out of control within.

For the rest of the evening, everything else I experience – conversations, driving, eating, drinking, smoking, trying to watch TV – absolutely *everything* I do, or perceive, is some distant, obscure narrative distorted and overruled by eyeball-close danger. I'm slipping deeper into the catatonic trance; the immersive shock makes all interaction with the outside world an almost out of body experience. I've fallen from a cliff but have yet to hit the ground: a sealed fate I have the horror of observing as it hurtles upwards. I try to rationalise but nothing works. The gut-level conviction of imminent danger simply will not budge. Hannah will surely discuss the incident with someone else, won't she? If I don't return to work tomorrow, will that look incriminating? If I do, this will surely now happen again and again – the stakes have just gone through the roof and each new blushing episode will arouse further suspicions, bringing those fatal recriminations closer. My life might not be in immediate danger just yet but it surely soon will be. Blushing is a *thousand* times more likely now the lid has come off. This is so unfair. I haven't harmed anyone. I hate being alive and feeling this scared each second of every day. It seems beyond anything nature ever intended. I go upstairs to my room and put on the subliminal 'Freedom from Fears' CD. The muffled voices can't make me any more freaked out than I already am. I'll try anything at this point. As the track plays, it mercifully takes the edge off some of the terror and, exhausted, I slip into shallow sleep for about half an hour. I wake when the track's finished with the burning shock still charging to every inch of my body; the stress hormones a corrosive acid, burning me up from the inside. Everything is on constant Red Alert. There's no peak to it, just a ringing and ringing and *ringing* like a fire alarm that can't be shut off. I'm hypnotised by an ascending danger-signal, hurtling straight upwards. There's no longer any scale or context; totally absorbed by these feelings, time, space and all other contexts are slipping away. Sooner or later the most unfair and untimely end will be upon me. Consciousness starts to divide: part of me *knows* it's all in my head but we're past the point where the other, catatonic part can be reasoned with. One part of my mind is almost bizarrely sanguine – glad this thing has finally happened and I can stop worrying about it; deal with it somehow…move forward – but another, more primitive area is listening to the inconsolable hysteria coming from my body and freaking out beyond all measure.

I rest as best I can, breathe deeply and try to calm down. Mum arrives home and I mention the problem to her. Although I struggle once more to fully communicate what it is I'm going through, just knowing I don't have to do this in complete isolation anymore brings some solace. I can't imagine the state I'd be in had this happened before I told my parents about these strange problems. Deal with this in total isolation? It doesn't bear thinking about. I can't face going to work tomorrow, but I know this problem isn't going away. I need my body to calm down so I can at least try to think. The following morning, after a few short hours of hollow, disturbed sleep, I awake to discover a thick, luscious blanket of white, celestial dust covering everything in sight, glimmering in the morning sun. It snowed heavily during the night. I have today off. Thank god.

All Bets Are Off

All Bets Are Off

The snow melted away within a matter of days. But the scalding, nervous heat in my psyche showed no such signs of abating. It just wasn't cooling off, even a little. The thought of returning to the council evoked a manic, stupefying dread, akin to visiting a simmering volcano. It just wasn't going to work. I gave the agency some bullshit story about finding another job that required an immediate start. They were understandably disappointed, but there was no way I could risk telling them the truth. Time for yet another, unplanned, 'clean break'.

I registered with a different employment agency and was allocated some part time hours at a plant nursery several miles outside of town. It wasn't the most stimulating job – standing outside in the cold winds, picking weeds out of potted plants – but the boss had no other employees at the time so I was mostly left to work alone and, being out in the middle of nowhere, it felt relatively safe. Relatively. Since the blushing incident with Hannah, company of any kind felt more dangerous than ever – in urban areas especially. But even in the quiet, rural backwater of the plant nursery, my brain remained convinced that every vehicle rolling off the narrow, country road, crunching to a halt on the gravelled car park, contained either undercover police an angry, well-armed cadre, ready for action. My heart pounded a thundering drum-and-bass rhythm every time any other humans visited the site; that rocketing sense of stalking-danger and imminent disaster peaking at the very sight of each new person. Nothing remotely bad happened, but, as each vehicle left the site, it seemed no more than another dangerously close call – one more digit in an unstoppable countdown to that inevitable visit that would surely spell the violent end. It was as though something in my consciousness was somehow calling it into existence. My mind and nerves were worse than ever before – worse, even, than they'd been in Edinburgh or at the County Council offices – hanging now by a single, brittle thread. It was increasingly obvious there was something very seriously wrong with me, something more than a problem that would eventually subside if ignored long enough or confessed to loved ones. But the thought of gambling trust in a stranger at the NHS, however qualified and experienced, called to mind those same visceral images of total, irrevocable ruin, only now they were *so* vivid I could practically hear the screams and smell the disinfectant of the psychiatric wards. I was by now bone-tired, jumpy and almost constantly nauseous. The electrified-tension and hyper-alertness that kept me awake each night in Edinburgh was back, and remained throughout the day, but now with an even higher, paralysing charge. It made everything still louder, brighter, and sharper, racking up the pressure of the throbbing tension-headaches in the left side of my brain. And, as ever, those heavy blocks of solid concrete lodged in my gut heaved with the weight of so much suppressed emotion, weighing down every thought, word and action. An unbroken curse. Nevertheless, I was grateful to still be able to work in some capacity. It was just safer to keep away from other people for now. And try not to think or feel too much about anything. At all. It always brought the heat of danger another inch closer.

Another Month, Another Job

After about a month, as the cold began to ease and the days lengthen with the advance of March, I was beginning to calm down, if only a little. Despite the resurgent shitstorm of the past few months, I'd retained a *slight* feeling of defiance, having confided in my parents, blushed at the council and lived to tell the tale. I was still clearly in a bad way, but not about to retreat into absolute isolation as this, I knew, would only worsen matters. In my spare time I forced myself to attend an evening drama class, and a community choir. Being in an enclosed space with so many strangers was a hard slog, but forcing myself to endure it for a couple of hours a week to rekindle old hobbies, while exhausting felt good and worthwhile. At any rate, it wasn't half as scary as being crammed into a stressful office for eight hours a day.

The weekly drama class proved quite therapeutic. Although not my original intention, I began using much of the ever-present internal turmoil as a resource. It was obviously never discussed with anyone, but if, for example, we were instructed to act fearful, I'd take my mind back to the rivet factory when those most harrowing intrusions first tore into consciousness, and tap some of the insane emotions for effect. Conversely, if we were told to act joyful, I'd let myself imagine the whole problem just suddenly, inexplicably and totally disappearing for good. It didn't, of course, but it was wonderful to pretend, if only for a moment. It did nothing to abate the problems but was nonetheless a little cathartic to finally express some of the bewildering emotions. At the end of each class, as we emerged into the evening air, although I still half expected to be greeted - and ended by an angry mob, I was also strangely emboldened, having channelled the terror *into* something, rather than just fighting, resisting and failing in the usual way. Outside, the lynching party still hadn't shown up, despite the incessant, adrenaline-fuelled mental messages that they'd arrive any second. Was this a way forward? A therapy that actually worked? There was a very strange side effect, however: a distant, peculiar, haunting image of a large, dark scab kept appearing on the periphery of my consciousness. It wasn't tearing in like the intrusive thoughts or frantically whispering danger as the blushing-and-lynching-fears did, it was just *there*, like an obscure memory from some strange, forgotten dream, hovering at the edge of awareness. I put it down to an overactive imagination after so much make-believe in drama class. Probably nothing. Hopefully.

In the meantime, the boss at the plant nursery was becoming a bit of an ogre. He'd taken on new members of staff and was starting to get short with everyone. There was much grumbling in the ranks. Crucially, he was giving me more and more hours which, in any other context would've been great, but sleep was still *very* difficult and I was only just starting to calm down. Time to look elsewhere. Group situations remained deeply unpleasant, but drama class was helping with confidence, so, if they were of a manageable size and the work was part time, it might just be doable.

I soon find myself standing among a small group of temps being given the tour of a new, state of the art call centre on the site of a modern factory across town. It was interesting for the first twenty minutes, even impressive. Then it became a little dull. By the time our tour was almost over, as stood, listless, in the lobby, hearing *all* about "the key philosophy at the very heart of the company", it was painfully boring. Still not sleeping well and highly nervous in such situations, my 'Interested-Face' was starting to slip. I glance at another temp – a slim, youngish, tired-looking, dark-haired woman in pin-stripe suit - and notice her face, too, has fallen. She points it obligingly at our trainer-induction-guide-person but the look she's wearing says exactly what I'm thinking: "When will this be over? Please, shut up or just shoot me. Make it stop." We exchange a glance and try not to smirk. This is going on *far* too long. The softly-optimistic monotone of our immaculately groomed guide is almost hypnotically boring; we're all just seconds away from nodding off right where we stand. Finally we get to sit and shadow the permanent staff. Smirking-girl and I go out for a smoke and get on really well. Her name is Lauren. Training starts on Monday. Throughout this entire, purgatorial process, amidst the boredom and the usual disgusting intrusions, paranoia, quiet panic and internal rituals; that strange scab-image grows a little closer, clearer…more haunting. Probably best to ignore it as much as possible. Gotta learn this new job.

Battle Scarred?

Over the weekend, I try to keep busy. I ignore it most of the time, but the scab-image grows ever more vivid and strangely eerily. It doesn't intrude, taunt, or scream danger like so much in my head, but as its clarity grows, it gets harder to dismiss. It's just *there*, like a haunting, obscure memory from another life. Curiosity compels an occasional 'glance'. It's vertical, serrated and symmetrical in structure, with jagged edges, like a loosely-sketched outline of chainsaw-blade. The scar tissue itself is mostly black, with patches of deep purple and scarlet around the edge, and a lumpy, contoured, rough, deeply-sore texture. A vanishing darkness envelops it. Intrusive thoughts will flash into my mind's eye out of nowhere; paranoia and fear can spread throughout brain and body like wildfire, and depression manifests with a vacuous, murky-ambience, sucking the life out of everything but...this? *This* image...this *thing*...has a wholly different...quality. It feels like it's coming from – or at least connected to – those grinding headaches in the left side of my brain; the area that wants to process something that just cannot be allowed, under any circumstances. Also, whilst technically in my head, it also feels somehow *outside* my body, slightly above my head and over to the left, as though suspended in an invisible aura of consciousness. It's alive...breathing...itching...the detailed imagery intricately connected to my deepest thoughts, emotions and sensations. A big, throbbing scar, compacted with strange psychic phenomena. Weird. Shit. It doesn't come and go or peak in any way, like so much other brain traffic – it's just constantly *present*; lingering in awareness, left over from an obscure dream. But this one doesn't vanish into vague obscurity over breakfast. It's Anomalous. Dark and resonant. Whenever I turn my attention to it, something inside echoes "*This* is the scar of your psyche. This is what you've done to yourself." – a notion that seems deeply and alarmingly true, deeper even than whatever is trapped all the way down in the visceral concrete. And yet it's intimately connected the concrete blocks;

the life of this strange psychic scab emanates from deep inside, like an eerie, still-living fossil. Glancing at the ethereal cipher, it hints at a truth too big, to imposing to bear; The Thing simply I can't face. An ocean of rumbling thoughts and impossibly intense emotions heave beneath it; ready to burst forth and sweep all in its path. As fascinating as it is, it quickly becomes something I dread to look upon. It heralds something so profound and powerful – it would surely finish me off. I recoil from the strange spectre and resolve myself to distraction with something else. Anything else.

Just Get On With It

Over the next week I fight to concentrate on the training course at the call centre, with a small amount of success. The work is more involved than previous call centre jobs, so it's fairly engaging, even occasionally distracting. Overwrought nerves and a manic brain have other ideas, but I'm used to that. During quieter mental moments, I focus as hard as possible, and resolve to just ride out the storm each time my mind starts doing somersaults, which is much of the time. There's nothing that can be done about it. Just get on with the work. The hours are part time so I can just about muddle through. Lauren and I become allies. Always stepping out together for a quick smoke, we soon discover a shared dry sense of humour and a similar motive behind taking this particular temp job: for both of us, it's a stop gap and nothing more. Although we're happy to work as hard as everyone else, we're both a little less enthralled by the training than we perhaps should be, and agree it's moving at a painful, unnecessarily slow pace. We've just got to get through the week. *So* easy to say. To do? Well, that's another matter entirely…

Throughout the week, at work and home, the haunting image looms larger in my mind's eye. Day by day it grows starker, presses further into consciousness, increasingly hard to ignore. Distant and obscure at first, it's fast becoming the exact opposite. Its presence is constant, like a perpetual déjà vu, bursting at the seams with god only knows what. That much closer and more vivid now, more of its nuanced, textured impressions become apparent. It's pulsating, interwoven and enmeshed with my own breath, sweat, hunger, thirst, tiredness and even sensory banal impressions like pins and needles. I *feel* it throb and tingle like a real scar, each itchy sensation shimmering with forbidden thought and emotion. I can practically smell its coppery stench; feel the powerful heat behind it. It's repulsive. Dark and compelling. My skin crawls every time I notice a little more of its aesthetic. It's a *part* of me, and…and…I *know* what it is. It's my unconscious mind finally boiling over into my waking thoughts. It's deeply and intrinsically connected to everything that's happened over the last four and a half years – maybe more…

By the week's end, the scab clearly isn't going anywhere, instead it just becomes more annoyingly apparent. The very thought of it stirs a cold, blistering dread, coupled with a compelling curiosity I've *never* had about the intrusive thoughts. This whole problem called 'my mind' seems as intricate and impossible to deal with as ever it did, but, there's something *there*, either within or behind the scab. I sense it; momentous and life-changing. I'm drawn to it, despite myself; a strange, compelling hunger. The elusive answer after all this time? The real reason my mind and nerves are so monumentally fucked up? The cause behind the horrible intrusions, depression, weed addiction, blushing, all mixed in with my spirituality, sexuality and so much more besides? It feels that way, but it just looks so intense, so dangerous. It's clearly not going anywhere and I'm so *deeply* tired of running. With a foreboding sense that I'm about to bite off *so* much more than I could ever chew, I resolve to at least try to deal with it.

Peering Down the Rabbit Hole

One evening, having unsuccessfully tried to ignore the eerie image for the best part of a week, I disappear into my room, sit cross-legged on the single bed, pull down the blind, lean back against the wall and close my eyes. I focus on the lingering scab in my mind's eye and start to describe it, internally, to myself; its physical appearance and all the weird notions and feelings that throb within it. "This is the scar of my life." "The damage that's been done." As I attempt to simultaneously observe and describe, one of the serrated edges peels back, just a little. A translucent, watery-yellow gas hisses out with furious decompression. I can almost smell it. Trapped emotion? Whatever it is, it feels important, but it's scary and tricky to fully describe. Perhaps I don't really want to. Hard to tell — it's so ominous. Once the gas has cleared, through the little hole in the scab I spy a thin, shining, sliver wire. See it, feel it, smell it, taste it. It's phenomenally tight, cold, hard and has the taste and smell of an old paperclip. Gives me the shivers. Another part of myself I don't want to look upon. It's something forced into place long ago, buried deep inside, clamped tight, slicing into my flesh. …It's my prison.

"Woah."

I say this aloud and quickly open my eyes. In that split second, when the shinning wire appeared, there was an unmistakable sense of a whole galaxy of entangled horrors, bursting with harrowing ciphers and symbols, ready to erupt. A bottomless pit, or at least something far deeper than I dare to go. And the prison? Am I already trapped inside it or will this bizarre process make false imprisonment from blushing more likely? In that moment, I feel with perfect clarity just how intricately connected all the imagery is with everything about my life I just can't face. I'm barely managing a part time job; nerves already as taut as they could possibly be, and my mind, while perhaps a little calmer than at the council, remains nonetheless tender after the blushing incident, still the same daily hell-storm of macabre-vileness it's been for years. Only now it's probably the most harrowing and disgusting it's ever been. Ever. The weakest, weariest, most jittery and fragile I've ever known it. There's no way I'd survive venturing down there into…whatever this shit is. No, no, no. Out of the question. I'll distract myself. Somehow.

Over the next two days, concentrating on anything at all is even more difficult than usual; almost impossible. At work I'm a jittering mess, struggling to maintain the usual façade, hold conversations, concentrate on work; at home I can barley watch the TV, even superficially. Something terrifying and momentous is happening: ever since first observing the scab, more and more obscure images have been spewing into consciousness. Counteracting them with the elaborate visualisations and arguments normally used on intrusive thoughts has zero impact. Cursing angrily is similarly futile. The idiosyncratic, ominous symbols constantly disrupt awareness, bursting out like freshly-drilled oil. Each one as intricate and alarming as the scab; nothing can be done to stem the eruption. Something powerful and threatening is rising inexorably from deep within. I'm being haunted by a thousand demons. My finger still in the dyke, only now the hole is too big and water's gushing all around me. I wish I'd just left that stupid image alone. I've started something now that I doubt can be stopped. It pushes relentlessly at all defences; a burgeoning rumble, soon to crescendo into an avalanche. My grip on reality might be finally and completely disintegrating once and for all. It looks like there's another private drama to ride out. This one seems different, though. In ways I can't explain…

Brace Yourself...

By Friday afternoon, as I drive home across town after the last day of training, the spectral images are in full flow and almost impossible to ignore. Something terrible is on the move, stirring to life, deep, deep down in those cold, concrete blocks. I've been both longing for and afraid of whatever's encased down there for years, and now it's finally shifting, whether I like it or not. It's at once exhilarating and mortally terrifying. This might finally be a way out of my troubles...but at what cost? Doesn't feel like there's much of a choice now anyway. Something unconscious has been triggered and is showing no signs of slowing down. Whatever it is, if I can't outrun it then I just want it over with. I arrive home, make polite conversation with Mum & Dad over a ritual cup of tea and disappear upstairs. I don't want them to know something's wrong...at least no more than usual.

Lying on the bed, I close my eyes and start to observe and describe the rest of the scab. Its dark colours, rough contours - even the vanishing darkness surrounding it – all thick with weird thoughts and emotions:

Some thoughts echo out from the dark ambience that envelops the image:

"This is the end of the road. There's nowhere left to run."

"The scab's made of compacted, half-dead emotions. Charred flesh of...of...my heart?"

"It's old and deep; poisonous and impenetrable."

None of these words feel like judgements or even interpretations. They simply present themselves as though emerging from another world. The imagery seems to encrypt a profound truth that can only be revealed by describing, as fully as possible, whatever appears. The more I describe, the more the weird insights emerge. Not analysing; just discovering. I don't want to be thinking any of this; it all just spews out from somewhere deep inside. As I behold and describe the nuances of the scar in more detail, more edges peel and yet more yellow gas hisses angrily out. Stress? Poison? Spirit? Disease? The usual intrusions, still very much active, join the macabre meltdown in an attempt to sabotage and obscure perception, taunting with their usual viciousness: *"This is bullshit", "You're making it up", "You're going to die because of this.", "It's not even a scar, you idiot".* I push on regardless, describing as best I can. It's pure emotion: dread and apprehension momentarily punctured; pent up feelings escape like ancient pockets of long-compressed gas. Through the murky, swirling, yellow gas, more 'truths' emit from the scab:

"This is how it was in the beginning. A scab of solidified panic. Anguish itself, pressed into hideous, distorted flesh."

Something occurs to me: although I've never forgotten that awful, life-thwarting day back at the factory, I've never quite faced up to just how horrifying, intense and terrifying it really was. A personal pandemonium. The scab is a symbol of how those first violent and sexual intrusions *really* affected me. It was like being run through with a machine gun, firing acid bullets that explode in the flesh, causing apoplectic pain…but not the release of death. Weary but intrigued, I continue. It's hard to describe and unlock the scab fully; its macabre, compacted content so intense. There's still *so* much I don't want to see. I never did. This is *why* the scab exists. This is where it's all gone. Unable to fully 'unlock' it, I peer through the areas that have already peeled and dissolved; the shiny metal wire from the other day is still there. I can actually feel the wire inside me, all over my body. It's imagery so deep and resonant as to be real. Then comes the realisation: it's not a prison, it's a *brace*. A metal brace of industrial-strength wires, covering every part of my body, from the soles of my feet, along every inch of flesh, locking in each joint, finger, and bone all the way up to my skull. The metal is forged from the purest fear and smokes with a transparent energy, like heat waves rising from tarmac. I shiver all over as I feel, smell and taste each flesh-searing wave of fear rippling inside. The brace's joints are fastened *hard* with plastic yellow screws, each wound so tight that the outer parts of wire that should cover, say, the front and back of my leg, are drawn so close they cut clean through flesh and bone and are almost touching one another. There's maybe an inch of space between them. A modern, industrial version of some awful, medieval torture device. Fucking hell. The brace compacts epic levels of emotion and sensation into a *tiny* network of cramped space, deep within my skeleton. Squashing…chocking human emotion…almost to death. But the bastard won't die. The intensity of the image is chilling; how profound and true it feels and the way I tangibly feel its impossibly-tight restraint, all over my body. I sense trapped humanity, quivering inside the tight frame, and the petrified, always-exhausted, zombie-like half-life I live outside of the brace. I've felt it throughout the last four and a half years. Every single day. I just couldn't admit to it – to what was really going on. As I describe each length of wire, each fastened screw, painful memories of those first, horrible intrusions seep out: god-awful, monstrous images tore in, pummelling mind and heart with relentless cruelty, my whole world torn apart, ripped open by wrathful lightning. Shock and awe became me. All those incendiary emotions and bodily reactions; their mortifying-intensity. Death itself. When I first feared for my life; when blood turned to flammable acid and my head became a violent, rattling furnace. The hairs on my skin stood up like electrified micro-wires. There was an edge to it all; an impossible-potency I just couldn't deal with, so I automatically repressed as much of the emotions as I possibly could, even as they erupted and burned the sky itself. It didn't achieve much. Wasn't enough to cope, but it's what I had to do. The brace is suddenly looser around my right leg. Over-taut flesh goes suddenly slack, reeling from years of pressure. Concordantly, my entire calf muscle rapidly pulsates as though a nerve is trapped. These complex, figurative images now causing actual, tangible, physical *movements*. Something's being released. Scary. Shit. Will my heart palpitate too? Bring on a heart attack? What am I unleashing here? What exactly is this? The unconscious? Demonic possession? Something deadly? It's too much. There's still so much more down there; a simmering lava of ciphers embodying every last bit of those aspects of my mental problems I can't face. I open my eyes and go downstairs. It was a mistake to do this. I'm not up to it. Not by a long shot. I've taken a big enough leap already. Let's hope it was enough and the whole thing will just stop. Please.

One Way Traffic

Throughout the rest of the day, the symbols and ciphers erupt in full flow, whatever I do. Walking about the house, trying desperately not to think about it, I feel the brace; the loose section around my right leg and the choking tightness of the unexplored areas, now buzzing, alive with buried thoughts, painful memories, and impossible feelings, all fighting for the surface. My unconscious is retching, swelling – ready to projectile-vomit out absolutely everything. Every last bit. Although at no point do any of the images become external, visual hallucinations, their powerful, hypnotic effect means they obtrude into every area of consciousness, including profound, *tangible* feelings all over my body. Intensely worried, I vacillate between distracting myself with television or music and briefly resuming the process in the hope that just a little bit more will be enough to calm it all down. Fat chance. A huge crack has appeared in the dam and water is gushing, fast, in one direction.

That night, lying in bed, thrashing around, waiting for sleep to spirit me briefly away from this strange, terrifying phenomenon, the brace continually obtrudes into consciousness. It's always been this way. Distraction in varying degrees during the day is easy enough, but once

I'm lying in bed, eyes closed and lights off, whatever the time and however tired I may be, there's just nowhere to turn. Weird mental phenomena of one kind or another invade every time. Exhausted, I sense resistance will keep me up all night, and so reluctantly, nervously, give over my full attention to the strange underworld once more.

The brace is still there, every suffocating inch of bone-penetrating wires and rigid screws contain more trapped memories of those first few days of the intrusions, when those murderous voices were still present and my blood curdled at each and every mortifying shock. I was sweeping the factory floor. Trying to hold on to the good, spiritual feelings of elation and keep out the worrying vibes of misery and despair. Up, down, up, down, up and down again. Over and over. It was unnerving, but I had to make it work. Then, suddenly, out of nowhere, images of rape, violence, abuse and the most heinous, vile offense were tearing into my head. I was beside myself. Terrified of blushing…being killed or hauled off to prison to be tortured and abused to death. I remember now just how bad it really was. How I was apoplectic with fear. Moments and memories: emotions, thoughts and car-crash sensations. Poisonous tension. Epic disgust. Abject horror beyond words. Adrenaline-soaked blood racing so fast it threatened to ignite my veins. I describe it all as it was but…not…not…the *thing*. That one thing I've been resisting ever since. Can't think it, let alone say it. I don't even know how. Too scared of what it might mean. As images, memories, emotions and abstractions are observed and described, the brace is steadily loosened all over – not enough to escape, but enough to move – and more weird, trapped-nerve-style palpitations judder all over the place. Fingers, neck, chest, arms, back, stomach, legs – some focused in small areas, others an entire limb. Rapid palpitations run all over as though I'm being electrocuted. The loosened brace now reveals what it's been restraining all this time: a glowing, yellow, ethereal hue; something essential to life; to being alive…being *human*. It's the sensitivity I was warned about. Vulnerability. Humanity. All such luxuries were trapped and restrained at all costs in the crucible of blind panic at the factory. I had to fight for control, with everything I had. And more. Breaking down and risking the suspicion of others was guaranteed suicide. I desperately wanted and needed help, but that fear of deadly consequences was *so* strong, so all-absorbing that I became scared of my own humanity itself – of that hopeless need to collapse on the floor and sob for help, for compassion. Fear provided the powerful super-fuel to repress it at all costs. To stay physically safe. The last few years of stone-cold numbness and mortal anxiety were the end result. As glimmers of feeling return, the edges of the concrete blocks start to crumble and fade a little. I'm scared. Still petrified of what might be done to me if anyone ever knew about the inhuman horror film forever playing in my head. Seeing this yellow hue of humanity, feeling the concrete begin to crumble, is truly an exhilarating wonder to behold – a first breath after almost drowning – but it's in no way reassuring. Yes, I'm human after all and yes, I'm still *just* as terrified as I always was. Intrusive thoughts rain in throughout, like falling balls of celestial fire. Thoughts that I'm evil; that I want to destroy others and that my thoughts can magically engineer terrible fates for everyone, including myself. I can't control it any more. God knows what's going to happen now. Thankfully, the trance-like release brought on by realising so much repressed life collides with deep fatigue and I drift off to sleep.

Unleashed

It wasn't enough. The next day begins with a heady mixture of nervous energy and jittering dread. The scab and brace are now fuzzy and loose, as though they've nothing more to reveal. I'd hoped yesterday's efforts would've been enough, but, over breakfast, a spectral carnival of further images races up into consciousness, each cipher intricately enmeshed with every thought, feeling and sensation: the sights and sounds coming from the TV, the walls of the room, the feel of the stool beneath me; even the taste of cornflakes. The whole world within and without. Saturation. Alarmingly real, so much so that anything going on around me barely registers, as if it's all happening in some other, far off dimension.

I sense that yesterday merely scratched the surface. Having just a glimpse of humanity return – knowing it's still there and didn't die off after all – is invigorating, lightens the load a little, but the payoff seems to be that the feeling of immanent, mortal danger is now coming to the fore like never before. The risk factor hasn't gone – just that much closer now. Unleashed at last. Those magical thoughts that can make things happen – cause a car crash or engineer a blushing trigger – are on the march, threatening to draw strength from this bizarre process. If a group of strangers brandishing baseball bats barged their way into the house right this second, I wouldn't be surprised. My blood would run cold with terror, but not surprise. After all, it'd be my own pathological fault. And still there's the 'thing' – that one thing I *still* can't bring myself to think or say. I. Can't. Do. It. I have to; there's no other way around it – I've always known that – but I just can't. I *won't*. It's wrong. It's not me. I'll never accept it. Perhaps embracing this process a little more will ease enough of the pressure and the thing can be avoided. For now. As horrible as the last four years have been, right now, if I could go back to cold, tired numbness, repression and straightforward anxiety, I would. But it's gone beyond that now. Beyond the pale. I can't choke off any more humanity for the sake of miserable, frugal safety. I've absolutely no strength left. No more ideas. I've been running on fumes ever since blushing in front of Hannah and just don't have any fight left in me. It's been going on for so long now. I can feel the futility of it all. The holding pattern has finally, irrevocably, broken. Something fundamental is drawing me inexorably down into the stale depths of my defective mind. Second by second, more and more cracks are appearing in the dam, splintering out in every direction. It's beginning to shake. This is it. It's about to burst. Let's get it over with.

I spend the rest of Sunday lost deep inside in a torrent of haunting, macabre symbols, emotions, memories and more worrying physical palpitations. Chards of glass that melt and reveal meaning when described; ethereal purple-green orbs, spinning with anxious energy, and the purple-skinned, yellow-eyed demon from that awful dream the first night after the intrusions – I see, observe and describe it all, taking the occasional break to eat or smoke. Each time I open my eyes, the tangible, real world hits my senses with vivid, crystal brightness. Out in the garden, sipping tea, smoking another roll-up, the world of solid forms and sensory information feels different: fresh air on skin; the sights, sound of birdsong, smells of the garden; the heat of the mug in my hands; steam rising up nostrils and the smoothing taste of tea – it's all coming steadily back…connecting somewhere deeper…registering once more. At last there's finally feeling beyond the shallow zombie-state I've grown so used to. Things inside are shifting, moving, stirring back to life. But still the ciphers relentlessly pull at every nerve, more real and poignant than anything else. Not so much as an inch of the fear has abated, in fact it's increasing, beginning to look like an almighty confrontation between this resurgent humanity and the deep, white-hot fear that's ruled my every waking moment for years, is now imminent. No idea which will win. Or if I'll survive. Utter disorientation and exhilaration in equal measure. No stopping it now. Down I go. Deeper, deeper and deeper still.

The Point of No Return

The scab and brace were the tip of the psychic iceberg. What follows in their wake, as I plummet endlessly down the rabbit-hole is a explosive eruption of more encrypted memories; those early heartbreaking moments of intrusions, saturated with combustible emotions and thoughts, pressed into a cascade of weird, unnerving symbols. Each image must be described as fully as possible, while intrusions continually interfere and sabotage in much the same way they did a few months back when meditation crashed and burned. Intrusions don't destroy the ciphers, though – after each disruption, the original cipher remains: resonant, transcendent, untouched by the pollution of intrusive thought. Describe, describe and describe some more. A runaway ghost train of symbols begetting more of the same, with me frantically describing it all, trying to keep up. More palpitations. All over. It feels that, for every inch of humanity reclaimed; danger edges a little closer just like The Snowman. The vicious mob-death now just inches away. Can I snatch back enough capacity to feel before the demon escapes? Before The Thing must be faced?

Still not enough. The Unspeakable Thing peers through the heart of each harrowing symbol: …the one thing I still can't allow myself to think or say, is just there; the fundamental building block of each and every emblem. A fatal race to the finish line; mental hieroglyphs slowly melting the visceral concrete as each symbol tries to communicate a truth I just can't face. So, more and more symbols abound; my mind encoding truth in a world of emblems. The truth can't be destroyed. Palpitations release years-long tension but draw in danger. Letting go is as suicidal now as it's always been. I'm coming back to life but the price could be life itself. Keep going. Describe the underworld just enough to pass through, regain what was lost and reach safety. There's nothing else to be done. Then I reach the bottom…

The erupting storm of images finally clears to reveal the last and most poignant one. Three, bright, conical, steel spikes rest, hammered deep into my brain, squashing all remaining grey matter in the tiny gaps between. Just like the brace, I feel their cold, hard texture, taste their bitter metallic tang – with *every* fibre of my being. *So* much appalling emotion, thought and sensation, all compacted into these painful, unnaturally heavy spikes. Their tangible resonance pulsates through cerebral veins. I'm close. Please, God, let there be enough of a release to calm it all down so The Thing… The Monster doesn't have to be faced. I describe once more…

The spikes are made of a hard, dense, unnaturally heavy metal. It has a strange mercury smell, there's a deadly psychic sickness compacted inside, *tight*. An otherworldly disease; the gruelling 'stuff' of suffering itself, tightly condensed, an inexplicable curse packed into metal, struck right through my brain. Almost scraping each other. They ache. It's all there: *everything* I resisted back at the factory; I couldn't cry. Couldn't break down on the floor in a quivering heap. Couldn't scream or beg. Violent and abusive monsters had invaded my brain, torturing me with voices and images of me attacking my loved ones. Stabbing. Twisting necks. Assaulting. Molesting. Insulting. Destroying them, totally, in the worst imaginable ways. The voices said the most awful things: to kill, to maim and mutilate…I *had* to hide it; had to grit my teeth and somehow wear a look of calm indifference while blood roared through my veins, pulsating the very skin of my teeth. Adrenaline cascaded out all over me, poisoning and mutilating everything it touched. I wanted to run. To weep. To die. My gut reaction was an impulse to stab myself to protect others, to make it all stop. No! Keep the mask steady. Danger! Then paranoia: could anyone see through the façade? More intrusions. More voices. Snapping, stabbing, tearing. Monsters frantically grabbing at my mind and soul. *I'm* a monster. What will others do if I risk telling anyone about this unbelievable horror? Where has it come from!? Why, why, WHY is this happening?! If *I* was mortified by it; how on earth would others react? The spikes shrink a little as aching brain tissue, so long squashed and compressed, starts to slacken. It's coming back. Vulnerability. The sensitivity that made me who I was. Who I *am*. It wasn't dead and gone, just squashed and squeezed beyond belief. With each description, more palpitations: toes, ribs, neck, stomach, fingers, ear canals, pelvic floor…even eyelids and eyeballs juddering. Something's being released. The fearful demon looms. The Thing. The confrontation cannot be avoided. For every drop of humanity recovered, the threat looms larger…closer. What will happen if I finally say it? Finally allow myself to think it? Will it come true? Am I really a hideous monster? Am I to be killed by a baying, righteous mob? Is this the end? I wish with all my heart I didn't have to do this. I wish I could just go downstairs, watch TV and not give a shit like the rest of the human race, but I can't. This fucked up brain of mine is my sworn enemy and we've finally come face to face. I can't believe I'm about to do this. Face The Thing. Say its name. This is it. No turning back now. Fuck. Here we go…

All Bets Are Off

"I'm a useless, pitiful, quivering maggot that doesn't deserve life. Not a man. Prey, ripe for the kill. The only reason I'm still alive is because they haven't found out about me. But they will."

With each tentative, reluctant word, the spikes shrink just a little, and a little more of the cold concrete crumbles. More life returns. But the darkness bears down. *"Say it"*.

"My thoughts can make things happen. Bad things. To other people. Road accidents, miscarriages, disease, murders, rapes. Every kind of suffering imaginable."

It's all bursting out now. Humanity, sensitivity, vulnerability and…and…fear. I've resisted the time-freezing fear, the anxiety and the terror with every single breath. Never allowed them to fully run their course. Anxiety now cascades violently upwards like an erupting volcano. Seven hundred degrees…

It's not enough. The nagging feeling pushes harder. If I stop now my mind will probably disintegrate, if it hasn't already. *"Say it."* Eight hundred and fifty degrees…

Something powerful swells within the concrete deadness. It's about to crack clean open.. The halting, morbid fear that's burned me at every turn for the last four and a half years is about to reach an almighty crescendo. A thousand degrees. I know what the problem is. I've known all along. Please, God, don't make me say it.

"Say it. Say it now. You can't control it anymore."

One thousand, two hundred degrees.

The swirl of ciphers and eerie brain-cinema fades to the background as I take a deep, long, sighing breath and at last, devoid of all alternatives, shaking my head in disbelief, I finally face my fear. Two thousand degrees…

"I *am* a monster. A vile fiend. I *want* to hurt people. Everyone. I want to insult, stab, kill, rape, torture, flay, molest and defile everyone. Because I'm evil and I get off on it."

The concrete blocks smash into a thousand pieces, dissolving into nothingness, releasing a brilliant, ubiquitous rainbow-brightness. Tears escape beneath my closed eyelids. And suddenly, it explodes in full force; *all* the humanity, love, fear, hope and despair I've been resisting all this time. A supernova booming with unstoppable force in all directions. The left side of my brain suddenly palpitates so rapidly I can actually feel brain matter violently juddering beneath my skull. What the fuck is happening to me? My brain is *moving*. Not metaphorically. Physically. It's actually fucking *moving*. Am I about to die? Whatever's about to happen, I want it over. There's nothing left to fight. I've lost the battle.

"God hates me. All of this is divine punishment for my weakness. I'm a failure in every way."

"I want to blush. I want people to talk about murderers, rapists and terrorists at work tomorrow so I can blush and they'll kill me. It's what I deserve. It's all I want in life. My destiny."

I can't believe I'm doing this, *saying this* and yet, after all that's happened, it's an indescribable relief. All the deadness and dread, the knots in my stomach, the headaches, painful muscular tensions – all suddenly evaporate. The dam is no more. My body palpitates all over, reeling in the sudden rushing release of *years* of deadening tension. I can *feel*. Not just sadness, weariness, anxiety and despair, but the whole range of human emotions. All the humanity, sensitivity, love, affection, inspiration and vulnerability come rushing back in an epic tsunami, bringing tears to my eyes, and in the midst of it all I know with absolute clarity *one* thing above all else: my *heart*. Not an image or cipher; not an intrusion, intuition, idea or a word. I don't *see* it in any sense of the word, but *feel* its blinding glow with every rejuvenating cell of my body; every breath, each drop of blood coursing through my veins. I feel it in the air around me, the walls, the ceiling, everything. I breathe it in…and out…and back in again. It's the truest thing I've ever known. It edifies and restores me. I thought it was long, long dead. Broken and gone, leaving nothing but a hollow shell of a human. But *here it is*, where it's been all along. And there's not so much as a speck of evil in it. None whatsoever. The intrusive thoughts continue as ever they did, but as I at last feel my heart, it outshines them, the ciphers, paranoia and *everything* else. I finally see what I've known all along. They're bullshit. Complete and utter bollocks. Nonsense. I don't know what these weird, horrible thoughts are, what causes them or why I'm *still* having them right this very second, but they do not now nor have they *ever* entered or emerged from my *heart*. There are a great many things I don't know, but *at last I see it*. I know who I am. I don't wish harm on anyone and would never act on such appalling and repulsive images or notions. *I'm* the one being harmed by them. They've hurt me in ways I could never have conceived; they've changed me – how I feel about the world and the prospect of living in it – but they'll *never* touch my heart. As the blinding brilliance of its love shines, from the depths of my psyche all the way up to the surface of my skin, I'm utterly speechless. Nothing can change it. The heart can only be repressed and ignored for so long. So there.

The Payoff

But it's not over yet. My heart's great rival, that all-encompassing, consuming, trancelike fear, has also been **completely** unleashed. It pushes back, with a near-cosmic force. Maybe the intrusions about me harming others don't matter, but what about those other things I can't control? What about those 'magical' thoughts that always taunt? It still seems they could make things happen, regardless of what's in my heart. Make things happen to others…and to me. They're not done with me yet. This brain is still broken. Even my newly rediscovered heart can't fix it.

I look again for the ciphers but now, instead of a trove of fluid, metaphorical images, I'm looking directly at my fear of the supposed process itself. No coded encryptions, no secrets to be revealed, no, what I see now is how my mind actually thinks this awful phenomenon really happens. The one thing I've been afraid of more than anything else in the world. I see that if it's not confronted, it'll wreak havoc with me forever. I see that now. My heart is on my side. Gotta do it 'till it's done.

From deep within the brownish-grey brain matter, from cold, hard bones and blind flesh, bright streams of orangey-yellow, creative energy dart out to the world. They make things happen before they can be countered with elaborate visualisations. This is what I've feared the most. These kinds of thoughts can give people diseases, engineer events, fatal accidents and even plant words in peoples' heads. I see how my mind *thinks* this happens, with perfect clarity. Powerful, yellow laser beams transmit words like "rapist", "terrorist" and "murderer" into others' heads, with quicksilver speed, so that sooner or later, they'll innocently say them aloud, and I'll blush at the worst possible moment. Then comes death. The worst kind imaginable. Painful, public and traumatically slow. Inch by inch by inch. My name will be dragged through the most vile dirt. The ideas themselves don't touch my heart – they never did - but the raw fear does. Fear of the physical and psychological torture that lies in wait. The heartbreaking effect it would have on my family. Like everything else, I have to call it out and say it or it'll play havoc with my mind and body and *still* this process won't be over. I want it over. I'm close.

"I *want* someone to say "rapist" tomorrow. I *want* to blush. I want *everyone* to see, to turn against me and kill me, before I have a chance to explain. Even if I did, no one would believe me. I want it to be over. With all my heart."

I know this isn't true. None of it. I don't want to go into work tomorrow and be violently attacked and killed for something I haven't done. I want to go in and have a delightfully boring Monday morning and come home with nothing in particular on my mind. If I am violently killed, at least now I can stop being violent to *myself.* Stop hating myself. Stop cursing myself internally and imagining knives chopping off my hand each time I have an intrusive thought of harming someone, because it makes absolutely *no difference.* They still come. I can stop picturing a gun shooting my brains all over the wall every time an inappropriate word flashes in. I may not be able to stop the disgusting, horrible intrusive thoughts, but I can stop hating myself for them. If I'm to die tomorrow, at least I have my heart back. I feared it was long gone; that I was already completely dead inside. Whatever the hell's going on here, at least now I truly know who I really am, despite all the crap in this diseased brain. Maybe it really is all just in my head. The problem is, my head is attached to my shoulders and goes everywhere I do. There's just no getting away from it. So I've faced it at last. The fear was *so* powerful, overwhelming, and there was nowhere left to run. And now humanity and foreboding swirl throughout mind and body like a sunlight thunderstorm. I'm still terrified. Terrified of what will happen tomorrow, now I've finally let it all go. But I'm not afraid of myself any more. I hope it really is all just a horrible illusion of this broken brain. I can't be sure. But I'll find out tomorrow, one way or another. I'd say, at this point, that all bets are off.

The Final Rush Hour, Part VII

The last set of traffic lights come into view, heralding the final stretch of road. They're green. I want them to change. For all the desire to get this thing over with, the body just doesn't want to die. It's designed to seek safety and survival at all costs so, yeah, a red light right now would be a bonus. One last moment of ambiguity, some small mercy. They stay green. I turn right onto the long stretch of road that runs past the housing estates, up to the industrial complex, where the moment of truth awaits. He we go. The green mile…or…the road to freedom.

Pristine car showrooms pass on the left. …Legs turning to watery-slush. …The post box on the right. …Am I about to pass out? I hope not. Would only delay the inevitable. …Now past the right hand turning onto the housing estate. …A white hot field of living-dread burns inside. A force of nature. Unstoppable. If they could harness this, it could power a city. I don't fight to control or resist. . …Over the mini roundabout. Let the epic torrent continue its eruption and sweep all in its path if that's what must happen. Blood racing at light speed. Nerves are flailing solar flares. Every reflex primed for action, ready to fight or flee before they can be intercepted by thought or intention. But they need not be. I won't run. Some deeper part of me is utterly serene; still as a Buddha at one with the storm. It's over. No more tricks up my sleeve; no creative ways to duck and dive, bargain, blag or avoid the inevitable. I laboured with every last morsel of strength to find a way around this problem – to sidestep the confrontation. But it was inevitable. I think deep down I always knew it'd have to be faced in the end. No more running. I'm already free. The strange, horrific cinema-of-doom in this weird brain is what it is. I've stopped fighting and so, somehow, for all the full-pelt Armageddon going on inside, the fight is over, and the Light remains, incandescent and untouchable, backlighting the chaos. It's a relief. The roof of the pristine, state-of-the-art factory at last comes into view behind the beautiful trees that outline its car park. Resplendent in full springtime bloom, their exquisite pink petals flutter playfully in the soft breeze, shaking off the morning dew; a tantalising, springtime orchestra. The world is such a breathtaking, beautiful place. It's wonderful beyond words to be able to feel that again.

I pull into the side road, adjacent to the factory, and park the car. My shaking fingers roll a fag before getting out; the *very* last opportunity to stall. There's something in my stomach like butterflies, only much worse. Moths? Bats? They dart around, wings cutting the sides of my shuddering stomach as it aches with their frantic, erratic dance. I climb out of the car and onto my jelly-feet that beg to run in the other direction. The tension is incredible. My brain sizzles with nuclear heat. It takes a gargantuan effort to force trembling muscles to cooperate, to stand, to coordinate the action of lighting my fag. Breathing even shallower now. Skin drum-tight and prickling all over. Sulphuric acid coursing through vein and bone.

 No people outside the entrance; no lingering, baying crowds. Every step towards the immaculately shiny, dark brown, mirrored reception is a surreal stagger of a body drunk on adrenaline. Bewildering detachment battles gut-wrenching immediacy. Almost an out of body experience, as though watching someone else crunch along this path, were it not for pain and danger trapping me within a bodily furnace. The sunlight has cleared the buildings opposite just enough to shine its ecstatic glow across the path to the approaching door. Its golden rays sublime, edifying. Whatever's about to happen, I now know who I am. What I'm capable of. And what I'm not. I don't have the ability to control the hateful circus in my head, but I'm not capable of acting out a single one of the intrusive thoughts. If I blush and get lynched, so be it. I can't control that either. Blushing doesn't make me who I am. I have my heart back. There are worse ways to go. Nonetheless, I can't help wondering how it's going to happen. For some reason it feels like it'll be out here, in the landscaped corporate garden of homogenised hedgerows, clean bark chippings, red brick walls and smooth concrete slabs. But there's no one here. Does the mob wait with baited breath on the other side of the door? Did all those horrible thoughts I finally turned loose manage work their hateful magic? Time to find out. Bones close to dissolving in a chemical cascade of terror, roasting muscles and burning, sweaty skin, I grasp the handle of the reception door and somehow haul it open.

Air swirls and whistles around the heavy door as it swings out into the morning air. I step inside. No mob here, either. A young woman sits behind the reception desk, staring intently at the screen. The immaculate, sterile reception area is otherwise empty. Sunbeams paint golden glows onto the windows. Yellow lasers beam the word "murderer" into her head. She looks up, smiles and hails me across the empty space with a cheery "Morning!" in a bright tone that matches the glowing morning. I stare at her for a second, but don't try to correct any of the intrusions or attempt to act calm. I smile back. Either she's not receiving the mental transmissions or she is but doesn't care. I'm deeply afraid but, because I'm not fighting it, I'm also free and alive. I respond with an equally cheery, "Morning!" Only today I'm not faking the amiability; not trying to hide any emotions or control any of the horrible thoughts, no, today…even amidst the rushing matrix of scalding terror and reborn humanity, it's nice to genuinely interact with someone, human to human. Weird, and in no way reassuring, but nice all the same. First hurdle? Passed.

No angry hoards in the corridor. I enter the office in a gushing fountain of anxiety, a cliff-edge feeling of 'This is IT', but, as I look around, everyone's sitting quietly, working away; no one looks up in disgust or shouts "There he is! Get him!" I make my way over to the small, enclosed enclave of desks that's been our training area for the last week-and-a-bit. I'm in freefall as I approach – this will surely be the place where it all kicks off? The fatal chain of events? Bring it on. Let the fear burn me alive, I won't turn from it. Liberated humanity swirls among the terror. I'm not giving it up, *ever* again. Under any circumstances. No more running, hiding or repression. I am what I am. Lauren looks up and smiles. Someone else shoots a casual glance. Everyone else carries on their Monday morning water-coolers. It obviously hasn't started yet – the rumours, the unfortunate conversations and awkward questions that will lead to that one final, fatal red face. I sit down and chat with Lauren, as a mild annoyance slips among the tempestuous ambivalence – it looks like I'm going to sit here and get on with work while waiting for the end to come. It would've been easier to face the fire straight away. But then, maybe there won't be one. Maybe it really is all in my head? Whatever. Let the annoyance mingle. There's room for everything today.

Our trainer soon arrives and we're set to work taking calls. This being our first day of live calls, there's nothing more to learn; we're just getting the feel for the work while she's on hand. So I take calls and occasionally chat with Lauren in the short intervals. It feels as if my whole body's made of erratic electricity: on fire with a dissonant orchestra of electrochemical screeching and singing; nerves and brain doing back flips, primed for someone to shout "Murderer!", "Pervert!" or "Terrorist!" at any given moment. Images of me harming others intrude, along with the awful words and the yellow beams zapping incriminating notions into the minds of others, every bit as horrible as they've been each second of every day for the last four and a half years. But I do nothing. Don't resist, correct or counteract them, and thus the heat of danger burns continually at my fingertips. All the while, the awakened humanity; the ability to feel, even amidst this hellish insanity, reverberates with magnificence in every direction. Feeling again is a revelation. Even mundane things. The colours of the graphics on the computer screen; the soft texture of the carpet, the chair; the idiosyncratic beauty of the chattering voices of colleagues, the subtle creases in scraps of paper, the smoothness of the shiny desk surface – everything around is a deafening, beautiful rapture of sensory delight, as though experienced for the first time and with immeasurable relish. The unleashing of everything inside me over the weekend appears to have included those wonderful old spiritual sensations, bursting forth in tandem with hypnotic fear, trepidation and just about everything else imaginable. The whole gamut.

Lunch break comes around. Still no calamity. Sitting in the small canteen with Lauren and the others, the fear starts to ebb, just a little. Maybe everything's going to be okay after all? Intrusions and joy continue. This is *the* weirdest day of my life. Fag break with Lauren is uneventful. It's really, really strange to not be mentally correcting intrusions while we chat; to not be constantly arguing with myself inside, while acting my socks off to appear 'normal'. It's strange, being scared to death while simultaneously awestruck by rapturous sensation of the whole world suddenly switched back on. I don't talk about it, but neither do I act. I'm just quietly waiting in the eye of the storm for it all to be over, one way or another. A few more hours of work remain. If I get to the end of this shift without some kind of awful tragedy occurring, then it'll be safe to say it really is all just bullshit. But the freefalling feeling isn't going anywhere just yet.

Lauren and I walk inside, another twenty minutes of lunch break left, to find the rest of our group, sitting in our little alcove, all facing one another, talking with our trainer. Ah ha. This is it. A small, enclosed space with a group of people, all facing each other. No way to sit on the periphery and no nearby window to gaze out of. Complete facial exposure. This'll be the place. The time. The final, fatal scenario. Bring it on.

Joy and Light fade a little to the background as a scalding head of steam swells within, ascending terror, ready for the onslaught. A new Ground Zero. I'm ready. Lauren and I take our seats to join the conversation. Polite smiles. Then someone speaks:

"We're having a few people over, next weekend, and we were thinking of hiring one of those chocolate fountains you can get now."

"Oh, yes! I've used those quite a few times, and they're really great. Everyone loves them!"

"Can you get different sizes, or is it just a standard one?"

"No, I think they do quite a range, as some people hire them out for weddings and big corporate events, as well as smaller parties, you see."

"That sounds great! How much do they cost?"

I can't quite believe my ears. I'm sitting here, enraptured in near-transcendent fear and foreboding, listening to quite possibly the most boring conversation imaginable. Chocolate. Fountains. An interesting subject for, say, five minutes? I wait with baited breath for the subject to change to a highly-sensitive news story, filled with trigger-words, destined to bring on that fate-sealing red face. But the chocolate fountain forum drones on for twenty, gruelling minutes. I'm petrified, elated, confused, inspired, annoyed and painfully bored. What a day.

Four o'clock finally approaches as the workday is all but done. The fear has by now settled into an odd background-cacophony. It looks like I'm probably going to live; that it really is all just in my head. Hallelujah! The violent tempest is almost over and the ship still intact. We're invited to hang around for a few hours overtime after our training has finished – only if we'd like – just to find our feet. I ask if it's mandatory. It isn't. So I'll be leaving at Four, thank you very much. Lauren is of the same mind. The lines quieten down and we chat a little. Finally, it's over. Freedom. Gladness. Sanguinity. Then, a couple of minutes before Four, Lauren mentions in conversation that a friend of hers was once date-raped. I blush like a hazard warning light for several seconds and she clearly notices. I try to carry on talking while she looks perplexed, taken aback. She seems suddenly distant. The shift ends and we can go home. Lauren and I usually walk and talk together on our way out of the building, en route to our cars, but now she's walking ahead, at a brisk pace. I catch up to her and attempt to chat a little but she seems ambivalent and evasive. We reach the end of the path and go our separate ways. It's over.

I unlock the car, climb inside and close the door. I rest my head against the steering wheel, close my eyes, take a deep breath, let out the longest sigh, smile and chuckle a little. It's not quite over. But it is, really. The fear was beginning to recede; it really did seem like a new dawn – genuine a clean break. That little blushing hiccup with Lauren has brought some of it back, and as potent and insidious as it is, it's dwarfed by the giddying elation coursing through every part of me. I lived. I feel. I called the bluff of each and every monster in my head and this was the best they could do, if indeed they did anything at all. I crossed the threshold, did the impossible and returned, from the point of no return. It's over.

The drive home is a delightful meander through a wonderland of exquisite sights, sounds and smells, delicate thoughts and blissful emotions, each one tangible and…elating. I traverse the city with delirious joy and a constant smile gently stretched across my face. This world is a *sublimely* beautiful place. And I'm alive. Inside and out.

2007: The Year That Was

2007: The Year That Was

I wish I could say that everything settled down after the events of late March 2007; that by standing in the face of fear, fear itself disappeared; that all the demons died off and everything thereafter was just great. But mental health problems are only solved with dramatic, penny-dropping moments of clarity and insight in the movies. The day after The Last Rush Hour, the agency rang, saying they'd spoken with their clients at the call centre, and they didn't want me back. Not sticking around for some healthy post-training overtime hadn't left a good impression. That was fine by me. Something much bigger and, frankly, far more important had happened. Now the drama was over, little else mattered.

Except it wasn't over. Not by a long shot. The deeply-sublime, numinous high of rediscovered humanity abated after about a day and a half, while the intrusive thoughts and scalding fears remained, present as ever. As the weeks and months rolled on, and I took another temp job at the local cake factory, the weird ciphers and symbols kept resurfacing, tugging at sensation and perception in the same way. It seemed that, having lifted the lid on a brimming unconscious, there was no way of closing it again. It had to run its course. And run it did. And run. And run. And *run*.

There were several similar incidents like the one described in 'All Bets Are Off' and, although none were quite so intense as that first weekend, they remained nonetheless distressing and confusing. Instead of freeing me from all the scary mental noise forever in my head, opening the floodgates of the unconscious only added to the problem. Attempts to ignore or resist the looming symbols always made them worse and, taken with the same old intrusive thoughts and mortal fears of blushing, they made everything that much worse. Long term, refusing to respond to intrusions with complicated thoughts, visualisations and words also proved impossible – their creative, dynamic edge always pushing forward, threatening. "Mum will die if I don't correct that thought", "I'll become a pervert if I don't counteract another", and so on. But, for all the mental deterioration, I retained the ability to feel. No more repression, however bad things were. It was no longer possible. The worrying concrete never returned; the invigorating fresh air of human emotion remained. Not that this eased the symptoms at all. On the contrary, with my unconscious now erupting all over the place, there was even more drama to deal with. The intense emotions of those first awful days of Ground Zero, back at the rivet factory, were now off the leash, stampeding in all directions. There's a reason they were repressed in the first place. But now there was nowhere to push them into; forcing them back down below consciousness only brought on more eruptions of ominous symbols and glyphs. I temped only as much as was absolutely necessary to cover bills, but continued forcing myself to drama class and community choir. The doctor still felt like too big a gamble – the problem itself still so weird, obscure and ripe for misinterpretation. Not to mention the dark scenarios that continued to grip mind and body at the thought of getting help. They were as present as ever. But, eventually, it became my only option…

No More Holding Pattern

Over time, as the unending barrage of impossible mental problems raged on, my resolve began to disintegrate. Having the ability to feel again was at first wonderful, but when emotions are so unbearable, so catatonic, *so* much of the time – even in everyday situations – they simply become another unmanageable burden. The fact that I'd been through so much; tried everything, including telling Mum and Dad, faced the demons and *still* the horrors raged on…it soon started to shift the suicidal-holding-pattern. I'd often wanted to end it all but, as explained in 'A Beautiful Dead End', could never have gone through with it for fear of the untold suffering it would undoubtedly cause my family. That was now changing.

Rapidly. I remained as loath as ever to cause said suffering, but soon began to feel as though suicidal feelings were actually starting to take me over entirely, to somehow absorb me totally…viscerally…burrowing deeper even than all the usual fears. As if I no longer had any say in the matter. The immeasurable sadness and sense of utter helplessness inside were now beyond any kind of resolution, a bottomless pit; a black hole sucking me inexorably in. This wasn't the panic-stricken feeling that something inside wanted to throw me out of the window, as had been the case after the psychotic breakdown of 'Reality Check', no, this was a still, pervasive, all-encompassing feeling that I was just going to end it all; I was somehow losing the ability to even *think* about fighting it. That was pretty alarming. That was what finally broke the holding pattern and sent me to the doctor with a view to telling them absolutely everything.

Pillar to Post

Doctor Hayle was a short, mild mannered lady, probably in her late twenties, who listened intently and concluded with "It does sound like you've got psychosis." She advised a visit from the Early Intervention Team, who came 'round within a fortnight. The large, businesslike, middle aged man who came over suggested the problem was Obsessive Compulsive Disorder. A psychiatric nurse, he recommended an outpatient approach; placing me under the supervision of the local psychiatric team, while I waited for Cognitive Behavioural Therapy. A letter soon dropped onto the front doormat confirming the date of my first appointment. I'd been assigned to Dr Bower.

Dr Bower was like the Wizard of Oz. We never actually met. The monthly appointments, lasting roughly one hour, were with a different junior doctor each and every month, and each and every month I had to explain my problems, from scratch, to a complete stranger once again.

Fluoxetine (Prozac) was prescribed. At the end of each session the junior doctor would disappear to discuss the dosage with Dr Bower and return with a new prescription, increasing the dose every four weeks until I reached the maximum possible amount. The diagnosis wasn't officially confirmed but there seemed to be a general consensus among each of Bowler's underlings that what I had was a combination of OCD and Social Phobia.

Fever Pitch

In August, several weeks after the first visit to Dr Hayle, my brain as was erratic and distressing as ever, and at around the same time I started taking fluoxetine, another blushing incident occurred, this time at the cake factory. It followed hot on the heels of another bout of describing weird unconscious symbols to myself, calling out the demons for the hundredth time, hoping this might ease things a little as had been the case before, but instead it coincided with another trigger-word appearing in casual conversation, obvious blushing and wide-eyed staring from the person in question. Unlike the similar moments with Hannah and Lauren earlier in the year, this one wasn't at the end of the working day but during a lunch break. I worked quietly for the rest of the shift, trying desperately not to panic as my body temperature sky-rocketed, dizziness and manic-tension set in; the world once again throbning with imminent, deadly threats, just a hair's breadth away. On returning home, I told Mum & Dad what had happened, but confiding in them did nothing to quell the rising panic. They went on holiday for a couple of weeks, during which time I stopped working and spent most of my time trying to talk myself out of the feeling that this was, finally, the cataclysmic end. *This* time the rumours would start and it was only a matter of time before things got out of hand. If I kept on blushing in this way, it seemed inevitable the deadly chain reaction would inevitably follow. There was now nothing that could calm me down, even a little. Every moment of every day, that electrified-trance feeling of accelerating danger that had been so all-consuming after blushing in front of Hannah at the council, was constantly present, and more intense than ever. No visualised, imaginative 'corrections' or ruminations; no deciphering of unconscious glyphs or elaborate self-arguments were able to touch it. At all. The catatonic fear had at last won out. My mind was finally collapsing.

After a fortnight it all came to a head. Not wanting to return to the cake factory, I applied to an Extras Agency, not expecting to get anywhere. My expectation had been in error as soon I was driving the one hundred and thirty miles down to Bournemouth for a costume fitting. Having had a minor panic attack the night before, while trying once again to clear the obtruding images rising up from my unconscious, followed by a couple of hours of sleep, the drive down there and back – without a Sat Nav – was exhausting. I'd been almost hysterically jittery during the fitting and had found getting to the site itself an infuriating pain in the backside. By the time I returned home, although my brain was still woefully fragile and burning up with trepidation, I was *so* tired that it felt like sleep was all but a certainty. I'd simply have to put head to pillow and fall into the sweet escape of slumber. Not so. Images and of that decrepit, old, purple-skinned, yellow-eyed demon I dreamt of on that first night in 'Ground Zero', when the intrusions and voices tore in from nowhere, were once again whispering a steady stream of soft terrors. Describing them in the hope their impact would lessen wasn't working. It seemed like there might actually be a real live demon inhabiting my brain.

That was it. While I'd experienced varying forms of panic before that day, this was on another level entirely. Full-blown panic attacks started erupting, peaking and then easing off, but, instead of trailing off completely, as would normally be the case, there was no return whatsoever to any kind of equilibrium. They simply came on and on and on and *on*, each more intense than the last. There was no end to it. I recall thinking to myself "So *this* is what going mad really feels like" just before telling Mum and Dad "You've got to take me to hospital, right now, please." I was by now on the floor, bent over my knees, head resting on the carpet, melting into a psychic-gloop of quivering terror, abject confusion and *total* despair. The only context left was the now all-consuming sensation of utter catastrophe: mental, physical and emotional anguish beyond time, reason or words. Pure, unadulterated panic. A nervous breakdown. At last.

Yogazone

After a couple of hours waiting in A&E, I was seen by a duty doctor who said, "Now, I don't want to do anything that's going to interfere with what the psych-team are doing, so I'm going to give you something to help you sleep and recommend you see your GP tomorrow." By the time we got home, around one in the morning, the sleeping pill was already kicking in – I stumbled from car to front door in a drowsy stupor. I went out like a light and didn't wake up until 2pm the next day. I returned to Dr Hayle, who said pretty much the same thing as the A&E doctor. She didn't want to interfere with whatever Dr Bower was doing – which, beyond writing prescriptions, wasn't much. I was given a prescription for zopiclone – a very strong sleeping tablet – and told to come back if things got any worse.

Zopiclone is a powerful medication. Within twenty minutes of taking it you're out like a light. The vaulting-panic was still very much present so it was nice to steal a full eight-to-ten hours of rest from my disintegrating brain. The side effects, in my case at least, included an intense, metallic taste in the mouth and nose like a kind of weird robot-cold, along with a heavy drowsiness that doesn't really let up, even following a good night's sleep. And, of course, I was still in a perpetual state of searing panic. The pills had helped wrest just a morsel of control back from the successive panic attacks, but they remained nano-meters away, threatening with each breath to invade and reclaim my mind once again, promising to shatter the paper-thin stability of zopiclone-induced stupor. Everything was now lost. Confronting demons had made the problem so much worse in the long run, and now, I'd simply *lost it*. So, in order to function at all; to be able to walk down the stairs in one piece; talk to Mum and Dad, or just sit in front of the TV without going into complete meltdown, I took to doing yoga.

I'd never been to a yoga class per se, but remembered a few asanas (poses) and exercises a singing teacher taught me several years beforehand, along with a handful of others from old dance classes and a home video, once borrowed from a friend. They were tentatively thrown together and practiced very, *very* slowly. A snail's pace would've seemed like a sprint. This wasn't about becoming more flexible or toning up; it was simply a case of finding something to help me get through the next moment. The intrusive thoughts, feelings of imminent danger and psychic meltdown continued throughout, but after about an hour of *phenomenally* slow and gentle yoga, I felt just about stable enough to leave my room and venture downstairs for a while. Within a matter of days, I was putting in roughly three to five hours each and every day. The intrusive thoughts, weird psychic images and ever-present sense of mortal danger raged on but I simply breathed deeply and slowly worked through the moves. It took about six weeks to finally emerge from the nervous breakdown and turn it all around. The full story of how I fought back, along with the ups and downs of the years that followed, could fill another book, but it was in those long hours of endless, slow-motion yoga, that gentle concentration and body-based mindfulness that I finally turned a corner. I can't imagine how I would ever have gotten out of that personal Armageddon any other way. 2007 was the year it all finally happened: the much-feared blushing incidents came on several occasions, triggering, not the anticipated vicious lynching (thankfully) but instead a steady mental breakdown; the year my swelling unconscious finally erupted like a bust water main; the year I finally went for broke by admitting both to myself and others the extent and severity of my mental health problems and seeking help; the year my nerves finally burnt out entirely and, most important of all, the year I was able to experience just how bad things really can get and what must be done to cope. It was 2007: the year that was.

On Reflection

On Reflection

As mentioned at the end of the previous chapter, the full story of the subsequent, post-diagnosis years of medications, therapy, self help and the ups and downs of recovery and long term mental health management could fill another book. That's not what this book is about. I wanted to tell the experiential, pre-diagnosis side of my story, as encountered and without reference to psychiatric labels. I also wanted to explore the various characteristics of the problems that persist to this day, by recounting those key moments that, looking back, played the largest role, or were at least the best example of certain issues. I hope that, having lifted the lid on that strange, horrifying world of undiagnosed and untreated mental health problems, the story has been told candidly and to the best of my ability. I'd like to spend this final chapter illuminating said problems with the hindsight afforded by treatment, and now, almost fifteen years of managing the problems, more or less successfully, including a little about my experiences of treatment.

Diagnosis, Treatment and the Lottery of the NHS

Although I never met Dr Bowler, the cognitive behavioural therapist I was referred to was really, really good. Michael Stout, the head of CBT at the outpatient unit in Worcester, was an experienced, enthusiastic professional. He really knew his stuff. Something of a treatment nihilist — that is, a professional not preoccupied with labels, preferring instead to simply treat symptoms as, when and how they arise — he effortlessly adapted his approach as issues presented themselves over the six months of regular sessions we spent together. Although still forcing myself to attend choirs and small amounts of social activities, I was nonetheless still fastidiously avoiding post-rehearsal trips to the pub and politely declining invitations to house parties. The fear of another Hannah/Lauren-style trigger and the subsequent breakdown that would follow remained powerful as ever. Michael encouraged me to socialise more often so we could discuss the difficulties before and after. We created blushing questionnaires, trigger-word behavioural experiments, and addressed intrusive thoughts with detailed thought records. Slowly but surely, over the six month period, Michael helped ease me back into the world. In treatment, finding a professional with whom you feel comfortable is of the utmost importance; I felt truly lucky to have been referred to Michael.

Shortly after the CBT course ended, I started working again, this time in a brand new café. It was an awful job. Many of the staff were inexperienced or poorly trained, the hours demanded were more than twice those agreed in interview, much of the equipment didn't work and breaks were a rarity. I rode it out as best I could, lasting longer than many other staff members who either left or were fired, but eventually it got too much and I went elsewhere, feeling perilously close to a relapse. Thankfully, my work with Michael had prepared me for the storm, and I just about weathered it.

A few years later, when holding down a job and managing this erratic brain became once again troublesome, I asked for another referral. This time I actually met the psychiatrist, Dr Dale, who was wonderful: an excellent listener who practically oozed compassion. She changed my medication, referred me for further therapy and finally gave that much hoped for, concise diagnosis: 'Obsessive Compulsive Disorder and Social Phobia with recurrent symptoms of Panic Disorder and recurring Depressive Symptoms.' Talk about having letters after my name!

The therapist I saw this time, however, was less than helpful. She often rambled, taking up much of the session, seemed directive (rather than collaborative, as Michael had been) and at one point, as I attempted to discuss what I thought to be the root cause of a certain problem, blurted out, "But that was twenty years ago!" Helpful. Despite all the weed, self-loathing and weird thoughts of those days at the Oakwood PRU, I did actually manage to achieve GCSE maths. I'm capable of counting to twenty and even, on a good day, beyond that. So that particular concern went unaddressed. The whole 'relationship' felt frustrating and unhelpful – not challenging and collaborative as had been the case with Mr Stout, no, as she spent more and more time mounting her soap box to deliver her lectures, it was clear these sessions were going nowhere fast. By this time I'd left another café job and started working for myself, looking after dogs, and so decided to take my chances without the 'help' of this particular professional.

There were a handful of times between 2002-07 when I did go to the doctor but was hyper-cautious, deliberately vague, didn't communicate just how bad things were and as a result didn't get the level of help so badly needed. The fears of being either lynched or locked up always left me feeling desperate, but also *very* tight-lipped. One doctor prescribed anti-psychotics that made me vomit; a psychiatric nurse gave me some generic pills that made me zombie-like, but the lumpy icing on the bone-dry cake was one complete and utter shithead – I'm sorry, but sometimes that's the politest way to describe some people – called Laura to whom I was referred, who just said nothing. Absolutely nothing. Zero. Her role was that of a Gateway Worker, someone to be seen over six sessions that would then decide how best to direct the patient. This wasn't explained at the time. She simply walked out into the doctor's reception, called my name and led me to a consulting room where we sat in silence. Didn't say hello, introduce herself or explain the purpose of the session. Just sat there, staring at me, saying nothing. It was gruelling, especially given how terrified I still was of opening up to anyone at all. When conversation did finally occur – always instigated by myself – she was rude and unhelpful. When I tried to explain the long hours taken up by the ruminations I was inexorably pulled into, her response was "It sounds quite luxurious…"

Yes. It's *luxurious* sitting up until five AM, struggling to convince myself my life isn't in any immediate danger. Luxurious. Piss off. This was another relationship that was terminated on my part and, as far as the NHS knew, I was just fine. A few years later I made several new friends via work and amateur dramatics, no less than three of which had also been referred to Laura, all had also terminated the process early for similar reasons and two made a formal complaint.

Treatment can be something of a lottery. Having the NHS, free at the point of use is of immeasurable value but, when it comes to mental health, the lottery of referral is a real problem. You might be assigned someone congenial and compassionate, keen to help, or you might get someone who'd be better placed as a Reality TV judge. I was lucky enough to meet Dr Hayle, be referred to Michael Stout and found Dr Dale really supportive, but some of those others encountered were worse than useless. They were, in fact, emphatically *detrimental*. I have friends with mental health problems that have had similar hit-and-miss experiences. There are NICE guidelines and BACP criteria for professionals but, when you find yourself alone in a room, your mental health in the hands of a complete stranger, it still so often seems more akin to a roll of the dice. Not an ideal situation when one in four people will find themselves dealing with a mental health problem at some point in their lives. Still, professionals like Michael Stout and Dr Dale are invaluable in the fight for mental health. We need *so* many more like them.

Psychiatric Pin-the-Tail-on-the-Donkey

Psychiatrists have an incredibly difficult job to do. The human brain remains the most complex phenomenon ever discovered. Ever. There's still so much about the mind that remains a mystery; diagnosing and treating those of us who struggle to live with our own minds is no small task, especially when so much of what psychiatrists have to work with is limited to what we are able tell them. I'm occasionally told I'm fairly eloquent. Certainly, English was always my strongest subject at school and college, and even I struggle to articulate myself on the subject of my own mental health; sometimes through that same old fear of stigma, but it's all too often due to the difficulty in just finding the right bloody words. Writing this book has been a hard slog; not just for the gruelling process of recalling to memory what were essentially the worst moments of my life ('Zenith' excepted!) and reliving them on paper, but also the creative of finding ways to describe the slippery, intangible world of inner experience. So hard to pin down and define and yet so immediate and paramount to all human experience. Describing the difference between the kinds of anxieties experienced at age five, fifteen and twenty five; the different forms of depression and panic and so on; it's been a challenge, to say the least. It's the first time I've really said it *all* out loud and, frankly, writing this book has brought me to the conclusion that my diagnosis is probably incomplete as there's much here that's never been discussed with a psychiatrist. I'll address that issue a little later on, but I'll start with the area in which I'm broadly in agreement with the professionals:

Obsessive Compulsive Disorder

OCD is characterised by deeply distressing intrusive thoughts that engender a debilitating level of anxiety. Intrusions can be about anything from germs and poisoning to inappropriate sexual images or visions of the sufferer having caused a horrific car accident and much, much more besides. While their content may vary wildly, the theme is always the same: the sufferer fearing they have caused or might cause untold harm and suffering to others, particularly those they care most about. The sufferer will scramble to 'neutralise' the intrusive thoughts with elaborate rituals or compulsions, such as hand washing, counting, ruminating or reactive visualisations, to name but a few. While such compulsions eventually bring a small amount of short-term relief, their effect on anxiety levels is increasingly negligible, and so they must be enacted for ever longer periods of time or have to be constantly reinvented to keep pace with the dynamic nature of intrusions. Crucially, while providing a meagre, short-term relief, compulsions consistently make the problem worse by assigning significance to intrusions, which leads inexorably to more and worse intrusive thoughts. Anxiety grows ever worse as the disorder robs the sufferer of more and more of their life over time. OCD is not a psychological problem, but rather, a psychiatric one, which, in my own view, is the basis of much that's misunderstood about the condition. In very general terms, psychiatric problems tend to be more complicated and robust than psychological ones. Psychological problems can usually be worked through with the help of a therapist and appropriate therapeutic model, but tend not to have official medical names, require medication or, in extreme cases, sectioning. Hence the name: *Psychiatric* ward. OCD isn't a psychological quirk that can be resolved with well meaning sound-bites about "learning to let go" or "loosening up"; it's a serious, complicated psychiatric disorder that requires a sustained, multi-pronged approach.

Looking back at all the elaborate weirdness described in relation to The Snowman in 'Something in the Shadows', it's clear to me now that much, if not all, of the problem in those days was indeed infantile OCD. Watching a program and feeling disturbed out for a little while is perfectly natural for any child, but a persistent and detailed, years-long distress over something as innocuous as a melted snowman seems a lot like OCD. The irrationality of it all: looking at a shadow wouldn't technically empower The Snowman and the little boy to start their tiny, shuffling steps up the garden – I had to be physically *in* the darkness for that – but nonetheless, even looking at a shadow from across the room felt risky. It was as though I knew my mind couldn't be fully trusted with the task of keeping them at bay, the anxiety like a strange contagion that could draw them near. Even at such a young age, I knew it was ridiculous and felt embarrassed to talk about it, but the emotions involved overrode everything else. The quicksand-feeling of OCD is so powerful as to be able to overpower an otherwise robust mind with a skyrocketing sense of doom. This was the reason I wouldn't even finish reading a paragraph in the TV guide that contained the phrase: "Thriller, starring…", let alone watch the program being described, as the prospect of reliving the fallout I experienced after watching Michael Jackson's infamous video at the age of nine seemed too terrifying. So it went on until the protracted, disciplined regime of prayer and concentrating myself to sleep over several months at the age of thirteen eventually brought it into remission. It returned with a vicious vengeance at the rivet factory in the summer of 2002, in the form of sexual, violent and generally misanthropic thoughts. Hearing voices, intense paranoia and fearing for your *own* life, however, don't really fall into the ball park of OCD. It's reflecting upon those additional symptoms that's led me to the conclusion my diagnosis is incomplete, as I do diverge from the mainstay of the condition on certain points:

Talking to other sufferers online and later meeting many in person at support groups and on organised trips, I learned a couple of things. Firstly, that some who've experienced the condition in a similar way to myself – the horrible, heartbreaking intrusive thoughts of harming others, specifically – become so afraid of causing said harm that they've been known to actually report themselves to the police for crimes they haven't committed. I once heard the story of a man who broke into a factory, late one night, as loudly and clumsily as possible, in the hope of getting caught and locked up; that's how afraid he was of harming his own family. It's important to point out here that OCD sufferers **do not** act out their intrusive thoughts; that's the whole reason for the 'Disorder' part of its name. The intrusions are distressing precisely because they represent the exact opposite of how the sufferer really feels towards others. In fact, many – perhaps even most – OCD sufferers tend to be very caring, sensitive people, often with a heightened sense of responsibility towards other people. If they *didn't* care so much, the thoughts wouldn't be intrusive; they'd just be thoughts, like any other, as is the case with psychopaths. If they did in fact act on them, that wouldn't be OCD; it'd be something else entirely. Nonetheless, the condition can be so terrifying that some sufferers go to elaborate and bizarre lengths to make sure their loved ones are extra safe, all because of those bastard intrusions. That wasn't the case with me. However morbid, disgusting and distressing the intrusions were, however much they hijacked my attention and emotion, brought me to my knees and had to be intercepted and 'corrected' in any, every and all ways possible, I never really believed anyone else was in danger. I knew I'd sooner drive my car off a bridge than act on any one of them. No intrusive thought could make me do anything I didn't want to do, however menacing they appeared. They had to be corrected in the usual OCD manner, to neutralise the horrible anxiety, disgust and guilt they'd elicit, but apart from the 'magical' thoughts escaping control and somehow causing untold havoc – from car crashes to miscarriages – there was never any question in my mind of me harming others. It just wasn't going to happen. I feared for what I might do to myself, but not to anyone else. That brings us nicely to the all-important anomaly: that deep, all-consuming fear of what others might do *to me*...

Social Phobia?

Social Phobia, sometimes called Social Anxiety Disorder is, as the name suggests, a debilitating anxiety disorder centred on social situations. Those with the disorder experience a level of discomfort in the presence of others far beyond what most would consider normal social nervousness. The social anxiety sufferer experiences a profound sense of dread before, during and after social interactions, to the extent that even something as simple as shopping or answering the telephone becomes deeply distressing. Key in the disorder is a fear of being judged harshly by others; being embarrassed or humiliated; blushing (bingo!), sweating or appearing incompetent or out of place. Avoidance of certain people, places or events becomes a huge problem, the condition can have a profound impact on self esteem and therefore on the sufferer's ability to perform at school or work, and form relationships. Certainly, much of this rings true in my case, but by no means all of it. Without meaning to sound flippant, in the grand scheme of things, I don't really care all that much what strangers think of me. Life's too short. From a young age I tended towards the belief that our opinions of others, and of the world at large, ultimately say more about us as individuals than whatever it is we're judging or commenting upon. That's not to belittle or trivialise the very real distress the condition causes sufferers – I've just been fortunate enough that such concerns never affected me in quite that way. That said, it clearly wasn't the case in those adolescent years, particularly in the events of 'My Little Green Friend', 'Reality Check' and 'A Study in Red'. In those days I was painfully self conscious and had huge self esteem problems; some of which were no doubt due to the bullying, some to the warped paranoia of weed use; some brought on by the struggle of coming to terms with my sexuality, largely in private and, of course, some was your usual run-of-the-mill teenage angst. But I overcame it. I've come to believe that the social difficulties experienced during and after the events of Ground Zero were of a different calibre, somewhere in the ball park of Post Traumatic Stress Disorder.

PTSD?

'Erythrophobia' is the clinical name given to the fear of blushing. In the context of social anxiety, it can manifest in all kinds of situations: talking to a passing acquaintance on the street or being introduced to someone new; being the centre of attention for even a second, or just about any other social interaction imaginable. It too is an anxiety disorder, an involuntary reaction born of the fight or flight response. It can be very unpleasant to live with. Sufferers try in vain to manage it with makeup, fake tan and social avoidance but, like so many anxiety disorders, the more it's fed, the worse it gets. Some people even have operations to narrow certain blood vessels to the face. Once again, this hasn't really been my experience. Even at the very worst of times, I could walk into a shop, look a stranger in the face and not blush. I've performed on stage on several occasions without blushing. And yet, it was overwhelmingly the one thing that those CBT sessions with Michael focused on. What brings it on in my case isn't fear of being harshly judged by others per se, but rather, a fear of what blushing might inadvertently *lead* to; of what others might actually *do* to me. In my case, fear of blushing and fear of trauma, and even death, go hand in hand.

One of the first things Michael ever said to me in our very first CBT session, was, "You've clearly got trauma issues." Talk of trauma, blushing and fear of a 'new trauma' were a recurrent theme, although the term Post Traumatic Stress Disorder never really came up. Perhaps that was because, as a Cognitive Behavioural Therapist, he wasn't in a position to perform a formal diagnosis and, me being under the invisible 'Wizard of Oz' Dr Bower at that time, one certainly wasn't going to come from him, either. Trauma 'issues' is a pretty vague term and obviously I'm in no position to diagnose myself, but in light of the stories recounted here, and knowing now what I didn't know back then, here's my take:

PTSD can develop following a traumatic event. This can include anything from time spent in a warzone to sexual or psychological abuse, experiencing or witnessing a horrific accident or natural disaster or a massive psychological shock, such as being diagnosed with cancer. The common denominator in all such events is that an individual's defences, boundaries, sense of safety and even sense of self are temporarily overwhelmed; they fear for their safety and even for their life. Not everyone who experiences a traumatic event will develop PTSD; there's a much higher risk for individuals over ten years of age and for rape victims, but the emergence of the condition following a trauma is never guaranteed. The precise reasons one individual will develop PTSD following a traumatic event while another won't aren't yet clear, but it seems to have much to do with the difficulty the brain and nervous system can have in fully shutting down their response to trauma, once the event has passed. The precise biological and psychological map of the problem is, at this stage, still very much a work in progress. On paper, some of the symptoms have much in common with OCD, and include:

- Disturbing intrusive thoughts and/or feelings
- Avoidance of cues or triggers that remind the sufferer of the traumatic event
- Rumination and hyper-vigilance
- Dreams/Nightmares related to the trauma
- Flashbacks
- Irritability and feelings of isolation and guilt
- Difficulty concentrating
- Insomnia, hyper-arousal (feeling on edge) and emotional numbness

Interestingly, the condition may not always develop immediately after the traumatic event. In many cases, it can take several years to emerge, appearing to manifest 'out of nowhere'. OCD tends not to invade dreams and the concern is usually focused on a fear of harming or causing harm to others, while PTSD seems to be very much a fear of the <u>individual</u> being harmed *again*, or that the harm is still somehow going on. OCD in particular can have a high incidence of co-morbidity (occurring at the same time as other conditions) and it's not uncommon for sufferers of OCD to also experience PTSD, although the former can emerge without the impetus of a trauma, whereas the latter, by definition, cannot.

Writing this book has brought several puzzling insights to my attention; Firstly, the apparently ill-fitting diagnosis of Social Anxiety Disorder. Were it not for the <u>mortal</u> fear of blushing, and its perceived potential to invite dangerous hostility, I doubt I'd have much of a problem around others. I don't blush out of social anxiety; I blush out of a fear of the power of those intense communal-emotions elicited by conversations about social taboos. It really doesn't matter what the subject is; topics like terrorism, murder and sexual violence are all, quite rightly, social taboos. They destroy lives and drive us to the very edge of the human condition, causing rage, despair, immeasurable grief and untold suffering. And they have absolutely nothing whatsoever to do with me. This strange fear I have is of somehow getting caught up in the emotional outrage of others; that such reactionary emotion and the almost predatory social consensus it can engender is a danger to me, not because I've done anything wrong, but because of the way blushing is often perceived. For years, from 'Ground Zero' right up to 'The Final Rush Hour' and beyond, I was convinced it was somehow connected to the OCD-style intrusive thoughts I was having of harming others; that I was deeply ashamed and embarrassed by them, which, of course, I was. If only the intrusions would stop, the blushing wouldn't be a problem, would it? But therapy with Michael helped identify areas that just didn't fit this assumption. Firstly, it was an occasional problem *before* the really nasty intrusions appeared and, second, I've often blushed at triggers that have nothing to do with my intrusive thoughts.

At a charity gig a few years ago, an amateur photographer friend of mine lost his expensive camera. His girlfriend came up to me with a flustered expression, asking, "Mike's lost his camera! Have you seen it anywhere?!" Feeling particularly on edge at the time, I blushed at this question. No, I hadn't seen it. About twenty minutes later, it transpired that Mike had left it in his car. All was well in the world. But for those twenty minutes, I was painfully paranoid. My blushing had clearly been noticed but not commented upon. But it had been *noticed*. I could tell by the perplexed expression on Kate's face. Would I be asked again? I was sure to blush. What if they couldn't find the camera? Did it look like I had something to hide? How far would this go? As far as I can recall, I've never had an intrusive thought about stealing someone's camera. If I have, I certainly wasn't having one at the time. I'd have remembered. It would've made the experience even worse.

In therapy, Michael explained that blushing taps into emotional memories. Let's say you fell from your bike as a child – clumsily, hilariously, and it made your friends laugh. It was embarrassing and you blushed. No big deal. You might then find, as an adult, that falling off your bike almost always causes a little blushing, even when there's no one else around. The emotional memory has been briefly aroused. Uncomfortable, yes, but not exactly debilitating. Except in my case, the root experience of my own blushing memory involved a prolonged, public humiliation that included several sexual assaults. No one else could see exactly what was happening, as it was under the table, but they knew – Adrian boasted about it there and then – and they laughed about it, encouraged it. I had no idea how far it was going to go. My face was being watched from all directions, and mocked the whole time. I was prey, being toyed with for entertainment; I felt I had to keep a brave face on things. But this is where it gets confusing: I've never had so much as a single *episodic* flashback to that event. By episodic, I mean a specific, detailed, visual flashback that feels as though the event is happening again, in the here and now. I repressed the horrible <u>emotion</u> of the whole experience as best I could *while* it was happening, to avoid either bursting into tears or laying into Adrian and making the whole situation that much worse. I felt like shit for the rest of the day but just put it all down to what I already knew: he was a vile shithead that I hated, in a school overrun with vile shitheads, including many of the teachers. Homophobia. Par for the course. Not much I could do but suck it up and keep my head down as usual. A few people asked me about it afterwards and I can vaguely recall being called into the Head of Hear's office a few days later and being questioned about it the incident but, as far as I was concerned, the whole episode raised the issue of my sexuality and that wasn't something I was prepared to discuss with anyone while still at school. Even talking about it seemed risky, not to mention uncomfortable, so my answers were deliberately monosyllabic. Just don't go there. I never forgot what happened but didn't dwell on it either. It was just another one of those horrible things that happened in that shithole school.

Years later, however, when the intrusions and voices started, I realise now that I was also experiencing flashbacks, but of an *emotional* nature. The fear that I might blush, that a baying lynch mob was just a few unfortunate incidents away, was so all-consuming, pervasive and <u>exactly</u> like the absorbing sense of danger I experienced, back in that music lesson at the age of thirteen. But because it was only the emotion and not the episodic details that came to the fore, I never made the connection. I repressed the emotion of what happened at school but not the episodic memory of the day itself. It was only years later, while practicing the rather harrowing CBT and ERP (Exposure and Response Prevention – a behaviourism approach) technique of writing down my intrusive thoughts in as much detail as possible for an hour a night, that something odd happened. Once the intrusions were down on paper, the process somehow merged with the weird overflow of unconscious imagery described in 'All Bets Are Off' in a kind of free-writing frenzy. I began describing my worst fears; how exactly the lynching might pan out –

when, where, who'd be present, what exactly would happen, how it would feel and so on. Night after night, week after week, I rinsed out all the unconscious fears on paper until it finally emerged clear as day: what I was really afraid of was what had happened in that music lesson all those years ago. I really had no idea of just how much it had affected me. I got sick to the back teeth of school, went off the rails, got expelled and encountered a whole other series of problems thereafter. C'est la vie. I didn't really think about it. I've come to believe this to be a good example of the downside of being a strong person. I used to be very strong. So strong in fact that I was able to fully repress the emotion of a sexual assault while it was still going on; so strong that I managed to force myself to suffer in silence for almost five years from 2002 to 2007 instead of just breaking down, letting it all out and getting the help I so obviously and badly needed. Every time I considered telling someone about the horrible circus in my head, the flashback of the emotion from that music lesson would flood in, urging me toward safety at all costs, in a way that was wholly different to OCD. Ruminating over the intrusive thoughts or the likelihood of trigger words coming in conversation was impossibly detailed and meticulous, but the visceral emotion that came on when the latter possibility felt likely was overwhelming, shapeless and terrifying. Combined with the ever-shifting maze of OCD, that feeling grew exponentially more intense. Being strong enough to keep things under wraps isn't always an advantage. In many ways, I'm glad my nerves burnt out in the end.

As mentioned earlier, PTSD can also arise as a result of a trauma in which an individual's sense of reality and self are overwhelmed. That's undoubtedly what happened in Reality Check, in the dusty humidity of the attic on that July afternoon. I think it was after that time that certain thoughts became scary and dangerous, and had to be avoided at all costs – strategized against to avoid repeating the experience of having reality itself unravel before my eyes. Certainly that feeling of my mental state being all too fragile, precarious and in need of constant attention remains with me to this day. Balancing spinning plates while walking on ice. It seems that the unprocessed traumas described in 'Thirteen…Unlucky for Some' and 'Reality Check' all converged on that awful day back at the rivet factory in 2002. Suddenly OCD, PTSD and a degree of psychosis burst onto the scene and I inexplicably found myself in a personal pandemonium. Were the events of those first few days the delayed onset of PTSD? It certainly looks that way. Recounting it all and reflecting on it now leads me to think it's time for another trip to the doctor, but trauma symptoms can be hard to describe in person as retelling almost always feels like reliving, even just describing a sense of danger can make it feel real again. While talking with the psychiatric nurse that diagnosed OCD, I mentioned the fear that others would treat me as dangerous, and before I could elaborate any further, he burst out laughing and said something along the lines of: "I think you can credit us with a bit more sophistication than that!" This was a little reassuring in terms of the OCD, but also meant we didn't discuss the lynching and abuse fears as, while trying, but remaining afraid, to open up fully, at this point I just clammed up. Talking about trauma can be hard. The advantage of writing about it is the ability to do so slowly, at an *almost* comfortable pace. This is what's led me to think another trip to the doctor is in order; I've not really reviewed the big picture until now. I confess to being a little ambivalent. The cynic in me says I'll be put on a waiting list for about two years, only to be given more CBT and told to keep on taking the same medication. And I have a certain amount of trepidation about playing the treatment-professional-lottery again. But, rationally, it seems there's little to lose and I can't know either way unless I try. I guess we'll see what happens.

After the Storm

So maybe I have PTSD as well as OCD. Perhaps there are still elements of Social Phobia in the mix. Life now is nothing like the events described in the bulk of this book. Six months of CBT with Mr Stout really helped with learning to manage my psychiatric problems. That, high doses of antidepressants, over the counter sleeping pills and a monumental amount of self help have brought me to where I am today. Not 'better' or 'fully recovered', but functioning. I work for myself, looking after dogs, and live independently. I still have the unpleasant intrusions, struggle to relax when talking with others; struggled to sleep without medication for over ten years and, whenever I've reduced or even stopped medicating entirely, that all-consuming nuclear-wind of danger returns with a vengeance, as though I've stepped back in time to the impossible 'dangers' of 2007. At time of writing, I've been single for almost nineteen years now and remain very uncomfortable with most kinds of intimacy. But I can feel. And listen to music. And read. Watch TV, have a social life. Things are nowhere near as bad as they once were, by any stretch of the imagination. There's still work to do. The events of 'All Bets Are Off' and 'The Final Rush Hour' as a whole do appear to have changed my nerves permanently. I'm generally a much more jumpy person than before, even more so than back in the dark days of 2002-07, but the payoff of having a nervous breakdown and living to tell the tale is that such experiences can be oddly liberating. I saw just how bad things can get; what I can and cannot change and what can happen if I don't take these problems seriously.

And to the Rest...

There are just a few other areas that need to be covered that don't come under the remit of OCD, Social Phobia or PTSD I'd like to discuss:

ADHD

This is a controversial one. If you want a phrase that sums up a lot of people's frustration with trends in education, psychology and psychiatry, it's ADHD. It is, in my own estimation, massively over- diagnosed. I was given the diagnosis by an Educational Psychologist after being expelled from school, but, as mentioned at the end of the titular chapter, received no treatment whatsoever. I've come to suspect it was a bureaucratic diagnosis by someone who believed that a Pupil Referral Unit was a better environment for a kid like I was at that time, and the label would help with admission. On the other hand, she could've just been plain wrong. I've since spoken to therapists, psychologists and psychiatrists on the matter and all seem to share my view that I don't have the condition. I've come to believe that my behaviour in 'The "ADHD" Days' was really about not feeling safe at school and doing whatever seemed necessary to cope. I was rude, disruptive and obnoxious because I was continually nervous, jittery and on edge and had lost all faith in the ability of teachers to keep control of kids like Adrian Watson, who, despite his behaviour towards me and other students, was never expelled. I didn't consciously make the connection at the time; I just felt a manic-anxiety at the thought of slipping back into that old role of the 'good boy'. Before that period, during the previous academic year, I had almost no problems with concentration or behaviour and was quiet as a mouse. On one occasion during my off-the-tracks school days, I spent a week doing work experience at the college library. Twitchy old Mr Farron – he that proved beyond ineffectual when Adrian was working me over for the class – came to check on me at the end of the week and stood, quite literally open-mouthed, staring at me, clearly taken aback at how well behaved and conscientious I was outside of the school environment. Perhaps he was expecting to find librarians in tears at my awful behaviour or discover

I'd not attended at all. Seeing me sitting quietly, getting on with my work and getting nothing but glowing feedback from the library staff left him speechless. Go figure. Dickhead.

I have friends who do have clinical ADHD and being around them has reinforced my view that I myself don't. The over-diagnosing of ADHD and subsequent backlash of cynicism from the public at large on the one hand, and the way this can mean other problems are overlooked and therefore not really dealt with on the other (as was the case with me), can lead to a lot of ignorance and stigma towards those who genuinely do have the condition. I've met many who don't even think it exists at all. Over-diagnosis is a worrying trend, but nonetheless, I can't imagine how it must feel to hear such ignorant and ill-informed assertions for those who do, in fact, have clinical ADHD.

Cannabis Psychosis

The events of 'Reality Check' and 'Ground Zero' seem to have encompassed, in addition to the above descriptions, a degree of psychosis, or at least of psychotic symptoms. The way reality disintegrated so quickly during the drug-induced breakdown in the attic seems consistent with what I've read of psychosis, as does the hearing of voices and the feeling that my mind had been torn open for all to see during those catastrophic moments at the factory in 'Ground Zero'. On both occasions I was under the influence of cannabis, but the warping of reality, in the eye of both storms, lasted long after the drug had worn off and were, as such, something far more serious than a little stoned freak-out. Four months after the events of 'Ground Zero', cannabis use already waning as it seemed to make all the terrifying thoughts that much worse, I caught a late night documentary about cannabis psychosis. It was a fairly new term at the time (2002) and much of what was discussed in the program hit home, although, mercifully, the voices hadn't lasted more than a day or so. For years – until meeting with the psychiatric nurse from the Early Intervention Team, in fact – I was convinced my problem was cannabis psychosis, but utterly bewildered when, after quitting the drug entirely, the symptoms hadn't abated. Everything then was about what had happened back at the factory; I made no connection to the events of high school, the weird night terrors of childhood or the depression at college. I'd messed my mind up with weed and that was all there was to it. Stop smoking the weed, wait long enough and you'll start to feel better. The only problem was, given the resilience and sophistication of the problems, it never got better and in fact seemed to deteriorate. Looking back now, especially while writing this book, I keep asking myself, "Why didn't I just stop? Back when I was sixteen and it became a serious problem?" Hindsight is a wonderful thing, especially after therapy and years of abstinence. I remember how distracted and on edge I was during occasional attempts to quit, during the days of college and that first relationship with Tom. The world was so loud and yet so dead; I felt too messed up to function much of the time and my head was a cacophony of white noise; I've come to the conclusion that I was self medicating. The overwhelming majority of those stoned years between the age of fifteen and twenty weren't the gentle, eye-opening moments of bliss described at the beginning of 'My Little Green Friend'; they were overwhelmingly just me, lying on my bed, ruminating in slow motion circles or just trying to focus enough to watch the TV or talk with someone. I hated being stoned after the breakdown of summer 1998; hated the fact that I could never function for long without it and especially hated myself for all the disgusting ways I used to find a hit. But until it made everything *so* much worse in August 2002, it did seem to take the edge off, if nothing else. The years of abstinence before getting diagnosed and medicating with fluoxetine were undoubtedly the worst of my life, even when compared to high school. At least now I'm medicating with something a little less risky.

The psychiatric nurse who diagnosed OCD asked a few questions about the voices: "What were they saying?" "Whose voices were they?" "Were they disembodied or did they come from your head?" "What did you think of them at the time?" And so on. It turned out that, while I may have had some psychotic episodes, it wasn't cannabis psychosis after all. The key? Lucidity. Yes, there was a lot of unpleasant crap in my head most of the time, but the fact that I knew it was a mental problem made all the difference. Sometimes I think it's worse, having all those horrors in your head and knowing there's something wrong. Ignorance is bliss, after all. Then I remember how it felt hearing those voices and feeling my grip on reality start to give, and I'm not so sure. Having experienced such things for a very short period of time, my heart truly goes out to the people living with those horrors day after day. I can barely bring myself to imagine it.

As for the uber-werid stuff that went on during 'All Bets Are Off', I decided to participate in a study on the effects of CBT on the early stages of psychosis. The study was mentioned by the psychiatric nurse towards the end of his seminal visit, and, as I was deemed in the 'at risk' category, it seemed like a good idea. All I had to do to take part in the study was show up at my local GP surgery once a month and discuss my mental health with a couple of trainee psychologists. We discussed that weird descent into the unconscious described in 'All Bets Are Off', and came to the conclusion that, whatever it was, it perhaps had me on the cusp of psychosis, but not quite psychotic. Probably. These things are spectacularly hard to define. As mentioned in the previous chapter, the weird ciphers kept on creeping into consciousness, demanding to be dealt with in a very different way to the intrusions. It went on for most of the year until, scribbling away one evening, I finally uncovered the *emotional* memory of what happened in that music lesson all those years ago, and how it really felt.

These days the phenomenon is still there, but doesn't intrude at all. The psychologist Carl Jung conceived of a self-help-and-analysis technique called Active Imagination – a secular and more scientific take on esoteric practices like shamanic journeying and the like – wherein one's imagination can be marshalled to access the unconscious mind. The curious thing is that, ever since the events of 'All Bets Are Off', I've had direct access to this strange world of forms, without any effort whatsoever. I can say something to my mind like, "Show me how I feel about writing this book" and detailed, evocative imagery suddenly springs up, without any conscious effort on my part to imagine anything whatsoever. These days, it can be turned on and off like a tap but back when it felt like my unconscious was overflowing, and having never experienced anything like it before, it was truly terrifying. As to why it happens, I've come to believe the fact that I have mild synaesthesia is probably a big part of it. Synaesthesia isn't a mental illness, but a benign neurological phenomenon where the mind automatically associates colours with, for example, letters and numbers. Five is red. The musical note 'G' is a light blue. Thursday is brown. Others experience it in much more detail than I, but when taken with the visual tendencies of this particular brain of mine, synaesthesia may go some way to explaining this odd path to the unconscious. Thankfully, it doesn't appear to be any form of psychosis.

Psychological Abuse

And finally…

The sexual abuse experienced at the hands of Adrian and Tom were unpleasant enough, but with regard to my not-so-beloved first boyfriend, I often wonder if it was actually all the mind games that had the deeper, more insidious and lasting impact. I've only really become fully aware of this phenomenon in recent years. I ran into an old housemate one autumn afternoon, and we made a date to catch up that evening. While sipping tea in his flat, he showed me a piece he'd written for an online support group about psychological abuse. As I read his considered piece, pennies kept dropping, light bulbs blinked to life. Seeing such behaviour described in black and white finally gave form to all the subtle and not so subtle tricks used by Tom and a few others encountered along the way. Terms like 'Gaslighting' and 'Dosing and devaluing' made a lot of sense. The sheer mastery of the psychological abuser is, on reflection, quite chilling. The practice of dosing a subject up with gilded complements over time, winning their confidence, and then slowly but surely changing the tone from adoration to 'helpful' interventions and eventually to downright verbal abuse, is very effective. The moment the abuser starts to feel they're losing you, the sugar-coated compliments start again, just long enough to regain their position. The rest of the world only ever see the amiable face the abuser presents at the beginning of the relationship, while the victim is treated to another side entirely. You need them. They're always right. You're lucky to have someone like them tolerate your irritating presence at all, let alone date you. Nothing you do is ever quite good enough. I've come across a few people like that in my time, one or two even worse than Tom, but he was the one I was closest to and thus the most damaging. Psychological abusers tend to seek out kind hearted, reasonable people who wear their heart on their sleeve, because they're the kind most likely to look for the best in others and not dwell on their shortcomings and flaws. It's a perfect match, at least from the abuser's point of view. As described towards the end of 'Fabulous, Darling!' Tom really got under my skin in ways so incredibly subtle and pervasive that the need for his unattainable approval lingered on for years after I kicked him to the kerb. I'm starting to believe that the importance of an awareness of this kind of behaviour is on par with teaching about the concept of sexual consent. The abuse can be so damaging. I mentioned at the beginning of this section how it can, in some ways, be more damaging than the physical abuse; after Tom's little "accident" that evening in his bedroom, I ached physically for about four days, but the fact he was even able to convince me that was an accident at all shows the power he had over my mind. The effects of the latter violation lasted a lot longer.

Gladly, a newfound literacy on this subject, following on from reading my friend's article, and doing some research of my own, has really opened my eyes. It's also increasingly discussed in the public domain on radio, TV, online, in soap operas and so on. This is great news. Knowledge is power. Suffice to say, that kind of crap will no longer be tolerated in my own life!

Final Words…

Final Words

If you've made it this far, I'd like to take this opportunity to thank you, from the bottom of my heart. To put it mildly, this has been a very strange book to write, and I can only imagine it must have been at least as strange to read. It's been quite an emotional rollercoaster, recalling and detailing what were among some of the best and worst moments of my life, and finding a way to convey them in as direct a manner as possible. When I first envisioned this project, I was more than a little enthralled by the creative challenge it posed; little did I realise it would push me to the very limits of my linguistic ability. Nor had I anticipated just how emotionally demanding the process of plumbing my own psychic depths would be. Thank you so much for indulging this weird project. I'm glad to have done it, and at least as glad that it's finally over!

It's my hope that this book will be, in some small way, a qualitative contribution to the burgeoning field of Consciousness Studies. It's a fascinating and still much-neglected area. But far, *far* greater than that, is my hope that this work may also help in the fight to reduce the isolation and stigma surrounding mental health issues. The mind can be a strange place to inhabit at the best of times. When it's in an unhealthy state it can be an unrelenting hell. Fear of being judged, not just for having mental health troubles, but also for the alarming things that can occur *within* a troubled mind is, I believe, still the main barrier to open and honest discussion. Were we to discuss with others the detailed contents of our own heads *all the time*, we'd surely find ourselves in a solipsistic, uncomfortable world of over-sharing. However, in those times when the mind is so deeply perturbed as to frighten us to distraction, then it seems something of a necessity. It can sometimes be as uncomfortable to hear about others' inner worlds as it can be to talk about our own but, I really believe, that as we learn to communicate on such matters we have a genuine opportunity, not only to reduce stigma, but to better understand one another as well.

Once again, thank you so very much for embarking on this journey with me. I wish you <u>all</u> the very best of mental health!

www.ingramcontent.com/pod-product-compliance
Lightning Source LLC
Chambersburg PA
CBHW061742250726
48657CB00001B/8